Parallel Curriculum Units for Social Studies
Grades 6–12

Parallel Curriculum Units for Social Studies
Grades 6–12

Jeanne H. Purcell | Jann H. Leppien

EDITORS

CORWIN
A SAGE Company

Copyright © 2010 by Corwin

All rights reserved. When forms and sample documents are included, their use is authorized only by educators, local school sites, and/or noncommercial or nonprofit entities that have purchased the book. Except for that usage, no part of this book may be reproduced or utilized in any form or by any means, electronic or mechanical, including photocopying, recording, or by any information storage and retrieval system, without permission in writing from the publisher.

For information:

Corwin
A SAGE Company
2455 Teller Road
Thousand Oaks, California 91320
(800) 233-9936
Fax: (800) 417-2466
www.corwinpress.com

SAGE Ltd.
1 Oliver's Yard
55 City Road
London EC1Y 1SP
United Kingdom

SAGE India Pvt. Ltd.
B 1/I 1 Mohan Cooperative Industrial Area
Mathura Road, New Delhi 110 044
India

SAGE Asia-Pacific Pte. Ltd.
33 Pekin Street #02-01
Far East Square
Singapore 048763

Library of Congress Cataloging-in-Publication Data

Parallel curriculum units for social studies, grades 6–12/Jeanne H. Purcell and Jann H. Leppien, Editors.
    p. cm.
Includes bibliographical references and index.
ISBN 978-1-4129-6539-2 (cloth)
ISBN 978-1-4129-6540-8 (pbk.)
  1. Social studies—Study and teaching (Elementary) 2. Social studies—Study and teaching (Secondary) 3. Curriculum planning. 4. Curriculum evaluation. I. Leppien, Jann H. II. Purcell, Jeanne H. III. Title.

LB1584.P24 2010
300.71—dc22
                                      2009033576

09 10 11 12 13 10 9 8 7 6 5 4 3 2 1

Acquisitions Editor:	David Chao
Editorial Assistant:	Sarah Bartlett
Production Editor:	Jane Haenel
Copy Editor:	Jenifer Dill
Typesetter:	C&M Digitals (P) Ltd.
Proofreader:	Susan Schon
Indexer:	Maria Sosnowski
Cover and Graphic Designer:	Rose Storey

Contents

About the Editors	vii
About the Contributors	ix
Introduction: A Brief History of the Parallel Curriculum Model (PCM)	1
1. Becoming a Geographer (Grade 6)	**13**
Heather Burke	
Background Information	13
Content Framework	14
Unit Assessments	15
Overview of the Unit	15
Lesson 1: Climate and Seasons	16
Lesson 2: Investigating World Populations	25
Lesson 3: Shop Around the Globe	30
Lesson 4: The Culture of Geography	39
2. Through the Looking Glass: A Unit for Reading/Writing/ Social Studies Intervention Classes (Middle School)	**45**
Dawn Vier and Lisa L. Ward	
Introduction to the Unit	45
Content Framework	46
Unit Assessments	50
Background Information	51
Unit Sequence, Description, and Teacher Reflections	52
Preassessment: What Makes Your Identity?	52
Lesson 1: Introduction—"Who Am I?"	53
Lesson 2: The Pursuit of Happiness	60
Lesson 3: Authentic Authors	65
Lesson 4: Sociocentrism	68
Lesson 5: The City	77
Lesson 6: The Great Depression	83
Lesson 7: A Sign of the Times	90

Lesson 8: Persuade Me!	94
Lesson 9: Planet Earth	97
References and Resources	101

3. Subversion and Controversy: Sociological Considerations of Humor, a Cross-Curricular Unit in Sociology and Literature (Grades 7 and 8) — 103
Kelly M. Dausel

Background Information	103
Content Framework	104
Guiding Questions for Each Parallel	104
Unit Assessments	108
Overview of This Unit	109
Unit Sequence, Description, and Teacher Reflections	110
Lesson 1: Introduction to Sociology and How Sociologists Think	110
Lesson 2: Humor in Society	117
Lesson 3: Humor in Communication	126
Lesson 4: Sociological Research	132
Lesson 5: Curriculum of Identity Creative Extension	147

4. True Story-Telling: How Historians Construct the Past (Grade 10) — 153
Catherine Little

Background Information	153
Content Framework	155
Unit Assessments	156
Overview of Key Lesson Ideas/Purposes	157
Lesson 1: Selective Memory	158
Lesson 2: Constructing History	171
Lesson 3: The Past Through Many Eyes	180
Lesson 4: Who Writes History?	199
Lesson 5: What Makes the History Books?	206
Resources	216

Index — 219

About the Editors

Jeanne H. Purcell is the consultant to the Connecticut State Department of Education for gifted and talented education. She is also director of UConn Mentor Connection, a nationally recognized summer mentorship program for talented teenagers that is part of the NEAG Center for Talent Development at the University of Connecticut. Prior to her work at the State Department of Connecticut, she was an administrator for Rocky Hill Public Schools (CT); a program specialist with the National Research Center on the Gifted and Talented, where she worked collaboratively with other researchers on national issues related to high-achieving young people; an instructor of Teaching the Talented, a graduate-level program in gifted education; and a staff developer to school districts across this country and in Canada. She has been an English teacher, community service coordinator, and teacher of the gifted, K–12, for 18 years in Connecticut school districts and has published many articles that have appeared in *Educational Leadership, Gifted Child Quarterly, Roeper Review, Educational and Psychological Measurement, National Association of Secondary School Principals' Bulletin, Our Children: The National PTA Magazine, Parenting for High Potential,* and *Journal for the Education of the Gifted*. She is active in the National Association for Gifted Children (NAGC) and serves on the Awards Committee and the Curriculum Committee of NAGC, for which she is the co-chair for the annual Curriculum Awards Competition.

Jann H. Leppien served as a gifted and talented coordinator in Montana prior to attending the University of Connecticut, where she earned her doctorate in gifted education and worked as a research assistant at the National Research Center for the Gifted and Talented. She has been a teacher for 24 years, spending 14 of those years working as a classroom teacher, enrichment specialist, and coordinator of the Schoolwide Enrichment Model in Montana. She is past president of the Montana Association for Gifted and Talented Education. Currently, she is an associate professor in the School of Education at the University of Great Falls in Montana. She teaches graduate and undergraduate courses in gifted education, educational research, curriculum and assessment, and creativity, and methods courses in math, science, and social studies. Her research interests include teacher collaboration, curriculum design, underachievement, and planning instruction for advanced learners. She works as a consultant to teachers in the field of gifted education and as a national trainer for the Talents Unlimited Program. She is coauthor of *The Multiple Menu Model: A Parallel Guide for Developing Differentiated Curriculum*. She is active in the National Association for Gifted Children (NAGC), serving as a board member and newsletter editor of the Curriculum Division, and is a board member of the Association for the Education of Gifted Underachieving Students.

About the Contributors

Heather Burke has a BS degree in elementary education and sociology and a Master's degree in reading and language arts. She is currently a stay-at-home mom. Prior to the birth of her children, she was an elementary school teacher for five years in Cheshire, Connecticut. She takes a particular interest in curriculum revision and technology integration.

Kelly M. Dausel teaches seventh-grade English at Kemps Landing Magnet School in Virginia Beach, Virginia. Her undergraduate degree, in middle grades education and with concentrations in language arts and social studies, was earned at Greensboro College. She recently completed her Master's degree in educational psychology at the University of Connecticut.

Catherine Little is an assistant professor in educational psychology at the University of Connecticut. She teaches courses in gifted and talented education and in the undergraduate honors program in education. She previously served as visiting assistant professor in gifted education at the College of William and Mary, and as curriculum coordinator at the Center for Gifted Education there. Catherine received her PhD in Educational Policy, Planning, and Leadership from William and Mary. Her research interests include professional development, teacher talent development, curriculum differentiation, and perfectionism. She presents regularly at state and national conferences and in local school districts, and she has written or co-written several curriculum units as well as book chapters and journal articles related to curriculum implementation and other issues in gifted education. She co-edited the text *Content-Based Curriculum for High-Ability Learners* with Joyce VanTassel-Baska. Catherine received NAGC's Early Leader Award in 2008.

Dawn Vier received her education degree in 2000 from the University of Nevada–Las Vegas. She taught second grade for three years while earning a Master's degree in curriculum and instruction, with an emphasis in literacy, also at UNLV. She worked with undergraduate students at UNLV in reading and writing curriculum and instruction intervention prior to becoming a Grade 6–8 reading and math support teacher. Currently she is the AVID coordinator/teacher for Grades 6–8 at Sky Vista Middle School in Aurora, Colorado. Teaching is her passion, guided by the belief that students cannot be taught until a connection with their teachers has been establish and cultivated; the tone and mood of classrooms absolutely determines the engagement of students.

Lisa L. Ward is currently a special education coordinator, reading intervention teacher, and speech-language pathologist. She is an experienced teacher of high-needs students at all levels of the education system, including students with learning disabilities, speech-language disabilities, hearing impairments, and multiple disabilities. Lisa has taught for 25 years in the public school system and as an adjunct instructor at the college level. Lisa received her Bachelor's degree in elementary education and her Master of Arts degree from the University of Northern Colorado in the area of acoustically handicapped, an endorsement in learning disabilities from Kearney State College, and a Master of Science degree from the University of Nebraska at Omaha in speech-language pathology. Her career highlight has been to implement and write curriculum using a gifted curriculum model with students who have disabilities. It is her belief that the PCM curriculum empowers high-needs students well beyond any conventional curriculum used today. Lisa lives with her husband and two daughters in Parker, Colorado, where she enjoys biking, hiking, skiing, and reading.

Introduction

A Brief History of the Parallel Curriculum Model (PCM)

When *The Parallel Curriculum: A Design to Develop High Potential and Challenge High-Ability Learners* was published (Tomlinson et al., 2002), the six of us who authored the work knew we had found ideas in the model to be interesting, challenging, and worthy of a great deal more thought and articulation. Since the original book's publication over six years ago, we have spent a great deal of time talking among ourselves and with other practitioners about the Parallel Curriculum Model (PCM). These colleagues were as passionate as we were about the nature of high-quality curriculum and the increasing need for such learning experiences for all students. Our colleagues offered us invaluable viewpoints, opinions, suggestions, and probing questions. We surely benefited in countless ways from their expertise and insights.

Our conversations led to the publication of two new books about PCM in 2006. Book I, *The Parallel Curriculum in the Classroom: Essays for Application Across the Content Areas, K–12*, featured articles that we hope clarified and expanded upon selected aspects of the model. We continue to hope that it helps educators think more deeply about important facets of the model and some of its nonnegotiable components.

Book II, *The Parallel Curriculum in the Classroom: Units for Application Across the Content Areas, K–12*, invited readers to consider eight curriculum units that were designed using PCM. As we compiled the units, we sought to answer the following question: What is necessary in the design process of any Parallel Curriculum unit?

We did not consider these units as off-the-shelf selections that a teacher might pick up and teach. Rather, we viewed the eight units as professional development tools that would be helpful to any educator who wanted to reflect on one way of creating thoughtful curriculum.

Over the last two years, we have continued to engage in conversations about the nature of curriculum models and how they can be used to create rigorous learning opportunities for students. As before, these conversations ultimately led us to two additional projects. The first was to create an updated version of the original publication. This second edition of PCM was completed in the spring of 2008 and is called *The Parallel Curriculum: A Design to Develop Learner Potential and Challenge Advanced Learners, Second Edition* (Tomlinson et al., 2008, Corwin). The second edition of the Parallel Curriculum Model extends our understanding of how this framework for curriculum development can be used to create, revise, or adapt curriculum to the needs of *all* students. In addition, it explores the concept of Ascending Intellectual Demand (AID) for all learners in today's heterogeneous classrooms.

The second project was the creation of a series of curriculum units, based on PCM, that could be used by practitioners. To address the varying needs of teachers across the K–12 grade span—as well as different content areas—we decided to create a series of five publications. The first publication is dedicated to the elementary grades, K–5. It features lessons and curriculum units that have been designed to address the needs of primary and elementary learners.

The last four publications span the secondary grades, Grades 6–12. Each of the four publications focuses on a different content area: English/language arts, social studies/history, science, and mathematics. It is our hope that the lessons in each publication not only underscore important and discipline-specific content, but also illuminate the four parallels in unique and enduring ways.

We could not have completed these tasks without the invaluable assistance of two new team members. Cindy Strickland contributed to both publications in 2006, and she also helped create *The Parallel Curriculum Multimedia Kit*. Marcia Imbeau is also a longtime user and trainer in PCM. She edited the K–5 book in this series.

THE PARALLEL CURRICULUM MODEL (PCM): A BRIEF OVERVIEW

A wonderfully illuminating fable exists about seven blind men who encounter an elephant. Because each man feels a different part of the beast, none is able to figure out the true nature of the gigantic creature.

Did you ever stop to think that students' perceptions about their learning experiences might be as limited as the perceptions the blind men had about the nature of the elephant? Perhaps, like the blind men, students learn only bits and pieces of the curriculum over time, never seeing, let alone understanding, the larger whole that is humankind's accumulated knowledge.

What if we were able to design curriculum in a multifaceted way to ensure that all learners understood (1) the nature of knowledge, (2) the connections that link humankind's knowledge, (3) the methodology of the practitioner who creates knowledge, and (4) the "fit" between the learner's values and goals and those that characterize practicing professionals? How would classrooms be different if the focus of curriculum was *qualitatively differentiated curriculum* that prompts learners not only to accumulate information, but also to experience the power of knowledge and their potential role within it?

The Parallel Curriculum Model suggests that all learners should have the opportunity to experience the elephant and benefit from seeing the whole. Moreover, as students become increasingly expert in their understanding of all the facets of knowledge, the curriculum should support students' developing expertise through "ascending levels of intellectual demand." This overview of PCM will provide readers with a very brief summary of the model and an opportunity to see how the sum of the model's component parts can be used to create qualitatively differentiated curriculum for *all* students.

THE PARALLEL CURRICULUM: A UNIQUE CURRICULUM MODEL

What is a curriculum model? Why are there so many models to choose from? A curriculum model is a format for curriculum design that is developed to meet unique needs, contexts, goals, and purposes. To address specific goals and purposes, curriculum developers design or reconfigure one or more curriculum components (see Table I.1) to create their models. The Parallel Curriculum Model is unique because it is a set of four interrelated, yet parallel, designs for organizing curriculum: Core, Connections, Practice, and Identity.

Table I.1 Key Curriculum Components

Curriculum Component	Definition
Content	Knowledge, essential understandings, and skills students are to acquire
Assessment	Tools used to determine the extent to which students have acquired the content
Introduction	A precursor or forward to a lesson or unit
Teaching methods	Methods teachers use to introduce, explain, model, guide, or assess learning
Learning activities	Cognitive experiences that help students acquire, rehearse, store, transfer, and apply new knowledge and skills
Grouping strategies	The arrangement of students
Resources	Materials that support learning and teaching
Products	Performances or work samples that constitute evidence of student learning
Extension activities	Enrichment experiences that emerge from representative topics and students' interests
Differentiation based on learner need, including ascending levels of intellectual demand	Curriculum modifications that attend to students' need for escalating levels of knowledge, skills, and understanding
Lesson and unit closure	Reflection on the lesson to ensure that the point of the learning experience was achieved or a connection to the unit's learning goal was made

THE FOUR CURRICULUM PARALLELS

Let's look at these parallel designs through the eyes of Lydia Janis, a Grade 5 teacher who develops expertise in using the four parallels over several years. We will focus on one curriculum unit, Lydia's American Civil War unit, in order to illuminate how it transforms to accommodate the goals and purposes of each parallel. For the sake of our discussion, we treat each parallel as a separate unit. In reality, teachers use the parallels fluidly to address students' talent development needs. At the end of this summary, we will speak directly to when and how these parallels are used. Readers wishing for a more detailed analysis of Lydia's work are referred to Chapters 4 through 7 in both editions of *The Parallel Curriculum Model*.

The Core Curriculum

Lydia Janis sat at her kitchen table and looked over her textbook objectives for the American Civil War unit, as well as her state frameworks. She was troubled. She realized that the textbook objectives were low-level: They simply called for students to identify and describe facts, such as "Describe how the Civil War began," and "Identify the differences between the North and the South." Her frameworks, on the other hand, required different kinds of knowledge and understanding: "Explain reasons for conflicts and the ways conflicts have been resolved in history," and "Understand causal factors and appreciate change over time."

Lydia realized that the content embedded in her frameworks—concepts and principles—lay at the heart of history as a discipline. These key understandings were vastly more powerful, enduring, and essential to the discipline than the facts in the textbook objectives. She decided, however, to keep her textbook and use it as a resource. After all, the information was right there on her shelf, she was familiar with the content, and the topics covered were fairly well aligned with her state frameworks. But Lydia decided to replace the more simplistic objectives found in the text with the objectives found in the state frameworks.

Lydia realized that the change in *content* necessitated changes in other curriculum components. Her *assessments* needed to match the content. Her assessment tools needed to measure—both pre and post—students' conceptual understanding in addition to basic facts about the time period. Her *introduction* needed to be retooled in order to both prepare students for the various roles they would assume during the unit (as analyzers of documents, data, maps, and events) and to lead them to the powerful understandings she had targeted.

Lydia's *teaching methods* could no longer be strictly didactic, such as with lecture and direct instruction, but needed to be more inductive in order to support students as they constructed their own understanding of the time period. Her *learning activities* needed to invite students to think about and draw conclusions about maps, documents, and related data. In order to accomplish all of these things, Lydia supplemented the textbook with other *resources*, such as primary source documents, college textbooks, and the video series, *The Civil War*. She imagined that she would have students who wanted to pursue *extension activities*. She gathered a few books about the Underground Railroad, Abraham Lincoln, and strategic battles. Finally, because she already knew that her students were at different stages in their ability to understand materials and content, she gathered print materials that varied in complexity from song lyrics and easy-to-decipher documents to several dense primary source documents so that *all* students could work at ascending levels of intellectual demand.

Lydia also altered the *products* that students would be expected to create. In a variety of grouping arrangements, they would complete document analysis worksheets, ongoing concept maps, and timelines to chronicle their deepening understandings about conflict and the causal relationship of events that led up to the Civil War.

Lydia reflected on her work. She had made significant changes to her teaching and to the levels of student learning available, and she was confident in her improvements. She felt the power of the Core Curriculum as a foundational curriculum.

The Curriculum of Connections

Later in Lydia's career, she became aware of initiatives for interdisciplinary teaching. She was puzzled by some of the units that were labeled "interdisciplinary." A unit on Mexico, completed recently by fourth graders, came to mind. Students learned and performed the Mexican hat dance, held a fiesta—during which they broke a piñata and ate tacos, viewed a display of Mexican money, and drew maps of the migration route of monarch butterflies. "Yikes," she thought to herself, "this unit is an illusion. It *looks* integrated, but it lacks a powerful theme to tie the activities together!"

Lydia sat looking at the Core Curriculum unit on the Civil War that she had created a few years ago. She thought about the concept that earlier had focused her work: conflict. It reminded her that history repeats itself across people, time periods, and cultures, as seen in the Vietnam War, women's suffrage, the Civil Rights movement, and the civil war in Bosnia. This principle, "history repeats itself," held so much power. She realized that she could use the macroconcept of *conflict* and the generalization *history repeats itself* as the content centerpiece to help students build authentic and powerful bridges between their understanding of the American Civil War and other times, events, cultures, and people.

Lydia made preliminary plans for her Curriculum of Connections unit. She prepared some assessment prompts, with accompanying rubrics, to assess students' understanding of conflict and the idea that history repeats itself. She developed preassessment and essential questions for the introduction to clarify the focus for this unit: "What is a war? Do all conflicts have a resolution? Does history repeat itself?" She knew that her teaching strategies would need to help students make their own bridges for the connections between the American Civil War and other events and time periods. She decided to emphasize synectics, metaphorical thinking, Socratic questioning, problem-based learning, and debriefing. Her learning activities emphasized analytic thinking skills to help students in the comparisons and contrasts they needed to make and to encourage analogy making. Her supplemental resources were more varied and covered more events, cultures, and time periods than the resources she had used in her old Core unit, and the materials that she developed to scaffold student thinking included many more graphic organizers, such as Venn diagrams and reader-response questions. She was pleased when she realized that the products, grouping strategies, and extension activities would remain similar to those she had used in the Core Curriculum.

For students needing support with this unit, Lydia developed more detailed graphic organizers; for those needing increasing levels of ascending intellectual demand, she thought of several unfamiliar contexts to which students could apply their new learning, such as the conflict in Ireland and the significance of revolutionaries like Nelson Mandela and Elizabeth Cady Stanton. She tucked away these ideas for later use.

Lydia reflected on the modifications she had made. "This unit will benefit all of my students, especially my abstract thinkers, who value the 'big picture,' and my scholars," she thought. "It holds so much promise...much different than the Mexican Hat Dance unit," she mused.

The Curriculum of Practice

That summer, Lydia realized she could polish the same unit even more. Even though she had seen her students engaged and learning deeply about the Civil War, she began thinking more about how talent develops—specifically, how students become acquainted with and skillful in the use of methodologies. "Now that students have the important ideas within and across disciplines, they need to learn how to act like a practitioner," she thought to herself.

So began Lydia's journey through the Curriculum of Practice. She sought out her state and national frameworks to identify the standards related to the role of the historian. To address them, she decided to invite students to read historical novels set during the mid 1800s and to record the characters' feelings, images, and perspectives, as well as to note how they changed throughout the story. Second, she decided to try to deepen students' understandings of these historical perspectives by asking them to read related primary source documents and find evidence to support the characters' feelings and attitudes.

For students to complete these tasks, she decided to focus her teaching on the skills of the historian: the steps of historical research, taking notes, determining bias, and analyzing point of view, to name a few. She decided to demonstrate or model these skills for students and then use more indirect teaching methods, such as Socratic questioning, to help students construct their own analyses of primary source material. To help students focus on the methodology of the field, she decided to invite a local museum curator to take part in the introduction of the unit.

Lydia subsequently decided to scaffold students' work with a learning contract. The learning contract required specific learning activities and also asked students to complete several short-term products and a culminating project, their historical research. Lydia provided them with a rubric to guide and assess their final work. Lydia knew her grouping formats needed to be fluid in order to honor students' interests and acknowledge that there were times when students needed to work alone or in pairs. This fluidity would be especially important if students elected to complete extension activities around self-selected research questions.

To accommodate students with sophisticated knowledge about the historical research process, Lydia prepared a list of more complex research topics that required ascending levels of intellectual demand, such as inviting advanced students to conduct oral histories on a topic of their choice.

Lydia reviewed the lessons that now reflected the Curriculum of Practice. "Wow," she thought. "So far, I have three ways to optimize learning." Lydia compared and contrasted the three sets of revisions to the Civil War unit: Core, Connections, and

Practice. "Each approach is unique and powerful," she thought. And she understood why teaching artful curriculum was a satisfying, career-long journey. "What will I discover next?" she wondered.

The Curriculum of Identity

It was a student who set Lydia on her next journey through the PCM. His name was Jacob, and she was amazed at his knowledge of American history. She envisioned this boy as a history professor, immersed in his own research about historical topics and mentoring others as they investigated questions not yet answered.

She spent time thinking about how she could morph her curriculum once more. The content for any Identity unit has a triple focus: her already rich Core Curriculum; the ideas, attitudes, beliefs, dispositions, and life outlooks of a professional; and the learning profile of each student, including his or her interests, learning style preferences, values, and goals. Her task, she thought, would be to increase students' awareness about the degree of fit between their own emerging sense of self and the profile of practitioners in the field.

Lydia developed a survey of her students' abilities, interests, grouping preferences, goals, and co-curricular activities. Next, she sketched out the stages that students might go through as they went from an early awareness of and interest in history to self-actualization *through* the discipline. "This tool will help me identify where each student currently is on this continuum so I can support his or her progress," she thought.

Now familiar with the many teaching strategies available, Lydia selected visualization as an important method because students would have to move back and forth between their past self, current self, and future self. She also knew that she would use problem-based learning, simulations, and coaching to help students come to understand their place in the Civil War unit as they acted as historians, authors of historical fiction, or war correspondents.

She envisioned her students in varied grouping formats as they spent time with learning activities that required self-analysis and reflection, prediction, and goal setting, among others. Ideas for products came easily to Lydia: completed learning profiles, responses to prompts that asked students to reflect upon and note patterns in their changing profiles, and responses to prompts that invited students to reflect upon the fit between themselves and those of the guest speakers (i.e., a local historian and journalist), who would take part in the introduction to the unit.

Lydia anticipated several extension activities, including explorations about notable leaders from the 1860s, as well as less well-known figures, such as the girls who dressed and fought as soldiers during the Civil War. As she gathered resources to support this unit and its potential extensions, she made sure that her collection featured a variety of introspective materials that would help students understand the beliefs, values, goals, achievements, and sacrifices made by practitioners and would enable students' comparisons between their own emerging beliefs and attitudes and those of the professionals.

Lydia reflected on her continuing journey with the Parallel Curriculum Model. Her journey elicited a clarity that comes only with time and persistence. She now deeply understood the model's power and promise. It held the power to awaken and support a teacher's passion and focused creativity. Equally important, it held such promise for uncovering and supporting the gifts and talents of *all* students.

Lydia imagined each of her students as a diamond (see Figure I.1). The model's four parallels—Core, Connections, Practice, and Identity—served as unique polishing tools to reveal the brilliance in each young person. The Core fostered deep understanding in a discipline, while Connections elicited the metaphoric thinking required to span the breadth of humankind's knowledge. Practice advanced the methodological skills required to contribute in a field, and Identity cultivated the attitudes, values, and life outlook that are prerequisites to self-actualization in any field.

Figure I.1 Lydia's View of the PCM

Reprinted from *Teaching for High Potential* (Vol. IV, No. 1, April 2002), published by the National Association for Gifted Children, Washington, DC. www.nagc.org

THE FOUR PARALLELS: WHEN AND HOW

We began this article by talking about seven blind men, their limited perceptions about an elephant, and their ultimate realization that "Knowing in part may make a fine tale, but wisdom comes from seeing the whole." Lydia's work with each of the parallels illustrates how different curriculum components can be modified to help students gain an understanding and appreciation for the whole of a particular discipline.

There are an infinite number of ways to draw upon the parallels. They can be used to *revise* or *design* tasks, lessons, or units. With a revised or designed unit in hand, a teacher can move back and forth across one, some, or all parallels in a single unit. Equally attractive, a teacher might use just one parallel to extend a Core unit.

Various individuals within a school can use the parallels differently. A classroom teacher can use the parallels separately for different purposes, or teachers can work collectively—within grade levels or across grade levels and subjects—to use the parallels to support the learning for all, some, or a few students. Furthermore, classroom teachers can use the parallels to modify learning opportunities for students who need something beyond the grade-level curriculum.

What is the driving force behind decisions about when and how to use the parallels? Decisions stem from teacher expertise, the learning goals, and, most important, the students themselves. We draw upon the parallels to make curriculum more meaningful, emotive, powerful, engaging, and more likely to advance energetically the abilities and talents of students.

The PCM holds the power to help students and teachers see the whole of what they are learning. It is our hope that curriculum based upon this model will optimize student learning and enhance the likelihood that all students will lead productive and fulfilling lives. We invite practitioners to read more about this model and to join us on a professional journey that we believe will yield that joy and wisdom that comes from seeing the whole. The possibilities are limitless.

THE FORMAT

The curriculum books that are part of our latest initiative share four features that will provide common threads to readers as they transition among the publications. First, each unit contains a section called "Background Information" that provides readers with a snapshot of the lessons or unit. If a series of lessons are provided—instead of a whole unit of study—the author may suggest ways to incorporate the subset of lessons into a larger unit. The author may also identify the parallel(s) he or she has elected to emphasize and his or her rationale for highlighting the Curriculum of Connections, Core, the parallel of Practice, and/or Identity. Authors may share their experiences regarding the best time to teach the unit, such as the beginning of the year or well into the last half of the year. Finally, the author may share what students are expected to know before the unit is taught, as well as resources that would support the teaching and learning activities.

The second common element is the "Content Framework." One of the nonnegotiables of PCM units is that they lead students explicitly to a conceptual understanding of the topics and disciplines on which they are based. Thus, each set of lessons or unit contains a list of concepts, skills, and principles that drive the teaching and learning activities. We also included the national standards addressed in each unit and lesson.

"Unit Assessments" is the third common feature. Within this section, authors have the opportunity to describe the assessments that are included within their lessons. Some authors, especially those who supplied an entire unit of study, included preassessments that align with a performance-based postassessment. All authors have included formative assessments. Naturally, scoring rubrics are included with these assessments. In many cases, authors describe the nature of students' misconceptions that surface when these performance measures are used, as well as some tips on how to address students' mistaken beliefs.

The final common element is the *two-column format* for organizing the lessons. In the left-hand column, authors sequence the instruction in a step-by-step manner. In the right-hand column, readers will hear the author's voice as he or she "thinks out loud" about the introduction, teaching and learning activities, and closure. Authors provide many different kinds of information in the right-hand column, including, for example, teaching tips, information about student misconceptions, and suggestions on how to differentiate for above grade-level or below grade-level students.

OUR INVITATION...

We invite you to peruse and implement these curriculum lessons and units. We believe the use of these lessons will be enhanced to the extent that you do the following:

- **Study PCM.** Read the original book and the other companion volumes, including *The Parallel Curriculum in the Classroom: Units for Application Across the Content Areas, K–12*; *The Parallel Curriculum in the Classroom: Essays for Application Across the Content Areas, K–12*; and *The Parallel Curriculum Multimedia Kit*. By studying the model in depth, teachers and administrators will have a clear sense of its goals and purposes.
- **Join us on our continuing journey to refine these curriculum units.** We know better than to suggest that these units are scripts for total success in the classroom. They are, at best, our most thoughtful thinking to date. They are solid evidence that we need to persevere. In small collaborative and reflective teams of practitioners, we invite you to field-test these units and make your own refinements.
- **Raise questions about curriculum materials.** Provocative, compelling, and pioneering questions about the quality of curriculum material—and their incumbent learning opportunities—are absolutely essential. Persistent and thoughtful questioning will lead us to the development of strenuous learning opportunities that will contribute to our students' life-long success in the 21st century.
- **Compare the units with material developed using other curriculum models.** Through such comparisons, we are better able to make decisions about the use of the model and its related curriculum materials for addressing the unique needs of diverse learners.

THE HISTORY BOOK INTRO SEGMENT, GRADES 6–12

This volume contains four units. The first unit was created by Heather Burke for students in Grade 6, and it is called *Becoming a Geographer*. Highlighting the Core Curriculum and the Curriculum of Practice, it is a set of four lessons that will take approximately 14 hours. Lesson 1, "Climate and Seasons," is designed to help students investigate earth's movement. Lesson 2 focuses on demographics and provides students with opportunities to explore how the terrain of a location affects the people that live in that area. Lesson 3, also highly interactive, invites students to explore the relationship between natural resources and people's wants and needs. The final lesson is designed to focus on the connection between geography and culture.

The second unit, *Through the Looking Glass*, was created by Dawn Vier and Lisa L. Ward for their middle school students who are served in intervention classes. This interdisciplinary reading/writing/social studies unit provides an in-depth analysis of the concept of identity through an examination of self, community, our nation, and the world. The semester-long unit encompasses all four parallels seamlessly, while providing direct reading and writing instruction and scaffolding in order to meet student goals. A multisensory approach to using resources is provided for our diverse learners, including short stories, videos, poetry, music, novels, articles, and picture books.

The third unit, *Subversion and Controversy: Sociological Considerations of Humor* was created by Kelly M. Dausel for students in Grades 7 or 8. The series of five integrated lessons focus on the Curriculum of Practice and the Curriculum of Identity. Students are provided with opportunities to learn common forms of humor and examine literature and video samples through the lens of a sociologist, considering the function, scope, and limitations of humor used in society. The lessons within this unit extend the students' use of the skills of inference and drawing conclusions about how literature reflects the role of humor in society, as well as the ways it, in turn, can influence an audience. In the research module of this unit, students study an aspect of humor in society by applying the methodologies used by sociologists to carry out their own studies.

The final unit, by Catherine Little, *True Story-Telling: How Historians Construct the Past*, is created for high school sophomores. The five lessons that comprise this unit focus on the work of the historian and on some of the considerations of context that influence history, including observation, interpretation, and perspective. All the lessons use the lens of the Progressive Era in American history as the context for exploring how the concept of historical significance emerges over time. *True Story-Telling* is a Core Curriculum unit because it emphasizes concepts and analysis skills that are central to history standards and the work of the professional historian. Clearly, this unit illuminates a strong link between the Core Curriculum and the Curriculum of Practice. The unit also addresses the parallel of Identity because it requires each student to use their personal experiences to claim their own place and role in making, interpreting, and recording history.

1

Becoming a Geographer

Grade 6

Heather Burke

BACKGROUND INFORMATION

Learning takes place only when there is a base of prior knowledge from which to build. It will be necessary for students to have certain foundational skills in order to attain success with this unit. A general knowledge of map reading and construction is assumed. Students should understand cardinal directions, scale, and the purpose of a map key. Knowledge of simple geography ideas, such as continents, countries, and lines of latitude and longitude, will also aid in student learning. The idea that maps can serve multiple purposes, such as displaying population, climate, and elevation, is a helpful concept for students to comprehend, yet is not necessary to ensure success while completing the unit.

When teaching this unit, it will be necessary for students to have access to an atlas appropriate to Grade 6 students. In addition to being grade-level appropriate, the atlas should include climate, population, economic, and natural resource maps as they are all dealt with during the unit. Computers with Internet access would be helpful because the students will conduct several independent research activities. If the students have not had much experience conducting research on the Internet, it may be necessary to conduct several brief mini-lessons about responsible use and how to evaluate Internet Web sites for quality and validity. The teacher should provide students with other tools and materials (e.g., clay, paints, poster paper) that will allow students to be highly creative and productive during classroom sessions.

A learning journal will also be an effective tool for the students to have while implementing this unit. The journal, as an organizational tool, will provide students with a place to record ideas, respond to guiding or prompting questions, reflect on their learning, and complete classroom assignments. The learning journal also affords the teacher the opportunity to measure student growth during the course of the unit and throughout the school year, and it also gives the teacher the occasion to correspond with her students on a one-on-one basis through writing. Learning journals, also called *learning logs*, achieve these goals across subject areas.

CONTENT FRAMEWORK

Organizing Concepts

Macroconcept(s)	*Discipline-Specific Concepts*	*Principles*
M1: Relationships	C1: Geography	P1: Geography is the study of the Earth's surface, climate, continents, countries, people, industries, and projects.
	C2: Economics	P2: The study of geography extends into the fields of science, economics, and cultures.
	C3: Cultures	P3: The Earth's climate depends upon its movement in space.
	C4: Climate	P4: The Earth's climate varies.
	C5: Rotation	P5: Climate affects the culture and economy of a place.
	C6: Revolution	P6: The geography of a place affects the population.
	C7: Axis	P7: The population of a place affects the economy and culture.
	C8: Population	P8: Wants and needs can be fulfilled in a variety of ways.
	C9: Demography	P9: The resources available in a particular area determine the types of goods produced.
	C10: Increase and decrease	P10: Geography has an impact on culture.
	C11: Natural resources	P11: Cultures vary around the world.
	C12: Wants	P12: Examining geography and culture helps us to understand a place.
	C13: Needs	
	C14: Goods	
	C15: Culture	
	C16: Language	
	C17: Religion	
	C18: Traditions	

Skills

S1: Make connections
S2: Reason deductively
S3: Determine cause and effect
S4: Develop hypotheses
S5: Analyze and interpret information/data
S6: Compare and contrast
S7: Read
S8: Infer
S9: Summarize

National Standards

SD1: Understands the characteristics and uses of maps, globes, and other geographic tools and technologies

Benchmark: Understands concepts such as axis, seasons, rotation, and revolution (Earth-Sun relations)

SD2: Understands the nature, distribution, and migration of human populations on Earth's surface

Benchmark: Understands demographic concepts and how they are used to describe population characteristics of a country or region (e.g., rates of natural increase, crude birth and death rates, infant mortality, population growth rates, doubling time, life expectancy, average family size)

SD3: Understands the physical and human characteristics of place

Benchmark: Knows the human characteristics of places (e.g., cultural characteristics such as religion, language, politics, technology, family structure, gender; population characteristics; land uses; levels of development)

UNIT ASSESSMENTS

Formative Assessments

A variety of formative assessments are included in the four lessons contained in this chapter. Student performances during classroom discussions and lesson activities provide the teacher with rich information that can be used to determine mastery of lesson and unit concepts, principles, and skills. References to formal and informal formative assessments are made throughout the lessons. Equally important, suggestions are provided about how to differentiate instruction based upon the data that has been collected.

In addition, multilevel rubrics that address several of the unit objectives accompany student assignments. The rubrics not only ensure that students are aware of the expectations of the assignments, but also serve as a tool to help the classroom teacher pinpoint the following: (1) where students already possess the required declarative and procedural knowledge and (2) gaps in the prerequisite declarative and procedural knowledge.

OVERVIEW OF THE UNIT

The four lessons highlighted in this collection come from a larger unit designed to be completed in approximately 14 hours. The entire unit focuses on all aspects of geography, beginning with an in-depth investigation of the "five principles of geography." Concepts such as the theory of plate tectonics, renewable and nonrenewable resources, using latitude and longitude to determine location, landforms, and layers of the earth are investigated. Lessons focusing on the relationships between geography and other disciplines are detailed in greater depth across all the learning activities.

This collection of four lessons focuses on climate, demographics, resources, and culture. Lesson 1, "Climate and Seasons," provides students with interactive learning opportunities to investigate Earth's movement (i.e., rotation and revolution) and how it influences world climates. Lesson 2, "Investigating World Populations," focuses on demographics and the principle that climate and physical terrain affect where people live. "Shop Around the Globe," Lesson 3, invites students to explore the connection between natural resources and peoples' wants and needs. Finally, Lesson 4, "The Culture of Geography," offers students the opportunity to investigate the connection between geography and culture.

This collection of four lessons not only focuses on the Core Curriculum, but also the Connections and Practice parallels. They allow the teacher to make decisions based on the needs of the students. The lessons provide the opportunity for the teacher to challenge all students by using interest-based projects, flexible grouping, and peer coaching.

LESSON 1: CLIMATE AND SEASONS (2 HOURS)

Concepts

C4: Climate
C5: Rotation
C6: Revolution
C7: Axis

Principles

P3: The Earth's climate depends upon its movement in space.
P4: The Earth's climate varies.
P5: Climate affects the culture and economy of a place.

Skills

S4: Develop hypotheses
S5: Analyze and interpret information

Standards

SD1: Understands the characteristics and uses of maps, globes, and other geographic tools and technologies
Benchmark: Understands concepts such as axis, seasons, rotation, and revolution (Earth-Sun relations)

Guiding Questions

- How does Earth's movement affect our climate?
- Why does Earth experience seasonal change?
- How are day and night determined?

Unit Sequence	Teacher Reflections
Introduction	
Explain to students that the subjects they study are not separate. They overlap each other, and during these next several lessons, they will be exploring some of these relationships. Explain that during this lesson they will be investigating the connection between geography and science.	*Students may have difficulty with the idea of relationships between the areas they study. In an effort to clarify this idea for students, I asked students to brainstorm some instances where the subjects overlapped. Offer some suggestions, such as reading a book during math, science, or a social studies class.*
Distribute several Post-it notes to each student, and write the term *climate* for students to view on a piece of chart paper or poster board. Ask the students to write words or ideas on their Post-it notes that come to mind when they think about the word *climate*. Ask students to write one idea or word on each note. Allow students several minutes to complete this activity and then ask students to place their Post-it notes around the term *climate* that has been written on the chart paper or poster board. The teacher should then walk the students through the grouping of the ideas the students contributed into a type of concept map. Add subcategories as you find related terms and ideas.	*This introductory activity is meant to elicit students' prior knowledge concerning the concept of climate. This activity will achieve its desired purpose if students are encouraged to discuss their ideas with a partner. I discovered several students discussing their ideas as I was moving around the classroom. My first reaction was to stress that this was an independent assignment. Yet as I listened to their brief conversations, I found that they were meaningful, focused, and added to student interest in the topic. I found it helpful to provide students with some prompting questions to stimulate the thought process.* *Students may have misconceptions about climate, yet this will provide an opportunity to modify the concept web at the conclusion of the lesson. In the interest of student motivation, I allowed these misconceptions to remain on the concept map and used them as an opportunity to check for student understanding at the conclusion of the lesson.*
Teaching Strategies and Learning Experiences	
Seasons Ask students what their lives would be like if we did not experience the seasons. For example, ask how would they feel if the temperatures were cold or warm all of the time. Allow them several minutes to discuss this with a small group or a partner. Share the students' responses as a whole class. Next, ask students why we experience seasons and allow them to discuss this with peers. Follow with a whole-class discussion and record student ideas on chart paper.	**Connections Parallel** *These questions allow students to connect their lives with the concepts in the lesson and teachers to gauge student knowledge in the area.* *Student discussions were very animated; most concluded that they enjoyed the seasons because they provided them with variety and kept them from getting bored of the warm or cold weather.* *After the whole-class discussion about the reason for the seasons, I made a mental note that a group of six students had a much deeper understanding of the concepts. These students were advanced learners and prime candidates for differentiation. Based upon my new knowledge of their advanced learning needs, I built differentiation into the remaining lessons.*

(Continued)

(Continued)

Unit Sequence	Teacher Reflections
Display two pictures of the Earth, one with the Earth on its axis and the other showing the Earth without the tilt. Ask students which picture is accurate. Engage students in a discussion of Earth's axis. Darken the room and have students work in small groups. Direct the students to shine a flashlight directly on a white piece of paper and then trace the circle formed by the light with a marker. Without moving the flashlight, ask students to slightly tilt the white paper away from the flashlight and trace this area with a different color marker. Ask the groups to engage in a discussion about the differences or similarities between the two shapes and their relationship to the sun's light shining on the earth. Ask students to answer the following questions in their small groups: 1. Which shape made by the flashlight demonstrates the way sun shines on the earth in the summer? How do you know? 2. Which shape made by the flashlight shows the way the sun shines on the earth in the winter? How do you know?	*Prior to conducting this experiment, I asked students why they believed the places on earth experienced seasons. I asked them to record this information in a learning journal. I engaged students in a discussion of the scientific process and stated that they had just formed a hypothesis, further stressing the connection with science. The students made several comments referring to how they formed hypotheses on a regular basis and did not make the connection.*
Place a model of the sun in the center of an oval created by the seated students. Explain to the students that the oval represents Earth's elliptical orbit around the sun. Ask one student to sit in the center of the oval with a flashlight. Explain to the students that they will be passing a globe around the oval to represent Earth's journey around the sun. As students are passing the globe around the oval, draw students' attention to the parts of the globe that are getting the most direct sunlight and the least direct sunlight. Following this simulation, ask students to draw a diagram showing the sun and the Earth during the different seasons.	*This simulation directly addresses the national standard dealing with understanding axis, seasons, rotation, and revolution. In designing the simulation, I wanted the students to be part of the demonstration and not just bystanders. With each movement of the globe, students are able to see which portions of the Earth receive the most direct rays of light and why the Earth experiences seasons. It also provides students with the opportunity to ask questions, make comments, and engage in discussions.*

Unit Sequence	Teacher Reflections
Differentiation: Invite students demonstrating understanding in this area to explore another activity while these simulations are taking place. Ask students to develop a 12-page calendar detailing the seasons in various places on the Earth. Provide atlases, the Internet, and various other resources to the students. **Climate** Distribute a climate map of the world to small groups of students. Ask groups to develop a definition of climate from looking at the map. Allow groups to share their definition and develop a working definition that combines elements of all groups' ideas. Ensure that students are able to read the climate map by moving from group to group or student to student while they are working on the preceding task and asking map reading questions such as the following: - What area of the world experiences a tropical wet climate? - What is the climate of Australia? - What is the climate type where you live? - What area of the world experiences subarctic climate? *Differentiation*: Place students who display inadequate map-reading skills in a small group. Provide a mini-lesson in which map-reading skills are covered. Once the students are familiar with the term *climate* and the reading of a map, ask students if they understand the terms present on the climate map: *semiarid, Mediterranean, humid subtropical*. Most students will not have much background knowledge of these terms. Divide students into small groups, assign them a climate type to research, and then teach the class. Students can choose the ways in which to display the information they have learned.	*I wanted the students with more advanced levels of prior knowledge to learn more about the seasons than why the seasons exist. The assignment gave students the occasion to conduct independent research and to compare and contrast different places in the world by looking at the season they experience. The students may not have the amount of time necessary to complete this activity, yet if they have time available throughout their day, it can be used constructively, or this activity can be used as a school/home connection assignment.* *I have found that simply giving the students the definition of a term has much less impact than asking them to draw conclusions and develop their own ideas about concepts. Even though students may develop misconceptions during the initial phase of the activity, sharing the groups' ideas as a whole class and writing a whole class shared definition will aid in eliminating those misconceptions.* *The small group interactions provided me with a great deal of information. Identifying students who required additional instruction made the learning experiences that followed more meaningful because students had the prior knowledge necessary to build new knowledge.*

(Continued)

(Continued)

Unit Sequence	Teacher Reflections
Using the jigsaw approach, have students form new groups with one climate type in each group in order to present their findings and teach their classmates.	*This jigsaw activity is very motivating for students because it allows them to do the teaching. I have also found that limiting the number of requirements actually promotes student creativity and interest. The activity lends itself to differentiation because the teacher can control student grouping. I find it useful and interesting to group advanced learners with students who would benefit from a bit of guidance in order to promote growth and intellectual development. I refer here to Vygotsky's idea of a "knowledgeable other" to guide students as they work within their zone of proximal development. The teacher also has the opportunity to group students who might benefit from small group instruction together in order to complete the assignment with the assistance of the teacher or other adults, while enhancing their confidence by having the chance to teach the other students in the class.*
Introduce the climate project that students will engage in over the next several lessons. (Please see the following three attachments that are included with this lesson and support this assignment: "Climate Map Project," "Become a Climate Expert," and "Become a Climate Expert Rubric.") Explain that they will be looking in more depth at different parts of the world, compiling information about these places, and determining the best way to convey the information learned. The project asks students to choose four different locations in the world to complete the requirement. Explain that they will be designing several different maps and gathering data to draw conclusions. For this section of the assignment, they will only be researching the climate. The students will be required to design a climate map that details the climate for each place that is researched. The students should include not only the place they researched, but also major surrounding cities and countries.	*I designed this multiple lesson project to address several standards, principles, concepts, and skills throughout the unit. This portion of the project addresses the principle concerning the various climates present on earth.* *I found it important to be forceful when I suggested that students choose four different climate types. This ensured that the learning they did in this and future lessons had the greatest impact.* *These questions serve the purpose of connecting the learning students have already done with the future direction of the lessons while preparing students for the learning they will be doing.*

Unit Sequence	Teacher Reflections
As students complete their maps, display the following questions and ask students to respond in their learning journals: • How might the climate of a place influence the number of people who live there? • Given the climate of a place, what might people do to earn money? • How might the climate of a place affect the things that grow there?	
Closure	
Revisit the Post-it note concept map made during the introduction. Ask students to sit close to the concept map and to examine it to see if they would like to make any changes. Encourage students to regroup, make new subcategories, modify or eliminate any inaccurate information, and add to the web.	*This closure activity allowed students to engage in their learning and truly see what they had learned throughout the lesson.* *At first, the students were a bit hesitant because they did not want to refute an idea a classmate contributed earlier in the lesson. I sensed this, and we had a brief discussion concerning the purpose of developing a concept map prior to learning about something and how revisiting it after the lesson helps us to examine the learning that has been done. Following this discussion, several students were brave and made some changes and additions to the concept web. The rest of the class followed their lead, and the concept map was revised with great success and amazing discussions amongst classmates.*
Engage students in a discussion based on the premise that geography and science are connected. Ask students guiding questions such as the following: • What did we discover about the relationship between geography and science? • Why is this relationship important for us to understand? • How does this relationship help us develop a deeper understanding of the subjects? • How does what we learned apply to our lives?	*This discussion is a necessary element to bridge the purpose of the unit design, the lesson introduction, and the lesson closure. The purpose of designing the unit was so students could see these relationships.* *The students were quickly able to see the connection between the subject areas. Following the discussion, I asked students to respond to some of these questions in their learning journals. This element enhanced the students' responses and demonstrated student motivation and understanding.*

CLIMATE MAP PROJECT

- Choose four locations in the world that you would like to research.

- Research these locations using an atlas and/or the Internet.

- Design a climate map for each location.

- The map for each location must include surrounding cities and countries.

- Each map must include the following:
  o title
  o labels
  o key with symbols
  o scale

- Upon completing your maps, answer the following questions in your learning journal:
  o How may the climate of a place influence the number of people who live there?
  o Given the climate of a place, what may people do to earn money?
  o How may the climate of a place affect the things that grow there?

Copyright © 2010 by Corwin. All rights reserved. Reprinted from *Parallel Curriculum Units for Social Studies, Grades 6–12*, edited by Jeanne H. Purcell and Jann H. Leppien. Thousand Oaks, CA: Corwin, www.corwinpress.com. Reproduction authorized only for the local school site or nonprofit organization that has purchased this book.

BECOME A CLIMATE EXPERT

Your group will research a climate type. Learn all you can about this climate, including the following:

- the characteristics of this climate (precipitation, average temperature, etc.)
- which plants grow in this climate
- what animals inhabit areas with this climate
- countries or areas of the world with this climate

You will teach your fellow classmates about your assigned climate; therefore, it is important that each group member becomes an expert. Follow the directions below to help prepare yourself for your expert presentation.

1. Research the climate type assigned to your group using some of the following resources:
    - http://www.blueplanetbiomes.org/climate.htm
    - http://www.physicalgeography.net/fundamentals/7v.html
    - http://www.uwsp.edu/geo/faculty/ritter/geog101/uwsp_lectures/climates_toc.html
    - http://www.mapsofworld.com/world-maps/world-climate-map.html

   These sites will not provide you with all of the information necessary to complete this assignment. You will need to do additional research using nonfiction texts and other Web sites.

2. Each group member is responsible for designing a presentation to share the knowledge gained through your research with your classmates. You may choose to present your information in any way you see appropriate. Be creative! Suggestions include the following:
    - a poster
    - PowerPoint presentation
    - overhead transparencies

3. Present the information you learned about the climate you researched and learn about the other climate types from your classmates in your assigned jigsaw group. The information you learn from them will be important for future activities, so be an active listener!

Copyright © 2010 by Corwin. All rights reserved. Reprinted from *Parallel Curriculum Units for Social Studies, Grades 6–12*, edited by Jeanne H. Purcell and Jann H. Leppien. Thousand Oaks, CA: Corwin, www.corwinpress.com. Reproduction authorized only for the local school site or nonprofit organization that has purchased this book.

BECOME A CLIMATE EXPERT RUBRIC

Become a Climate Expert Rubric

Criteria	4	3	2	1
Content	Accurately identifies the characteristics of the assigned climate type, including average temperature, precipitation, plants, and animal life.	Adequately identifies the characteristics of the assigned climate type, including three of the four components described in the column to the left.	Incompletely identifies the characteristics of the assigned climate type, including two of the four components described in the column to the left.	Inaccurately identifies the characteristics of the assigned climate type, including one or fewer of the four components described in the column to the left.
Group work	Each group member has a clear understanding of their responsibilities and actively participates in group discussions and research activities.	Each group member has a general understanding of their responsibilities and participates in group discussions and research activities.	Some members of the group have a general understanding of their responsibilities and participate in group discussions and research activities occasionally.	Group members are not aware of their responsibilities and frequently hesitate to participate in group discussions or research activities.
Presentation	Each group member designs a creative presentation that includes all the necessary content to teach classmates about the assigned climate type.	Each group member designs a clear presentation that includes most of the necessary content to teach classmates about the assigned climate type.	Group members design a basic presentation that includes some of the necessary content to teach classmates about the assigned climate type.	The group presentation needs additional work to ensure clarity and comprehensive content.

Copyright © 2010 by Corwin. All rights reserved. Reprinted from *Parallel Curriculum Units for Social Studies, Grades 6–12*, edited by Jeanne H. Purcell and Jann H. Leppien. Thousand Oaks, CA: Corwin, www.corwinpress.com. Reproduction authorized only for the local school site or nonprofit organization that has purchased this book.

LESSON 2: INVESTIGATING WORLD POPULATIONS (4–5 HOURS)

Concepts

C8: Population
C9: Demography
C10: Increase and decrease

Principles

P6: The geography of a place affects the population.
P7: The population of a place affects the economy and culture.

Skills

S5: Analyze and interpret information/data
S1: Make connections
S2: Reason deductively
S3: Determine cause and effect

Standards

SD2: Understands the nature, distribution, and migration of human populations on Earth's surface

Benchmark: Understands demographic concepts and how they are used to describe population characteristics of a country or region (e.g., rates of natural increase, crude birth and death rates, infant mortality, population growth rates, doubling time, life expectancy, average family size)

Guiding Questions

- What factors cause large populations in some parts of the world?
- How does climate and physical terrain affect where people live?
- How does the geography of a place satisfy the needs of the people who inhabit it?

Unit Sequence	Teacher Reflections
Introduction	
Explain to the students that during the previous lesson they examined the relationship between geography and science, and during this lesson, they will be exploring the connection between geography and math. Ask students to predict ways in which geography and math may go hand in hand.	*The idea of relationships is central to this unit. I found it necessary to highlight this relationship prior to beginning the lesson to keep the students focused on the main purpose of the unit. By asking the students to predict the relationship between math and geography, I was hoping they would begin to understand ways to make these types of connections.*
Conduct a class discussion to determine if any students have ever moved residences. Ask those students who have moved to volunteer the reasons for their moves, and	*The aim of this discussion is to allow students to make a personal connection with the lesson concepts and to begin to introduce the idea that people populate certain areas for specific reasons.*

(Continued)

(Continued)

Unit Sequence	Teacher Reflections
record this information on a piece of chart paper. Ask all students to brainstorm additional reasons that people move from place to place. Record the responses as well.	

Teaching Strategies and Learning Experiences	
Explain to the students that they will be working in small groups, and write the term *population* for all to see. Provide each group with a sentence strip or long piece of paper. Ask each group to write a rational sentence that includes the word *population* on the sentence strip. Provide several minutes for the groups to devise the sentence. Post each group's contribution for all to see. As a whole class, read each sentence and lead students in a discussion to develop a preliminary understanding of population. Explain that the following learning activities will focus on expanding their knowledge of population and its importance in the world.	*This learning activity is a variation of the "possible sentences" vocabulary strategy. It asks the students to devise a sentence around a term with which they have little or no familiarity in the hope that they will be able to make meaning through the context and teacher guidance. Unless students have previous background knowledge surrounding the concept, they are not expected to make meaning of the word through this activity. The sentences will be revisited and revised at the end of the lesson. Examining the sentences at the lesson's conclusion will aid in demonstrating student learning and growth through the following learning activities.*
Population Distribution	
Differentiation: Differentiate the following learning activity by dividing the students into smaller groups based on prior knowledge. Provide one group of students who are at or above grade-level expectations with world population maps. Provide another group of students who are at or below grade-level expectation with United States population maps. Prior to the lesson, decide which students will be receiving the world or U.S. maps and distribute them accordingly. The students can complete this activity independently or with a partner. Explain to the students that the maps that they have in front of them are population maps and show where people live. Review the map key and features of the maps. Write the following questions on a piece of chart paper. Students should record their answers in their learning journals.	*I intended that the learning activity would address the portion of the national standard on distribution of human populations and encourage students to engage in higher-level thinking skills. By differentiating the maps, the teacher can challenge students who excel in this area and nurture those who are not adept at thinking on this level.* *I found that the world map did provide a challenge for the students. Some students were overwhelmed by the challenge. I asked these students to first draw some conclusions using the United States map and some teacher assistance. To build on the learning they achieved, I then asked them to go back to the world map and make another attempt. Many of the students that I originally assigned the United States map still had a great deal of difficulty. I used this as an opportunity to conduct a small group and directly guide the students in answering the questions and drawing the conclusions.*

Unit Sequence	Teacher Reflections
• What are some areas with the highest population? • What do these places have in common? • What are some areas with low populations? • What do these places have in common? • What landforms are present near places with a high or low population? • Refer to a climate map. Do you notice a connection between climate and population? What do you think this means? Upon completion, divide students into groups based on the maps they investigated. Ask students to share the conclusions they drew from this investigation. **Demographics** Prior to teaching this lesson, it is necessary to compile demographic information on your town/city and state and surrounding towns/cities and states. The census Web site (www.census.gov) is a useful site that provides this information. Display and explain population-growth data for your town or city. Using Microsoft Excel, make a bar and line graph that shows the population increases. Ask students to explain why graphing this information is helpful. Display the data of the surrounding towns or cities, and ask students to compare this to the data from their town. Graph this information using Microsoft Excel. Ask students why the populations in some towns/cities are larger or smaller than their town. Display a political map of your state. Ask students to examine the comparison graphs and try to make a connection between the information on the political map and the population data. Repeat this process comparing the state in which you reside with states in other parts of the country. Stress that a majority of	*I wanted the students to share their findings simply because there was so much they could have learned from these maps. I wanted them to achieve higher levels of understanding by interacting with their peers.* *I designed this learning activity to address the Grades 6 through 8 benchmark corresponding to the national standard. I chose to use a more direct approach to teaching the concepts and skills coinciding with the standard since students had never previously examined or analyzed demographic information. I highlighted the connections between the population of a place and the area, the proximity to a large city, or the presence of a particular landform that promotes or deters people from settling there. I also wanted to take the opportunity to model how to design a graph using Microsoft Excel. The students will be asked to use this program to make similar graphs to display data with reference to the four places they examined earlier in this lesson.*

(Continued)

(Continued)

Unit Sequence	Teacher Reflections
the U.S. population resides in the east (with the exception of California), even though Midwest and western states are larger. Ask students to make a connection between landforms and population.	
Provide small groups of students with demographic data regarding several states in the United States, such as life expectancy rates, birth rates, and family size. Ask the students to graph this information using an appropriate graph type.	*Differentiation:* In designing this activity, I saw it as steps toward independence. The previous section of this lesson was teacher directed; in this portion, the students had a support system in the form of a small group. In the final activity, they will independently apply what they have learned. Yet the ability to differentiate is present. I was available to assist and reteach with a small group of students who were having a great deal of difficulty. I also compiled some demographic data that was more difficult to interpret for students who displayed important learner differences. I did not encounter a need for differentiation during this lesson.
Upon completion, students should independently respond to the following questions in their learning journals: • Why is demographic information collected? What purpose does it serve? • Why is a graph a good way to display this information? • Who might use demographic information as a part of their job?	These learning-journal entries provided me with important assessment information and presented an opportunity to dialogue with the students in writing. I was able to determine whether they had any misconceptions concerning the lesson standards, concepts, or skills. I also observed their ability to assimilate and apply their learning.
Theme Park Development Project Segue into the upcoming Theme Park Development Project (Lesson 3) by reminding students about the purpose of the Climate Map Project completed in Lesson 1. The Theme Park Development Project will build upon students' understanding of climate and will be completed in Lesson 3.	I chose to explain the specific information for this project after the students had already completed the first set of requirements in the previous lesson. I wanted to determine whether adding a real-life scenario to the project would increase student motivation. I went a step further and informed them that they must work to find a location for the next Disney Theme Park (or Olympics). This motivated the students. They said they found it exciting to be doing something that a grown-up would do. The discussion evolved into what types of careers people who are interested in geography might have. We explored the Web site www.aag.com to further explore these ideas.
In the Theme Park Development Project, students take on the role of a researcher for a development company. This company is looking for a location somewhere in the world to begin production on their newest theme park. The students' job is to provide the development company with all of the necessary information to aid in the decision making process. In order to submit their	Share with students that their only job is to think about the location for their Theme Park. Remind them that they will have plenty of time to work on the project in the upcoming lesson, "Shop Around the Globe."

Unit Sequence	Teacher Reflections
findings to the development group, they must design a mode of presentation, such as PowerPoint. Distribute and discuss the rubric detailing the criteria for success on this project. Key elements of this rubric include accurate and detailed maps, quality of presentation, and knowledge gained. Ask students to gather their project information from the previous lesson. Explain to the students that for this portion of the lesson they will be responsible for the following: - Designing a population map for each of the four places they choose for this project. - Finding demographic data for each place. - Graphing the demographic data for each place using Microsoft Excel. The CIA World Fact Book Web site is a good source for the students to find the demographic information necessary to complete this assignment.	***Differentiation:*** *I asked students who exhibited a high level of interest in this area to further explore a career they found appealing. I also asked them to inform the class about their learning in an effort to pique their classmates' interest in the area.* *I found that the discussion about the purpose of demographic information was very helpful. The students had difficulty understanding why death rates were recorded and why it was important to know if a population increased or decreased. They wanted to know how this demographic information was going to help them with their project. The students missed the connection between death rates and population growth/decline. Following a discussion where I guided the students in making these connections, the purpose seemed much clearer to them.* *This portion of the lesson completed the gradual release of the support framework used throughout the lesson. The students applied the knowledge they gained from the previous two sections of the lesson independently. Not all students were ready to complete this assignment without teacher guidance. I formed a small group to work closely with, and I provided the necessary guidance. Most of them achieved the desired level of independence by the end of the lesson.*
Closure	
Display the sentences the students composed at the beginning of this lesson during the "possible sentences" activity. Ask small groups of students to revise their sentence to make it more accurate and/or descriptive. Engage students in a conversation about the relationship between geography and math. Ask students to think about the following ideas: - What math skills did you use while you were experimenting with population and demographics? - Why were these math skills important to the study of geography? - Do you think you will use the information you learned from this lesson again?	*Asking the students to revisit the sentences they wrote at the beginning of the lesson provided them with the opportunity to examine the learning they had accomplished. It also provided necessary assessment information, along with the student project and learning journal entries, to measure whether the lessons' concepts and principles had been successfully reached.* *The discussion brought focus back to the central theme of the unit. It provided the students with the opportunity to establish another relationship and further develop their understanding of geography.* *The students found the exploration of geography careers especially informative and useful to their lives. It seemed to take geography from a subject in school to the real world and gave it new meaning for the students.*

LESSON 3: SHOP AROUND THE GLOBE (3 HOURS)

Concepts

C11: Natural resources
C12: Wants
C13: Needs
C14: Goods

Principles

P8: Wants and needs can be fulfilled in a variety of ways.
P9: The resources available in a particular area determine the types of goods produced.

Skills

S6: Compare and contrast
S3: Determine cause and effect
S2: Reason deductively

Standards

SD3: Understands the physical and human characteristics of place

Benchmark: Knows the human characteristics of places (e.g., cultural characteristics such as religion, language, politics, technology, family structure, gender; population characteristics; land uses; levels of development)

Guiding Questions

- How do people in the United States get the things they want and need?
- How do people in other parts of the world meet their wants and needs?
- How do the types of natural resources available in a place affect the types of goods produced?

Unit Sequence	Teacher Reflections
Introduction	
Explain to the students that this lesson, like the previous two, focuses on relationships and will focus on the relationship between geography and economics. Ask students if they are familiar with economics or economy. Allow students to write in their learning journals for several minutes regarding their expectations for this lesson.	*In asking students to write in their learning journals about the lesson expectations, I hoped to see students beginning to make connections and see relationships. I also wanted to identify the students' prior knowledge of economics. A majority of the students were unable to make any viable predictions based on the fact that they didn't have any background knowledge in economics.*
Ask students to identify some of the things they need to survive. Make a list of the students' responses on chart paper. Engage students in a discussion regarding the places they go to get the things they need. Explain to the students that during this lesson they will be exploring the ways people in different parts of the world meet their needs.	*I designed this introductory activity to bring the students' prior knowledge to the forefront and provide a base for the new learning of the lesson.* *The students understood the differences between wants and needs. I prepared to review the differences, but the information gained during this activity provided me with enough evidence to allow me to move on with the new learning.*

Unit Sequence	Teacher Reflections
Teaching Strategies and Learning Experiences	
Display pictures of malls, marketplaces, and supermarkets in the United States. Ask students to pretend they had never been to these places before and to describe what they notice. Record the observations on chart paper. Draw students' attention to the number of choices Americans have when trying to meet their needs and wants.	*Because students showed so much excitement when learning about the various careers centered on geography, I took this opportunity to point out that they participated in an activity that an anthropologist might carry out. I felt that analyzing the world they lived in challenged them. I carefully guided students to help them change their perspective. It was as if they didn't notice the world they lived in. I found it necessary to take the time to allow the students to draw these conclusions in order for them to benefit from the activities that follow.*
Display a picture that illustrates how people in another area of the world meet their needs. Ask students what information they can obtain concerning how people in this place meet their needs. Record student observations on a piece of chart paper.	*For the purpose of this learning activity, I found it helpful to choose a country that is very different from the United States. My goal for this portion of the lesson was to guide the students in their effort to learn about the economies in different parts of the world. Because I wanted them to be able to draw these types of conclusions in small groups during the subsequent learning activities, I chose to highlight a culture quite different from our own. I found the students drew conclusions more easily because they were more apparent.*
Display a large Venn diagram, the two pictures, and the student generated lists from the previous learning activities. Using the think aloud strategy, model the thought process behind comparing and contrasting the information gained from the two pictures analyzed above. Ask questions such as the following: • Which had the most diversity? • Which could charge more for the same goods? Why?	*Student-generated Venn diagrams often focus on very superficial comparisons. With this learning activity, my intention was to model for the students a thought process that focused on the important ideas instead of the easy. I did not expect that the students would abandon the practice of only looking for obvious similarities and differences, yet I hoped to provide an example of a different thought process. I hoped that students would apply what they learned from the think aloud to their subsequent learning.*
Present the students with political, economic, and agricultural maps. Together with the students, analyze these maps to determine the cause for the differences in the means by which the people in the United States and the other chosen country meet their needs. Examine the impact of location, technological advancements, wealth, natural resources, and agriculture on these two countries or places.	*This learning activity requires students to assimilate information from a variety of sources and expects students to think at a very high level. Because the nature of the activity is teacher facilitated, I found that all students would benefit, on some level, from the type of thinking being explored during the activity.*

(Continued)

(Continued)

Unit Sequence	Teacher Reflections
Ask students to respond to the following questions independently in their learning journals: • What are some factors that contribute to the ways people meet their needs? • How does geography affect the way people meet their needs? Present small groups of students with pictures of marketplaces, malls, and grocery stores from around the world. Each group should receive four pictures and a recording sheet designed to provide students with a place to organize their thoughts and ideas. Prior to allowing the students to work in their small groups, present the directions and criteria for success to the students. • Examine one picture at a time. • Record your group's observations concerning how needs are met in this picture. • Use your atlas to research the location of this picture. Be sure to investigate the geography, climate, population, agriculture, land use, and any other maps you find useful. • Record this research on the recording sheet. • Use the observations and research to draw conclusions about the economy of this place. • Repeat with the remaining pictures. • Choose two pictures to compare and contrast using a Venn diagram. Supply each student with a Venn diagram. Ask each student to independently compare and contrast the two locations he or she did not compare as a group. Allow students to use their recording sheets to aid them in completing this assignment.	*Although the lesson is not complete, I wanted to gauge the students' understanding of the concepts and generalizations that we had focused on to this point. Due to the level of difficulty, I wanted to ensure that the students were given the proper amount of scaffolding before they were asked to attempt to draw these types of conclusions on their own.* **Differentiation:** *Based on the previous classroom discussions and the learning journal entries, I chose to differentiate this lesson in a variety of ways. I grouped together students who required more assistance and provided this group with pictures of areas that were familiar to them to allow obvious conclusions to be drawn. I also spent a considerable amount of time with these students to assist them in further achieving independence with this type of thinking. I also limited the number of places these students examined. This group observed only two locations and additional pictures from each location in order to make it easier for them to make observations. Although I did see an improvement with these students, they still required further attention during later stages of the lesson.* *To challenge those students who displayed the ability to engage in this higher level thinking activity, I chose more obscure pictures from various areas of the world. I also provided these students with access to the Internet in order to conduct research that was more thorough. I encouraged them not only to investigate maps, but other sources of information as well in order to learn more about the area they were examining. During this research, students found their own pictures to aid them in completing this assignment.* *The students who benefited from small group instruction during the previous activity again completed this assignment in the small group setting, with a great deal of teacher assistance. My intention was to limit the amount of frustration these students encountered while still allowing them to do the same learning as the remainder of the class. I did not expect mastery. I aimed for meaningful exposure.*

Unit Sequence	Teacher Reflections
Ask students to respond to the following questions in their learning journals: • What did you learn by examining the pictures from the various locations and several different types of maps? • What did you enjoy about this activity? • What did you dislike? • What would you have changed? • What did you find most challenging?	**Identity Parallel** *I used this learning-journal entry to assess the students' understanding of the lessons concepts, principles, and generalizations. I also wanted to gain feedback concerning their feelings about the learning they had achieved. A majority of the students felt challenged during the lesson. The consensus was that they enjoyed the small group aspects of the lesson and felt they learned from their classmates' thoughts and observations. Many stated that they felt overwhelmed when trying to organize all the information they gained from the maps and then trying to learn from them.*
Theme Park Development Project (See the Project Description and Rubric that accompany this lesson. Share the rubric with students so that they have a clear understanding of the expectations.) Explain to the students that they will be applying their new knowledge of economics to their theme park development project. List the following directions on a piece of chart paper and review with the students to ensure they are aware of the expectations for the assignment. • Examine political, economic, agricultural, and land use maps for each of your locations. • Design one map for each location that includes important information about the economy of this location. *Optional:* Conduct Internet research to find pictures showing the economy of this area to include in your proposal.	**Practice Parallel** ***Differentiation:*** *I intended this project to be a tool for students to apply their new learning independently. A majority of the students achieved a great deal of success with the project and found it very motivating. A small group of students seemed to be overwhelmed with the requirements for the project. I asked these students to choose one or two locations they felt most interested in and focus only on those. I did not feel I was compromising in making this adjustment. These students fulfilled the same requirements on a smaller scale and displayed an understanding of the lesson's major concepts, principles, and generalizations.* *The optional portion of the assignment provided an opportunity for above-average students to take their learning to a higher level. In addition, I felt it would give students with a high level of motivation and interest in this project an opportunity to achieve beyond my expectations.*
Extension Engage students in a conversation about where the things they use in their everyday lives come from. Discuss the connection we have to many different parts of the world through the things we use every day. Ask students to check the labels on their clothing, shoes, video games, electronics, and food in their refrigerator or pantry, and design a map showing how they are connected to the world.	**Identity Parallel** *One of my goals in writing this unit was to make it relevant to the students' lives. I used this learning activity to demonstrate to the students their participation in the world economy. I suspected that they felt somewhat disconnected from the lesson content. I wanted them to see how they fit into the big picture and how the learning they did during the lesson pertained to their lives.*

(Continued)

(Continued)

Unit Sequence	Teacher Reflections
Differentiation: Ask these students to try to find a connection between the types of goods produced in particular locations and the economy of these places.	
Closure	
Engage the class in a discussion about the different economies they have learned about during this lesson. Prompt students using some of the following questions: • Why are economies in various places different? • What effect does location have on an economy? • What effect does climate have on an economy? • What effect does population have on an economy? • What did you learn about the economy of the United States? • How does this new learning affect your life? • How will you use this new learning?	*The purpose of this classroom discussion was to measure the learning the students achieved during this lesson and to identify any misconceptions present. The misconceptions I did uncover, I addressed while the students worked independently on their "Theme Park Development Project." These conferences allowed me to gain insight into the student's thought processes and to address the misconception in context.*
Ask students to respond to the following prompt in their learning journals: • What is an economy?	*I included this learning-log entry in the conclusion to assess whether the students developed an understanding of the main concept in this lesson. I felt it was important that they be able to articulate their understanding of this idea in order to move on to the next lesson. In addition, I felt that this would prepare them for the final discussion concerning the relationship between economics and geography.*
Divide students into small groups and present the following question to the group: • What is the relationship between geography and economics? Ask each small group to develop between one and three ideas and then write them on a piece of chart paper. When the students have completed this assignment, engage the whole class in a discussion around the posted ideas.	**Connections Parallel** *The purpose of this closure activity was to address the central theme of the unit and to bring the students' focus back to the relationships. It was my intention to allow the students more responsibility in establishing the connections in their small groups. I was available for support. I joined in on each small group conversation and provided the groups with the necessary guiding questions to steer their thinking in the right direction.*

THEME PARK DEVELOPMENT PROJECT

Task

You have just been hired as a researcher for a development company. They are looking for the perfect location for their newest theme park. Your first task as a researcher is to provide your superiors with the necessary information to aid them in the decision making process. You will be conducting additional research on the four locations you began researching for the Climate Map Project. You will compile your information for this assignment into a proposal. The proposal will include the maps and graphs designed during the project, a persuasive essay, and a presentation. Listed below are the additional requirements for the Theme Park Development Project:

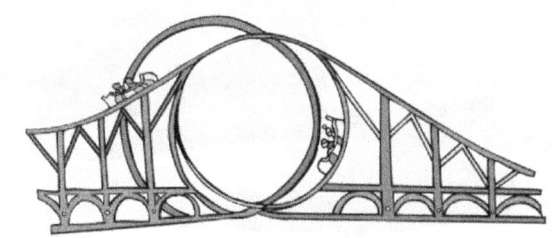

Population

- Design a population map for each location.
- The map for each location must include surrounding cities and countries.
- Each map must include the following:
    - title
    - labels
    - key with symbols
    - scale

Demographics

- Research the demographic data for each location (life expectancy, birth rates, family size, etc.).
- No more than three areas should be explored for each location.
- The CIA World Fact Book Web site is a source that will aid you in your research.
- Graph the information you have obtained using Microsoft Excel.

Economics

- Examine political, economic, agricultural, and land use maps for each of your locations.
- Design one map for each location that includes important information about the economy of this location.
- Each map must include the following:
    - title
    - labels
    - key with symbols
    - scale
- *Optional:* Conduct Internet research to find pictures showing the economy of this area to include in your proposal.

Culture

The development company would like to highlight the culture of the location chosen for the theme park. You will be responsible for researching the cultures of each of your locations and suggesting ways in which the elements of culture can be incorporated into the theme park. Possible areas to research include the following:

- religion
- language
- customs
- family structure
- music
- diet

You must also present the development company with language and religion maps for each location and the surrounding cities and countries. Each map must include the following:

- title
- labels
- key with symbols
- scale

Final Requirements

In order to submit your findings to the development company, you must fulfill the following requirements:

- Rank the locations researched from the best location for the theme park to the worst location.
- Write an essay persuading the development company to choose your recommended location.
- Organize all of the material produced (climate, population, economic, and culture maps and demographic graphs) throughout the project and determine the best method for presenting the information to the development company.

Copyright © 2010 by Corwin. All rights reserved. Reprinted from *Parallel Curriculum Units for Social Studies, Grades 6–12*, edited by Jeanne H. Purcell and Jann H. Leppien. Thousand Oaks, CA: Corwin, www.corwinpress.com. Reproduction authorized only for the local school site or nonprofit organization that has purchased this book.

THEME PARK DEVELOPMENT PROJECT RUBRIC

Theme Park Development Project Rubric

Criteria	4	3	2	1
Information, analysis, and application	The researcher is successfully able to draw conclusions from the conducted research and make a decision based on the research.	The researcher is able to draw partial conclusions from the conducted research and make decisions based on the research.	The researcher draws inaccurate conclusions from the conducted research.	The researcher is unable to draw conclusions from the research conducted.
Finding relationships	Accurately links climate, population, economic, and cultural resources to the goods, services, and livelihoods of a region.	Adequately links climate, population, economic, and cultural resources to the goods, services, and livelihoods of a region.	Inaccurately links climate, population, economic, and cultural resources to the goods, services, and livelihoods of a region.	No attempt is made to find relationships between climate, population, economic, and cultural resources and the goods, services, and livelihoods of a region.

(Continued)

(Continued)

Criteria	4	3	2	1
Maps and Graphs	All maps include required elements (title, labels, key with symbols, scale), are accurate, and are neatly presented. Graphs include title and labels and accurately portray research.	Most maps include required elements (title, labels, key with symbols, scale), are accurate, and are neatly presented. Graphs include title and labels and accurately portray research.	Some maps include required elements (title, labels, key with symbols, scale), are accurate, and are neatly presented. Most graphs include title and labels and accurately portray research.	Maps do not include the required elements and are not accurate or neatly presented. Graphs do not include title and labels and do not reflect the research.
Presentation	Presentation materials are visually appealing and appropriately display information.	Most presentation materials are visually appealing and appropriately display information.	Some of the presentation materials are visually appealing and may or may not appropriately display information.	Presentation materials are not relevant to the conducted research or visually appealing to the audience.
Organization	Organizes information and materials logically.	Organizes information and materials in an acceptable order.	Little organization of information or materials.	No organization of information or materials.

Copyright © 2010 by Corwin. All rights reserved. Reprinted from *Parallel Curriculum Units for Social Studies, Grades 6–12*, edited by Jeanne H. Purcell and Jann H. Leppien. Thousand Oaks, CA: Corwin, www.corwinpress.com. Reproduction authorized only for the local school site or nonprofit organization that has purchased this book.

LESSON 4: THE CULTURE OF GEOGRAPHY
(3–4 HOURS)

Concepts

C15: Culture
C16: Language
C17: Religion
C18: Traditions

Principles

P10: Geography has an impact on culture.
P11: Cultures vary around the world.
P12: Examining geography and culture helps us to understand a place.

Skills

S7: Read
S8: Infer
S5: Analyze and interpret information/data
S9: Summarize
S1: Make connections
S3: Determine cause and effect

Standards

SD3: Understands the physical and human characteristics of place

Benchmark: Knows the human characteristics of places (e.g., cultural characteristics such as religion, language, politics, technology, family structure, gender; population characteristics; land uses; levels of development)

Guiding Questions

- What is culture?
- Why is it important to learn about other cultures?
- How does the geography affect culture?

Unit Sequence	Teacher Reflections
Introduction	
Explain to the students that the relationship they will be exploring during this lesson is the relationship between geography and culture. Engage students in a conversation as to how these two concepts may be connected. Prompt the students with the following guiding questions: • How would the culture of a place be affected if it were located on top of a mountain? On an island? • What effect might a very low population have on a culture?	**Connections Parallel** *Once again, I felt it was necessary to highlight the central concept of relationships to begin the lesson. This discussion focuses on all of the areas we have focused on thus far in this unit. My goal was for students to see that the relationships were not isolated but, rather, all connected in some way. I attempted to initiate this connection in the introduction so the students would have it in mind throughout the course of the lesson. I planned to revisit these same questions in the conclusion.*

(Continued)

(Continued)

Unit Sequence	Teacher Reflections
• What effect might climate have on a culture? Might a country with a warm climate have a different culture from one with a cold climate? Why? • How is the culture of a place affected by having a poor economy?	
Teaching Strategies and Learning Experiences	
Introduce the following scenario to the students: A student from another part of the world is coming to visit our classroom for a few days. This student will also be traveling to other parts of the United States. The United States is very different from her home country. What things about the U.S. would you teach this student in order for him or her to have a successful experience in this country? Record the students' responses on chart paper. Divide students into small groups to role-play their interaction with this student. One student should play the role of the student from another country. Following the role-playing, bring the class together and pose the following questions: • What did you discover about the culture of the United States from this activity? • How is the culture in the United States different from other cultures around the world? Introduce a fiction or nonfiction book from a country of your choosing. Choose a country that you display an interest in and share your interest with the students prior to the reading. List the following on a piece of chart paper: • religion　　• food • language　　• family • government　• population • technology　• land use Review the terms to ensure the students are familiar with them. Ask the students to keep these concepts in mind as you read the book aloud.	*The purpose of this introductory activity was to motivate the students and spark interest in the upcoming learning activities. The activity also elicits students' understanding of their own culture and prepares them to think about other cultures.* *I wanted the students to realize that the United States is very diverse and a blend of many different cultures.* **Differentiation:** *Students who display interest in this area may want to explore some of the causes for the diversity in the United States.* **Connections Parallel** *When designing this activity, my intention was to provide students with modeling and support with the lesson's concepts, principles, and generalizations.*

Unit Sequence	Teacher Reflections
Read the book aloud to the students, pausing to ask guiding questions that lead the students to draw conclusions regarding how these concepts apply to the country in question. Record the information learned about the country on the chart paper corresponding to the appropriate term. In most cases, the chosen book will not address all of these areas. Ask the students to recommend additional sources to examine to help learn the desired information. Research this country according to the students' suggestions. Display a physical or landform map of the country and ask the following questions: • Is there a connection between the physical characteristics of this country and the culture? • What impact might the population have on the culture? • How is this culture similar to the culture of the United States? How is it different? • What impact does religion have on a culture? Multiple religions? Provide students with magazines and access to the Internet. Ask students to design a collage that represents the culture they learned about in the previous learning activity. Encourage the students to be as creative as possible. Remind students of the activity at the beginning of the lesson, where they aided a student from another country. Explain that you are going to turn the tables on them. Instead of teaching a student from another country about the United States, they are going to be the student from the United States visiting another country. Assign a country to pairs of students. Explain to the students that they will be researching this country to identify specific aspects of their culture, such as language, religion, family structure, customs, literature, technology, economy, population, and land use. Provide students such resources as the Culture Shock series of books. The following Web sites will also be very useful to the students: • http://www.oxfam.org.uk/coolplanet/ontheline • http://www.peacecorps.gov/kids	**Connections Parallel** *Reading the book aloud to the students provided me with an opportunity to review basic research and note-taking skills that I found a majority of the students lacked. After completing the research, I asked the students to apply the new knowledge and draw fact-based conclusions about this culture. It was my intention for the students to make connections with the learning done during the previous lessons in this unit.* ***Differentiation:*** *This question provided me with an opportunity to explore current events with the students. Students who displayed an interest in this area examined newspapers and appropriate Internet news sites to learn about the impact of religion on cultures. Students who completed this investigation chose to share their learning by role-playing and through the writing of their own newspaper articles. I encouraged them to be creative and share their learning in any form they felt appropriate.*

(Continued)

(Continued)

Unit Sequence	Teacher Reflections

Following the research, assign the following tasks:
 	
• You have learned many new things about this culture. Now imagine that you have spent several weeks in this country and write a personal narrative about your experiences in this place.
• Compare and contrast the culture you explored with the United States using a Venn diagram.
• *Differentiation:* Answer the following questions in your learning journal:
   o Did the population of this country have an effect on the culture? If so, how?
   o How did the climate affect the culture?
   o How did some of the customs or traditions of this culture originate?
   o Does the economy affect the culture in any way?
   o Are there any defining physical features that contribute to the culture in this country?
	This learning activity directly addresses the standard that requires students to understand the human and physical characteristics of places. The activity was authentic and meaningful to the students. The availability of multiple sources of information provides the students with the opportunity to evaluate the material and determine what is relevant and important for their learning.
	
	These learning-journal entries provided me with necessary information in assessing the students' ability to evaluate and apply the learning they have achieved during the unit. I wanted the students to not only master the content of this unit but to also engage in higher level thinking activities that would affect any area they were trying to make sense of and understand.

Engage students in a conversation about the feelings they would have if they actually had to go to a country they knew nothing about. How would they handle these feelings? What would they do to prepare themselves for their trip? Where would they want to go? Why? **Extension** Share the book *Material World*, by Peter Menzel, with the students. Explain that the author of this book asked average families from various countries to move all of their belongings outside of their home. The author(s) then photographed the family and their belongings and provided cultural and demographic information regarding the country. Choose picture(s) to display and discuss what these pictures tell the reader about the culture of that country. The pictures and cultures are compared and contrasted.	*I compiled the student-written personal narratives into the class's own "Culture Shock" book. It was bound and placed in the classroom library for all students to enjoy and learn from.*

Unit Sequence	Teacher Reflections
Theme Park Development Project Explain to the students that for the final piece of their Theme Park Development Project, they will be investigating the cultures of their locations. Provide the students with the following criteria to aid them in completing this portion of the project. Explain that the development company wants to highlight the culture of the location they choose in the theme park. The students will be responsible for researching the location's culture (religion, language, customs, family structure, music, diet, etc.) and suggesting ways in which these elements of culture can be used in the theme park. To support these suggestions, the development company must be presented with maps depicting the various languages spoken in this location and various religions present in this area. In order for the students to submit their findings to the development company, they must fulfill the following requirements: • Rank the locations researched from the best location for the theme park to the worst location. • Write an essay persuading the development company to choose your recommended location. • Organize all of the material produced throughout the project and determine the best method for presenting the information to the development company. Gather a group of other teachers, the principal, guidance counselors, or other students to play the role of the developers. Allow the students to present their findings.	**Identity Parallel** *The departure from the core curriculum detailed here is an effort to allow the students to explore their feelings and ideas about the lesson content. I wanted them to analyze how they would handle this situation if it actually were to happen to them. I hoped that this would lead to an internalization of the lesson's main concepts.* **Connections Parallel** *The* Material World *book is a fascinating vehicle from which to examine cultures from around the world. The book could support an entire unit exploring cultures. I found that providing the students with any amount of exposure to this book was beneficial. The students gained so much insight by comparing their home and belongings with those of a country in Africa.* **Practice Parallel** *Once again, this project allows the students to apply the skills and concepts addressed during the previous portions of the lesson independently.* ***Differentiation:*** *The requirements for the students to complete this project are very lofty. I did not hesitate to eliminate the persuasive essay from the requirements for those students who seemed overwhelmed by the assignment.* *The students responded positively to having people other than their classmates as an audience for their presentations. It made the experience more authentic for the students and they were highly motivated to produce high-quality presentations.*
	**Closure**
Engage students in a conversation concerning their feelings about the Theme Park Development Project. What did they like? Dislike? Did they find the requirements overwhelming? What would they change? Would they ever seek a career in this line of work?	

(Continued)

(Continued)

Unit Sequence	Teacher Reflections
Remind the students of the questions regarding the relationship between geography and culture that they were asked at the beginning of this lesson: • How can the culture of a place be affected by being located on top of a mountain? On an island? • What effect might a very low population have on a culture? • What effect might climate have on a culture? How might a country with a warm-climate culture differ from a cold-climate country? • How can the culture of a place be affected by having a poor economy? Conduct a whole-class discussion using these questions as a guide. Ask students how their thoughts regarding these questions have changed since the beginning of the lesson.	*I utilized this conversation to gauge the degree to which the students achieved the goals I set for this lesson.*

2

Through the Looking Glass

A Unit for Reading/Writing/ Social Studies Intervention Classes

Middle School

Dawn Vier and Lisa L. Ward

INTRODUCTION TO THE UNIT

At Sky Vista Middle School in Aurora, Colorado, students are exposed to the Parallel Curriculum Model in general education core classes, electives, and through intervention classes. The intervention model we provide serves students who are below proficient in reading and writing. Regardless of whether they have a special education label, any student needing academic support attends both their core class and a supplementary support class. These classes are tiered into three levels that mirror the federal guidelines for the Response to Intervention model (RTI) and our state proficiency levels (see a diagram of this model [Figure 2.1] on page 51). Our students are placed in these classes via state and district testing and teacher recommendation. To ensure appropriate placement and effectiveness of instruction, progress monitoring is continued throughout the duration of each class.

Students in the two most intensive levels of intervention include students on Individual Education Plans (IEPs) and non-identified students scoring at levels of *unsatisfactory* and *partially proficient* according to our Colorado state assessments. Students on IEPs include students with learning disabilities, speech-language disabilities, emotional/behavioral disorders, and physical disabilities. It is important to note that students with disabilities need not only skills intervention, but also vocabulary and concept development to enrich the gaps in knowledge that most seem to present.

Being a skills-based class, our ultimate goal is to bring the students to reading and writing proficiency (grade level). In doing so, our use of PCM takes on a slightly different life within this type of classroom with concept-based instruction. The Core lessons demand that we instruct students in areas of their deficits, which include reading fluency and comprehension, vocabulary development, and writing with voice, correct word choice, organization, content, and sentence fluency. PCM allows us to embed these skills into big ideas that broaden our students' awareness and thinking. Even though lessons may use a specific parallel for their design, we are constantly embedding core reading and writing skills throughout every lesson. After two years of implementation, Sky Vista is one of only two middle schools in our district that made AYP (annual yearly progress) on the Colorado Student Assessment Program tests (CSAP). Our "double dosing" model has proven to be not only effective, but inspiring and motivating as well. Students in intervention classes typically despise reading and writing because of their record of failure and their years of struggle. In this model, students love the idea of being challenged while improving their skills, rather than the "kill and drill" support model known in previous years.

CONTENT FRAMEWORK

Organizing Concepts

Macroconcepts	*Discipline-Specific Concepts*	*Principles and Generalizations*
M1: Identity	Community, groups versus individual, conformity, status symbols, loyalty, acceptance, norms, taboos, environment, globalization, information age, technology, global warming, ecological responsibility, stewardship, sustainable development	P1: People develop and change identities throughout their lives.
M2: Change		P2: Our identities change and are shaped by our environment and experiences.
M3: Communication		P3: Our identity is partially determined by genetics/nature.
M4: Voice		P4: Writers' voices reveal much about their identities and reflect their personality, time, culture, and so on.
M5: Perspective		P5: Our roles/responsibilities within a society help to create who we are.
M6: Cause and effect		P6: Identity is dynamic, multifaceted, and cuts across all cultures.
M7: Conflict		P7: Identity is the lens through which we base our perspectives.

Macroconcepts	Discipline-Specific Concepts	Principles and Generalizations
M8: Prejudice		P8: Identity is determined by multiple forces and influences.
M9: System		P9: Genetics, environment, experiences, cultures, race, perspectives, gender, and time all shape identity.
M10: Transcendence		P10: Group dynamics shape identity.
M11: Altruism		P11: Groups have individual identities.
		P12: Groups often require conformity to norms or standards set by that group.
		P13: Communities and cities can have very unique and individual identities that influence who we are.
		P14: The Great Depression and the Dust Bowl altered the identity of America politically, economically, socially, and culturally.
		P15: Hardships and catastrophic events lead to both positive and negative changes due to coping, making sacrifices, working cooperatively, and government programs.
		P16: Relationships exist between "then" and "now."
		P17: Cultural identities are developed, and they change over time.
		P18: Time periods have trends and themes associated with them.
		P19: Conclusions can be drawn about society and culture from these trends and themes.
		P20: These identities are shaped by intentional acts and chance occurrences.
		P21: Artists' voices reflect and can shape culture, personality, time, and opinions.
		P22: Word and sentence choices influence people's thinking.
		P23: Conflict leads or lends itself to change.
		P24: Conflict influences individual decisions and actions.
		P25: Preserving our environment and resources is integral to human, plant, and animal survival.
		P26: People, communities, and countries have certain responsibilities to ensure a continued, viable environment.
		P27: Political and economic conflicts occur in the balancing of human development and wilderness/environmental preservation.

Skills

Reading Skills

S1b: Summarize and synthesize fiction and nonfiction

S1c: Locate and paraphrase main ideas and supporting details from fiction and nonfiction

S1d: Infer, using information in a variety of texts and genres

S1g: Identify the meaning of unfamiliar words in context, using word recognition skills and context clues

S5a, 5b: Use organizational features of printed and electronic text to locate information

S6a: Read and respond to a variety of literature that represents perspectives from places, people, and events that are familiar and unfamiliar

Writing Skills

S2a: Write in a variety of modes, such as narrative, expository, descriptive, and persuasive, for various audiences and purposes

S2b: Organize writing using a logical arrangement of ideas

S2c: Use language that supports and enriches the idea

S2g: Develop ideas and content with relevant details, examples, and/or reasons

S4d: Recognize an author's or speaker's point of view and purpose

National Standards

Reading/Language Arts Performance Standards from the National Council of Teachers of English (NCTE) and the International Reading Association (IRA) include the following:

SD1: Students read a wide range of print and nonprint texts to build an understanding of texts, of themselves, and of the cultures of the United States and the world; to acquire new information; to respond to the needs and demands of society and the workplace; and for personal fulfillment. Among these texts are fiction and nonfiction, classic and contemporary works.

SD2: Students read a wide range of literature from many periods in many genres to build an understanding of the many dimensions (e.g., philosophical, ethical, and aesthetic) of human experience.

SD3: Students apply a wide range of strategies to comprehend, interpret, evaluate, and appreciate texts. They draw on their prior experience, their interactions with other readers and writers, their knowledge of word meaning and of other texts, their word identification strategies, and their understanding of textual features (e.g., sound-letter correspondence, sentence structure, context, and graphics).

SD4: Students adjust their use of spoken, written, and visual language (e.g., conventions, style, and vocabulary) to communicate effectively with a variety of audiences and for different purposes.

SD5: Students employ a wide range of strategies as they write and use different writing process elements appropriately to communicate with different audiences for a variety of purposes.

SD6: Students apply knowledge of language structure, language conventions (e.g., spelling and punctuation), media techniques, figurative language, and genre to create, critique, and discuss print and nonprint texts.

SD7: Students conduct research on issues and interests by generating ideas and questions and by posing problems. They gather, evaluate, and synthesize data from a variety of sources (e.g., print and nonprint texts, artifacts, and people) to communicate their discoveries in ways that suit their purpose and audience.

SD8: Students use a variety of technological and information resources (e.g., libraries, databases, computer networks, and video) to gather and synthesize information and to create and communicate knowledge.

SD11: Students participate as knowledgeable, reflective, creative, and critical members of a variety of literacy communities.

SD12: Students use spoken, written, and visual language to accomplish their own purposes (e.g., for learning, enjoyment, persuasion, and the exchange of information).

Making Sure the Parallels Remain Central in Teaching and Learning

Curriculum Component	Component Descriptions and Rationale
Content	Learning objectives for the Core Curriculum parallel address both reading and writing skills at independent and instructional levels and an understanding of how reading and writing are powerful tools of expression. The big ideas for the Curriculum of Connections parallel address identity, change, communication, power, systems, and conflict. These ideas cross disciplines as well as time. Students become authentic authors and critical readers in the Curriculum of Practice parallel when they research, draft, edit, revise, and publish their very own work. The Curriculum of Identity parallel is continuously addressed through a dynamic and multifaceted lens ranging from self-identity, to community, to the nation, to the world.

(Continued)

(Continued)

Curriculum Component	Component Descriptions and Rationale
	The unit is intentionally designed using eight mini-units. Lessons within the mini-unit can be taught to meet student needs without the pressure of following a sequential order; however, the order of the mini-units themselves should be kept intact as the students progress from self-awareness to global awareness.
Assessments	Students are placed in intervention classes based on our state assessment (CSAP), district assessments (ALT/MAP), and teacher recommendation. Pretesting takes place when a student begins an intervention class using the Test of Word Reading Efficiency (TOWRE) or Qualitative Reading Inventory (QRI) to acquire a baseline level of reading development. Fluency and comprehension progress monitoring is used at least four times per quarter to measure growth.
Introductory activities	The introductory activities ask students to explore and analyze their own self-identity by making connections and comparisons to other unique identities. In addition, they recognize specific roles that create and shape who they are and who they will be in the future.
Teaching strategies	A variety of strategies—which include multisensory information presentations, technology-based research, cooperative and active learning, class discussions, debates, and problem-based learning—are employed to meet the varied needs of the students.
Grouping strategies	Several strategies are used: grouping by reading level, skill level, or by interest level; and a purposeful skill combination group to provide struggling students a model for higher-level thinking and production.

UNIT ASSESSMENTS

This chapter contains a variety of diagnostic assessments. A preassessment is used at the beginning of the unit to determine the readiness level of the students in two areas: students' core knowledge about identity and their ability to construct a coherent and well-organized essay.

Several other performance tasks are designed to provide the teacher with ongoing data about students' progress. Students are invited to create an Interview Reflection of a Depression-era adult, construct a "Year of Your Birth" newspaper, and write a persuasive essay debating a national or world issue. Writing assignments and learning reflections on a smaller scale, used throughout all the lessons, are also used to monitor student progress.

BACKGROUND INFORMATION

The Sky Vista staff developed and adopted big ideas that we considered cornerstones of our implementation of the PCM: Change, Power, Conflict, Identity, Systems, and Communications. These concepts serve as organizational toolboxes into which curricular ideas can be embedded. This unit provides an in-depth analysis of the concept of identity through the examination of self, community, our nation, and the world. The semester-long unit encompasses all four parallels seamlessly, while providing direct reading and writing instruction and scaffolding in order to meet our goals. A multisensory approach to using resources is provided for our diverse learners, including short stories, videos, poetry, music, novels, articles, and picture books. In the Core Curriculum parallel, students are guided through lessons on skills to become proficient readers and writers. Within the Curriculum of Connections parallel, students explore different time periods and major historical events. They examine how important events in history impact the identity of a specific time and place. This helps support much of the curriculum that is being covered in our Grade 8 language arts and social studies classes as well. The Curriculum of Practice parallel provides opportunity for students to become true authors by writing, editing, revising, and publishing an authentic book, thus connecting their views on identity through the writing process. Through the reading of a myriad of authors—and the writing of poems, articles, and newspapers—students explore how their individual identity is created and changed,

Figure 2.1 Response to Intervention Model (RTI) Description

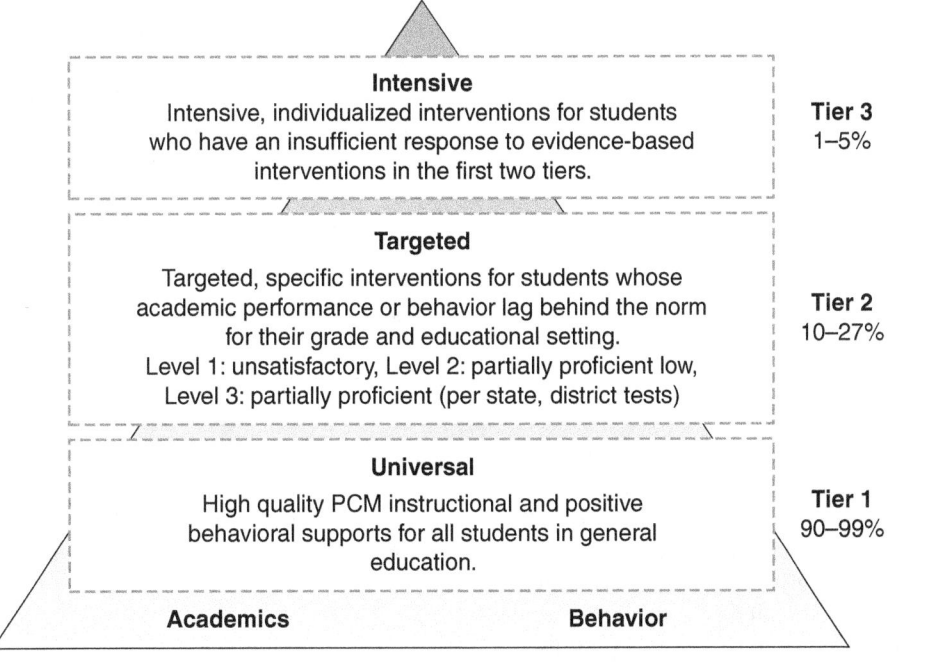

thus incorporating the Curriculum of Identity parallel. It is important to note that the lessons in "Through the Looking Glass" are known as mini-units. We call them mini-units because of the length of time required to complete each, which ranges from a week to as long as four weeks. We retained the word "lesson" at the beginning of each mini-unit to be consistent with the other units in this volume.

UNIT SEQUENCE, DESCRIPTION, AND TEACHER REFLECTIONS

PREASSESSMENT: WHAT MAKES YOUR IDENTITY? (1 CLASS PERIOD: 45–60 MINUTES)

Unit Sequence	Teacher Reflections
Preassessment Question Pose the following question: What makes up your identity? Have students respond to the question with an essay that discusses at least three aspects that create identity. Students will be given plain white paper as well as lined paper.	*This preassessment activity allows students to preview ideas for the upcoming unit and gives the teacher baseline data on the students' core knowledge about identity and their ability to construct a proficient essay.* *Students are given lined and plain paper to see if they have a grasp on the entire writing process, from brainstorming to drafting.* *A four-point "eye-ball" rubric (unsatisfactory, partially proficient, proficient, advanced) is used to review and analyze students' ability to brainstorm, organize, use correct conventions, and develop content and ideas. At this point in time, we do not stress spelling because many decoding-struggling readers wrestle with encoding as well and we merely want the flow of high-level thoughts and ideas. This rubric is not a formal one; it is informal only and designed to give the teacher a general sense of students' starting points.*
Debriefing and Group Discussion Upon completion of the essay, students will debrief and discuss ideas from their essays. An Identity Concept Wall will be posted where students will list ideas, words, thoughts, or questions relating to the big idea of identity. As a class, we will revisit this concept wall many times throughout the unit.	*The concept wall will provide ongoing evidence and a dynamic record of the changing, developing thoughts and ideas students develop throughout the unit.*

LESSON 1: INTRODUCTION—"WHO AM I?" (1 WEEK)

Concepts

M1: Identity
M5: Perspective
M2: Change
M6: Cause and effect
M4: Voice

In developing this unit, beginning with self-identity seemed to be the best way to hook our students. Middle school students tend to live in a self-absorbed world, which allows them to connect almost everything to their own lives. Once interest in the unit is established, a broader sense of identity can be further developed.

Principles

P1: People develop and change identities throughout their lives.
P2: Our identities change and are shaped by our environment and experiences.
P3: Our identity is partially determined by genetics/nature.
P4: Writers' voices reveal much about their identities and reflect their personality, time, culture, and so on.

Skills

S2a: Write in a variety of modes, such as narrative, expository, descriptive, and persuasive, for various audiences and purposes
S2b: Organize writing using a logical arrangement of ideas
S2c: Use language that supports and enriches the idea
S2g: Develop ideas and content with relevant details, examples, and/or reasons
S4d: Recognize an author's or speaker's point of view and purpose

Standards

SD1: Students read a wide range of print and nonprint texts to build an understanding of texts, of themselves, and of the cultures of the United States and the world; to acquire new information; to respond to the needs and demands of society and the workplace; and for personal fulfillment. Among these texts are fiction and nonfiction, classic and contemporary works.
SD2: Students read a wide range of literature from many periods in many genres to build an understanding of the many dimensions (e.g., philosophical, ethical, and aesthetic) of human experience.
SD3: Students apply a wide range of strategies to comprehend, interpret, evaluate, and appreciate texts. They draw on their prior experience, their interactions with other readers and writers, their knowledge of word meaning and of other texts, their word identification strategies, and their understanding of textual features (e.g., sound-letter correspondence, sentence structure, context, and graphics).
SD4: Students adjust their use of spoken, written, and visual language (e.g., conventions, style, and vocabulary) to communicate effectively with a variety of audiences and for different purposes.
SD5: Students employ a wide range of strategies as they write and use different writing process elements appropriately to communicate with different audiences for a variety of purposes.
SD6: Students apply knowledge of language structure, language conventions (e.g., spelling and punctuation), media techniques, figurative language, and genre to create, critique, and discuss print and nonprint texts.
SD12: Students use spoken, written, and visual language to accomplish their own purposes (e.g., for learning, enjoyment, persuasion, and the exchange of information).

(Continued)

> (Continued)
>
> **Guiding Questions**
>
> - What makes us who we are?
> - What creates our identity?
> - What makes people the same? Different?
> - Can you tell who someone is just by looking at them? If someone you already know suddenly changes their appearance, have they changed their identity? How?
>
> These questions help assess the level of understanding of identity within the Core parallel. Our main goal is to have students develop and expand this concept.

Unit Sequence—Core Curriculum	Teacher Reflections
Introduction	
Play a "Who Am I?" PowerPoint presentation in which there are 10 to 12 photos of unique and interesting people. Have students write in their personal journal books about *who* they think these people are and what clues helped to make their predictions using the Who am I? PowerPoint Worksheet included at the end of this mini-unit.	*Create a PowerPoint presentation: Place unique pictures of individuals from varying walks of life, ages, cultures, and so on, in a wordless PowerPoint presentation that is without bias so that students can reflect on their own perspectives and knowledge about identity. First, students are asked to write who they think the people are. Then, they individually appraise their developing ideas about identity.*
As a whole class, view each picture again, sharing ideas students had regarding the identities of the people in the photos. Students must be ready to defend their predictions about identity using their own perspectives and connections. Some questions might include: • Who are these people? How can you tell? • How does their appearance define who they are? What clues in their surroundings help to identify who they might be? Do they have more than one identity? Is it possible this person has an identity opposite from the one you perceive?	*In this class discussion, students' individual ideas will be questioned, defended, and expanded. The discussion should be guided by our guiding questions in order to focus and develop student understanding of identity, stereotypes, and the role of environment and experience in shaping identity.*
In small groups, have students brainstorm how the following factors contribute to a person's identity and continue to add these ideas to the identity concept wall. Example concepts: race, gender, family, socioeconomic status, location, education, failures, successes, experiences, innate abilities, friends, relationships, religion, culture, language, and so on.	*This is not a teacher generated or driven list. Students will construct and develop their views on identity and what creates and shapes identity throughout the entire unit. Ideas expressed on this wall will serve as a springboard and reference point for the ongoing development and discussion of ideas.*

Unit Sequence—Core Curriculum	Teacher Reflections
Teaching Strategies and Learning Experiences	

Unit Sequence—Core Curriculum	Teacher Reflections
Students are given the following direction: *Brainstorm in your journals a list of at least 30 events and/or experiences that you have had up until now in your life.* Using a highlighter, highlight only the events that have had a significant impact on who you are today. Ask students to select one of these significant events and to explain what change took place and to share it with their peers. Using only the highlighted events, students then create a personal timeline showing these events in chronological order. On the back of the timeline, students use a chart (three-column) to list 20 nouns, and 20 adjectives, and 20 verbs that describe who they are. (Use the I Am Poem: Outline Worksheet to guide the brainstorming. It is included at the end of this mini-unit.)	*Students will not necessarily realize right away which experiences were or are significant. Brainstorming a list of all experiences will lead to students eventually selecting events that actually caused a change in their identity.* *It is important for students to be able to identify significant events in their lives that caused change. Sharing experiences helps students connect to commonalities with each other and with the population as a whole.* *Give students time to truly reflect on who they are. A general list of 20 nouns, adjectives, or verbs is not the goal of this activity. Students are encouraged to deeply explore qualities that define them, both positive and negative. It is difficult for anyone, especially middle school students, to critically analyze their character or personality traits. Insisting that students take the time to genuinely reflect during this assignment will produce a much more meaningful end product.*

NOUNS	ADJECTIVES	VERBS
Reader	Funny	Illustrate
Student	Adventurous	Play
Uncle	Organized	Design
Friend	Lazy	Create
Son	Risky	Google
Soccer player	Honest	Reflect

Unit Sequence—Core Curriculum	Teacher Reflections
I AM Poems/Bio-Poems Activity Before beginning to construct their own identity poems, students are given one to two class periods to investigate and explore identity poems written by various authors. Have students explore poetry in groups of four, using the following question to guide their discussion: How do the authors express their identity in their writing? How are the poems like the photographs from the first exercise? (See the Where Am I From Poetry Handout included at the end of Lesson 1.)	*Have a fund of poetry books and individual poems available for students to access throughout this entire unit. This collection will grow as the unit develops. You will find that students begin to depend on these resources and should be exposed frequently to good authors. This also allows for a diversification of reading material at varying levels of difficulty and interest, which is necessary in a classroom with many diverse reading and ability levels. (See Mattie Stepanek (2002) and Shel Silverstein (1994) references to poetry books at the end of this unit.)*

(Continued)

(Continued)

Unit Sequence—Core Curriculum	Teacher Reflections
Using sticky notes, students record conclusions about a writer's identity and perspective. They must be able to defend and explain their thinking in this process to others in their group by drawing upon evidence from the texts. As we walk around and observe student groups, we pose the following questions to analyze how well they are processing these ideas within their groups (especially looking for evidentiary clues): • How did this author use voice to express her or his identity in her or his writing? • What clues let you know who this person is? • What is this author's perspective about their identity(s)? • Does the author express any changes in her or his identity? • Do you see an identity in a poem that either relates to your own identity (similar) or is the opposite of your identity? • How could you use voice to express your identity through writing?	*This is also a time to instruct students on how to read a poem—which is entirely different than reading a piece of text, fiction or nonfiction. Students are instructed to read a poem three times. The first time is for decoding purposes only. This first read gives students a chance to say and identify all the words and to view the stanza format. A second reading focuses on fluency and rhythm. The third reading is specifically for comprehension. A fourth reading might even be used to seek evidence. Students use vocabulary, phrases, punctuation, and stanzas to create meaning.*
<div align="center">**Closure**</div>	
Students use their chart, timeline, concept wall, and ideas from group discussions and poetry to create their own Identity poems. As they work on these poems, ask them reflective questions about the following concepts: • Does your voice share your perspectives? • Has your voice revealed to your readers both how you have changed and the cause and effect of those changes? • Have you included in your poems how your identity has changed over time? • How does your writer's voice reveal your identity and move the reader beyond the stereotypical views of middle school students? Poems go through the entire editing process, producing a final draft for a class anthology. Students jointly develop a cover for the anthology, truly making this authentic work.	*An exact format does not need to be followed in order for students to express their identity. They are encouraged to choose a poetic format that they like. We have noted that some below-proficient students are unfamiliar with poetry and often give us a paragraph/story style. On a skills-based level, students are encouraged and reminded to utilize previously taught writing devices. (Example: rhyming, alliteration, repetition, stanzas, full circle endings, etc.)* *Students have gained awareness of their identities and are able to express who they are in writing.* *Blank books can be purchased from Studenttales.com. Books are prepared with a cover and a dedication, and they are sent to this publisher for binding. We kept one as a class book and donated the other to our school library (see also Authentic Authors mini-unit).*

WHO AM I? POWERPOINT WORKSHEET

Describe *who* each person is. *What* clues tell you this? What *inferences* did you make? (Number for as many pictures as you use.)

1. _____

2. _____

Your thoughts:

I AM POEM: OUTLINE WORKSHEET

20 Nouns Describing Who You Are	20 Adjectives Describing You	20 Verbs Describing What You Do

On the back, draw a timeline of important events in your life:

Copyright © 2010 by Corwin. All rights reserved. Reprinted from *Parallel Curriculum Units for Social Studies, Grades 6–12*, edited by Jeanne H. Purcell and Jann H. Leppien. Thousand Oaks, CA: Corwin, www.corwinpress.com. Reproduction authorized only for the local school site or nonprofit organization that has purchased this book.

WHERE AM I FROM POETRY HANDOUT

Where I'm From

by Penny Kittle

I'm from Belmont Street in Portland
just an alley away
from tall evergreens and vine raspberries in Mt. Tabor Park.
I'm from skinned knees and stubbed toes,
shooting hoops until the streetlight came on above the backboard
to call us home.
I'm from the pussy willow tree that draped long, spindly branches
over the
greenhouse roof creating a fort for me in the shelter of green.
I'm from "Time for dinner!" and "What can I get you to eat?"
lump-free mashed potatoes and gravy
roast beef and whole turkeys
bloated brussels sprouts and waxy limas I hid in my napkin
because the dog wouldn't eat 'em.
I'm from sugar cookies with elaborate icing
and cakes with multi-tiered roses.
I'm from homemade jams and donuts boiling in oil
then shook in a brown paper bag a quarter-full of cinnamon sugar
when friends spent the night.
I'm from a double bed I shared with my sister
whispering secrets across the covers
giggling in unison
until she went to high school.
I'm from Elton John records on a plastic orange record player
I'm from the Beach Boys
The Jackson Five
the Beatles
and always Elton
until I grew tougher and taller and discovered heavy metal.

Retrieved on May 20, 2009, from http://www.heinemanndrama.com/shared/onlineresources/002154/MyQuickWritestextsamples.pdf. Reprinted with permission.

LESSON 2: THE PURSUIT OF HAPPINESS (3 WEEKS)

Concepts

M1: Identity
M5: Perspective
M2: Change
M6: Cause and effect

This unit module was developed with the understanding that a deep examination of many different identities would lead to not only a strengthened awareness of one's own identity, but also to a realization that all identities can make a contribution to society and create a lasting effect on the world.

Principles

P1: People develop and change identities throughout their lives.
P2: Our identities change and are shaped by our environment and experiences.
P3: Our identity is partially determined by genetics/nature.
P5: Our roles/responsibilities within a society help to create who we are.

Skills

S2b: Organize writing using a logical arrangement of ideas
S2g: Develop ideas and content with relevant details, examples, and/or reasons
S4d: Recognize an author's or speaker's point of view and purpose

Standards

SD1: Students read a wide range of print and nonprint texts to build an understanding of texts, of themselves, and of the cultures of the United States and the world; to acquire new information; to respond to the needs and demands of society and the workplace; and for personal fulfillment. Among these texts are fiction and nonfiction, classic and contemporary works.
SD3: Students apply a wide range of strategies to comprehend, interpret, evaluate, and appreciate texts. They draw on their prior experience, their interactions with other readers and writers, their knowledge of word meaning and of other texts, their word identification strategies, and their understanding of textual features (e.g., sound-letter correspondence, sentence structure, context, and graphics).
SD6: Students apply knowledge of language structure, language conventions (e.g., spelling and punctuation), media techniques, figurative language, and genre to create, critique, and discuss print and nonprint texts.
SD7: Students conduct research on issues and interests by generating ideas and questions and by posing problems. They gather, evaluate, and synthesize data from a variety of sources (e.g., print and nonprint texts, artifacts, and people) to communicate their discoveries in ways that suit their purpose and audience.
SD11: Students participate as knowledgeable, reflective, creative, and critical members of a variety of literacy communities.
SD12: Students use spoken, written, and visual language to accomplish their own purposes (e.g., for learning, enjoyment, persuasion, and the exchange of information).

Guiding Questions

- What is identity?
- What shapes, creates, or changes identity?

- What makes identity dynamic and multifaceted?
- How does identity shape perspective?
- Can people have conflicting identities?
- What are our roles/responsibilities in society?
- How does society treat people who are different from what we consider the norm?
- What is the norm? Who decides?

The discussions around the guiding questions were very interesting and impacting for both teachers and students because we had many students from different cultures and backgrounds who shared narratives about having conflicting identities (e.g., dealing with Chinese culture in an American society). Invite and encourage students to share personal identity experiences. You will be amazed by what they bring to the table.

Unit Sequence—Curriculum of Connections	*Teacher Reflections*
Introduction	
Watch *Unknown White Male* video/DVD (see references). After viewing, have a class discussion using a two-column note form. Focusing questions: • What parts of his identity did he lose? • What parts of his identity did he keep? • What parts of his identity were innate to his person? • What parts of his identity were created by his experiences? • Is there a connection between Questions 1 and 2 and Questions 3 and 4? Why or why hot? Example of class chart: **Aspects of Identity** | *Lost*	*Maintained*
Experiences	Abilities
Memories of family	Race
Relationships	Age
Job	Language
Environment	Personality (some)
Name	Family		*This video can be used here to continue the process of understanding what shapes identity or as a culminating activity at the end of the unit.* *This video follows the path of a man who awakens one day with all episodic memories completely erased (global amnesia): his name, his residence, his family . . . everything about who he is. The documentary follows his journey to discovering his past and rebuilding his future. It is an intense look at the significance of identity and the many facets of identity people take for granted.* *Don't rush this discussion process. Really encourage students to step into the shoes of the main character. "What would it be like if you had this type of amnesia? What would it be like for* your *family? How would* you *recover?" Multiple class discussions and journal entries will deepen students' perspectives and develop ideas about identity.*

(Continued)

(Continued)

Unit Sequence—Curriculum of Connections	Teacher Reflections
Teaching Strategies and Learning Experiences	
Students read several biographical articles on different eccentric identities of your choice. As students read, they examine different aspects of each person's unique identity and record this information on a handout chart (Character Identity Poems Handout, included at the end of this mini-unit). As a class, students add to a large version of the chart posted in the classroom. Students work with partners to discuss the guiding questions and use the chart to explore and record the impact of culture, gender, age, experience, environment, and time on identity (both its development and changes). Students will find evidence and explain and defend their conclusions. They will begin to notice similarities and differences between different identities. The Jamestown series offers a set of questions after each story, including main idea, basic recall, sequencing, vocabulary, and drawing inferences. Students will respond to the questions at the end of each story.	*Stories are taken from the Jamestown Critical Reading series "Eccentrics." Stories are written at a level appropriate for Grades 6 to 8 and include mini-biographies on the following eccentric people: Black Bart, Dennis Rodman, Vincent Van Gogh, Carry Nation, Snowflake Bentley, and Salvador Dali.* *Vary the type of reading groupings and formats that students engage in for each story: reading aloud, silent reading, partner reading, small group reading, and teacher read alouds. While students respond well to routine, struggling readers also need to be constantly engaged during reading instruction. Reading the stories the same way each time leads to monotony, boredom, and finally frustration.* *Students who need reading and writing support tend to be more visual than auditory learners and tend to rely on graphic organizers to organize information, remember facts, and process core concepts. Posting a class chart, as well as giving out an individual handout, gives students constant access to the ideas and concepts being discussed. It can also serve as a model for skills such as bulleting, listing, summarizing, paraphrasing, and so on.* *According to the RTI model, in addition to monitoring fluency rates, comprehension progress monitoring is done to evaluate students' response to intervention. The comprehension questions following each story are a perfect tool to monitor students at their grade level because they closely resemble the types of questioning found on our statewide exams.* *Students with reading and writing difficulties often struggle to locate information in the text and defend their answers in a cohesive way. Often they "fill in" with what they assume. As oral practice, we will often pose statements such as "Van Gogh was a tortured soul," and have students prove the statement by providing direct evidence from the text.* *In staying with our Core Curriculum model of reading fluency, students read each selection three or four times. This aligns with current research, which suggests that multiple readings increase fluency, which in turn increases comprehension. These readings include silent reading, read alouds, partner reading, and home readings.*

Unit Sequence—Curriculum of Connections	Teacher Reflections
Extension Activities View the three "Starry Night" paintings of Van Gogh, listen to or read the words to "Starry, Starry Night" by McClain. Interpret or analyze aspects of Van Gogh's identity via his art. Students should begin to recognize that all different types of identities make meaningful contributions to our society, not just the typical identities most often studied in school. Have students select an eccentric identity to research, including all the identity aspects discussed in the previous eccentric identities. Identify a person in current times that may not be eccentric but has contributed or is contributing to society. How does their identity shape this contribution? How is their contribution shaping the city, country, or world?	*Even though students in our classes are struggling readers and writers, many are also highly motivated by grades and furthering their own knowledge. Students will often suggest to us ideas they have on extension activities, and they are free to take these on. This quest for continual improvement, hunger to be productive, and ongoing quest to expand their interests is something rarely seen in traditional special education or intervention classes.* *Students are learning about themselves, their uniqueness, and about acceptance of others' contributions in light of and in spite of differences.*
<td colspan="2" align="center">**Closure**</td>	

As a culminating activity to this mini-unit, students are asked to interview adults within the school community (outside sources if necessary or desired). Students will develop a list of questions to ask adults prior to the visits. Students are asked to think about the guiding questions as they create questions for the visitors, such as "Did you ever have conflicting identities? What experiences changed your identity over time? In America/U.S.?" Students broaden their knowledge of identity to encompass the ideas of culture and family. They also come to understand that different countries have very separate identities of their own and realize how difficult it is for people to balance and assimilate into a new culture. After the interviews, debrief the "Ah-ha" moments as a class: - What were revelations for you? - What did you connect to your own life? - What were their triumphs over adversity? - What adversity have you had to overcome? - What do these individuals' struggles reveal about our acceptance of what we consider different? - What can be universally stated about people's identities that we all share in common? - What then makes us unique? - How does choice become part of your identity?	*Within the school or community, identify adults from various cultural backgrounds. Invite them to the classroom to share their personal experiences and revelations about their challenges and life changes and their understanding of their own lives/identities. We invited an immigrant from Mexico who shared with us her fears as her family lived "illegal" for a time when she was in school; we also invited a man from the Ivory Coast who faced economic challenges and a Pakistani woman who faced challenges in America given her strict cultural standards and customs. Students were awed as the visitors (people they knew) gave insight into their struggles to assimilate yet maintain their own identities.*

CHARACTER IDENTITY POEMS HANDOUT

Name: _____

I think the poem _____

written by _____

is a reflection of _____ identity because:

_____
_____
_____
_____
_____
_____
_____
_____
_____
_____
_____
_____
_____

Write a convincing paragraph specifically explaining *why* this poem reflects the character's identity. Use specific details from the poem and from the short story about the character.

Attach a copy of the poem or write the poem on the back.

LESSON 3: AUTHENTIC AUTHORS (3–4 WEEKS)

Concepts

M1: Identity
M4: Voice

This unit module is developed through the Curriculum of Practice parallel and invites students to become true authors. Students engage in researching, drafting, revising, editing, and publishing their work. They also meet with illustrators, discuss illustration mediums, and finally attend a book signing of their final product—a true practitioner experience.

Principles

P6: Identity is dynamic, multifaceted, and cuts across all cultures.

Skills

S2a: Write in a variety of modes, such as narrative, expository, descriptive, and persuasive, for various audiences and purposes
S2b: Organize writing using a logical arrangement of ideas
S2c: Use language that supports and enriches the idea
S2g: Develop ideas and content with relevant details, examples, and/or reasons
S4d: Recognize an author's or speaker's point of view and purpose

Standards

SD2: Students read a wide range of literature from many periods in many genres to build an understanding of the many dimensions (e.g., philosophical, ethical, and aesthetic) of human experience.
SD4: Students adjust their use of spoken, written, and visual language (e.g., conventions, style, and vocabulary) to communicate effectively with a variety of audiences and for different purposes.
SD5: Students employ a wide range of strategies as they write and use different writing process elements appropriately to communicate with different audiences for a variety of purposes.
SD6: Students apply knowledge of language structure, language conventions (e.g., spelling and punctuation), media techniques, figurative language, and genre to create, critique, and discuss print and nonprint texts.
SD7: Students conduct research on issues and interests by generating ideas and questions and by posing problems. They gather, evaluate, and synthesize data from a variety of sources (e.g., print and nonprint texts, artifacts, and people) to communicate their discoveries in ways that suit their purpose and audience.
SD12: Students use spoken, written, and visual language to accomplish their own purposes (e.g., for learning, enjoyment, persuasion, and the exchange of information).

Guiding Questions

- What is this person's true identity?
- What experiences shaped this person's identity?
- Has their identity always been the same?
- What caused the changes?
- How have success and failure shaped their identity?

The Authentic Authors unit module can be written using any topic. Writing biographies lends itself to a unit exploring identity. These guiding questions should be used to help students maintain an identity focus.

Unit Sequence—Curriculum of Practice	Teacher Reflections
Background Information to Share About How Biographical Accounts, Narratives, and so on Are Constructed by Scholars	
	Prior to the introductory activity, share the following information with students to help them understand how and why biographical accounts help us to understand various people and the events that shaped their lives. Often, the philosophical, ethical, and aesthetic dimensions of human experience help students to understand a time period and vice versa.
	Biographers analyze and interpret the events in a person's life. They try to find connections, explain the meaning of unexpected actions or mysteries, and make arguments about the significance of the person's accomplishments or life activities.
	Biographies are usually about famous, or infamous, people, but a biography of an ordinary person can tell us a lot about a particular time and place. They are often about historical figures, but they can also be about people still living.
	Many biographies are written in chronological order. Some group time periods around a major theme (such as "early adversity" or "ambition and achievement"). Still others focus on specific topics or accomplishments.
	Biographers use primary and secondary sources: letters, diaries, newspaper accounts, other biographies, reference books, or histories that provide information about the subject.
	When you begin to write a biography, there are a few steps to take:
	1. Select a person you are interested in researching.
	2. Find out the basic facts of the person's life. Start with an encyclopedia and almanac.
	3. Think about what else you would like to know about the person and what parts of their life you want to write most about. Some questions you might want to think about include:
	• What makes this person special or interesting?
	• What kind of effect did he or she have on the world? Other people?
	• What are the adjectives you would use most to describe the person?
	• What examples from their life illustrate those qualities?
	• What events shaped or changed this person's life?
	• Did he or she overcome obstacles? Take risks? Get lucky? Would the world be better or worse if this person hadn't lived? How and why?

Unit Sequence—Curriculum of Practice	Teacher Reflections
Introduction	
Students browse through many biographical picture books. (See references for suggested biographies.) Using two-column notes, students keep track of ideas they want to use in their own books.	*The teacher should read a book out loud to begin browsing time, as well as doing a book talk on several other books each day. The teacher will read many biographical books aloud to give students multiple models for the book they soon will begin writing.*
Brainstorm a list of people students can choose to create their own informational picture book. This list could allow students to self select the biographies or for the teacher to list historical people tied to a particular social studies unit.	*Student choice on the subject of their research manifests project motivation and commitment. Students may need to be guided toward a subject whose identity may be more challenging to research.*
Students begin research on the person of their choice. Examples students have used in the past include Oprah Winfrey, Howard Schultz, Bethany Hamilton, Betty Ford, and Patricia Polacco.	*Students use several different types of graphic organizers to research and record findings (timeline, outline, circle map, Cornell notes).*
Teaching Strategies and Learning Experiences	
Students use their research to create a fictional story about their person while incorporating nonfictional facts.	*During the browsing time and book talks done by the teacher, a class survey of the different formats of informational picture books is collected.*
Students become authentic picture book authors as they continue through the entire writing process, including drafting, peer-editing, teacher-editing, revising, and final drafting.	*Toggle books, such as* The Magic School Bus, *toggle back and forth between a fictional story and nonfiction facts. Other books, like* Snowflake Bentley, *tell a biographical story while listing nonfictional facts in the margins of the picture book; still others create a biographical story using nonfictional facts with some fictional aspects to keep the story fluent. (Based on the life of…)*
	Students choose which format they want to write their biography in and select a picture book to be their "base text." This base text will help guide students in the direction of their own book. They can borrow formatting and organizational ideas from the author and apply them to their own stories. (Credit will be given to the author of the base text.)
Meeting With Collaborative Illustrators From the Art Class Students meet with art students to discuss medium ideas for illustrations. The author has to "sell" their book to the illustrator. Illustrators choose which books they want to illustrate and the illustration process begins in the art elective teacher's class. Our art teacher had students study a specific illustration medium and time period, thus illustrating the book using their research topic.	*Students can illustrate their own books; however, the illustrations tend to be time consuming. We have found spending several days, sometimes even weeks, on illustrations can lead to ineffective use of time during our exceptionally undersized 45-minute class periods. Also, meeting with potential illustrators and discussing medium ideas puts the young author in a realistic position of a true author and illustrator relationship.*

(Continued)

(Continued)

Unit Sequence—Curriculum of Practice	Teacher Reflections
Closure	
Completed books are published by the Studenttales.com publishing company. Publishing takes approximately one month. Authors and illustrators attend a book signing where their hardback books are presented to the public (friends and family) for the first time.	*Authors, illustrators, parents, and fellow teachers are invited to a formal book signing. Authors and illustrators sit at large tables and sign their copies for family. Refreshments are provided and students do read-alouds, book-talks, and answer questions from the crowd. It is truly a powerful night.*

LESSON 4: SOCIOCENTRISM (2–4 WEEKS)

Concepts

M5: Perspective
M1: Identity
M7: Conflict
M8: Prejudice

Discipline-Specific Concepts

- Groups versus individual
- Conformity
- Status symbols
- Loyalty acceptance
- Norms
- Taboos

In this lesson, students begin to deepen their views and perspectives about identity and explore the identity of groups. They progress from an intrinsic observation toward identity, to the realization that identity is more than just who we are and can change depending on the groups with whom we involve ourselves, such as cultural, professional, religious, familial, and peer groups.

Principles

P10: Group dynamics shape identity.
P11: Groups have individual identities.
P12: Groups often require conformity to norms or standards set by that group.

Skills

S1b: Summarize and synthesize fiction and nonfiction
S1d: Infer, using information in a variety of texts and genres
S6a: Read and respond to a variety of literature that represents perspectives from places, people, and events that are familiar and unfamiliar
S2a: Write in a variety of modes, such as narrative, expository, descriptive, and persuasive, for various audiences and purposes
S2c: Use language that supports and enriches the idea
S4d: Recognize an author's or speaker's point of view and purpose

Standards

SD1: Students read a wide range of print and nonprint texts to build an understanding of texts, of themselves, and of the cultures of the United States and the world; to acquire new information; to respond to the needs and demands of society and the workplace; and for personal fulfillment. Among these texts are fiction and nonfiction, classic and contemporary works.

SD2: Students read a wide range of literature from many periods in many genres to build an understanding of the many dimensions (e.g., philosophical, ethical, and aesthetic) of human experience.

SD3: Students apply a wide range of strategies to comprehend, interpret, evaluate, and appreciate texts. They draw on their prior experience, their interactions with other readers and writers, their knowledge of word meaning and of other texts, their word identification strategies, and their understanding of textual features (e.g., sound-letter correspondence, sentence structure, context, and graphics).

SD4: Students adjust their use of spoken, written, and visual language (e.g., conventions, style, and vocabulary) to communicate effectively with a variety of audiences and for different purposes.

SD5: Students employ a wide range of strategies as they write and use different writing process elements appropriately to communicate with different audiences for a variety of purposes.

SD6: Students apply knowledge of language structure, language conventions (e.g., spelling and punctuation), media techniques, figurative language, and genre to create, critique, and discuss print and nonprint texts.

SD12: Students use spoken, written, and visual language to accomplish their own purposes (e.g., for learning, enjoyment, persuasion, and the exchange of information).

Guiding Questions

- How does one's perspective shape or alter truth?
- How does what others think about you affect the way you think about yourself?
- What is group identity and what are the individual's responsibilities to that group as well as the groups' responsibilities to the individual?
- How does perception motivate behavior?
- What are consequences for nonconformity in groups?

These questions are asked with the intent that students develop an understanding that there is a reciprocal relationship between groups and individuals. There are also issues of conformity to a group and consequences when someone breaks the norms or taboos of that group.

Unit Sequence—Curriculum of Connections	Teacher Reflections
Introduction	
First, have students brainstorm all the groups they think they belong to and then name them.	Students generally share their family, church, sports, culture, school, age, race, and so on.
Next, have students look up and discuss the following words with partners and come to consensus in a group about them: conformity, status symbols, taboos, and stereotypes.	Different grouping adds differentiation to your lesson, and often kids get in the habit of partner-sharing to verbalize and check their thoughts with a peer.

(Continued)

(Continued)

Unit Sequence—Curriculum of Connections	Teacher Reflections
Finally, hand out the Anticipation Guide Worksheet, included at the end of this mini-unit, to discuss with students as they prepare to read *The Outsiders*.	*This works well both as a handout and if scanned and used through a projector where students can process as a whole group after writing their answers individually. Students have a chance to share their perspectives.*
Teaching Strategies and Learning Experiences	
Read the novel *The Outsiders*. Have students find powerful quotes throughout the book and defend their responses to them (see Reading Response Quotes Worksheet included at the end of Lesson 4). • Find quotes from different characters to bring out evidence of characterization. • Find quotes on different types of conflict and defend the type (external/internal). • Find quotes that answer the essential questions concerning group dynamics/actions. • Find quotes that support the book's themes: family, power, prejudice, loyalty, and sacrifice, and so on. • Find quotes to support a specific reader's response (see Reader's Responses Worksheet, included at the end of Lesson 4). In student composition journals, have students construct paragraphs that answer topical and book-specific questions, comparing and contrasting, and so on. • Compare the social norms of the Socs versus the Greasers. • Compare Pony Boy's and Darry's relationship prior to their parents' death and after their parents' death.	*This is a very engaging book for this age group and lends itself to reading as a large group, with partners, and individually. Breaking reading into different formats keeps resistant readers very engaged and motivated. It also adds differentiation (regarding reading levels, concept levels, and even gender), which can lead to more interesting discussions, etc.* *Different chapters can have different focus questions/quotes.* *With this book, you can focus on necessary skills throughout and use evidence journals as their form of record keeping.* *Each student has their own composition book which is used for warm-ups, reader's responses, question pages, and so on. This is a unit that lends itself to a variety of short written responses and reflective writing.*
View the film *The Outsiders* and move to the culminating activity.	*In many classrooms, a movie is saved until last as a reward for finishing a book. In this mini-unit, the movie is used to enhance the book by watching it in parts along with the book. Struggling readers who have difficulty using imagery can often connect to the text better when they are provided a visual reference.*

Unit Sequence—Curriculum of Connections	Teacher Reflections
Closure	
Review and discuss the groups to which students belong. Hand out the worksheet on Sociocentrism—both the chart and the sheet called Questioning Our Sociocentrism Worksheet that are included at the end of this mini-unit. Read through the information on sociocentrism together as a class and then discuss how *The Outsiders* reflected this concept and its effect on one's identity. After students discuss their thinking, select one group on which to focus questions as a model as they complete the chart. After processing one group's questions, students are left to individually finish the chart as a summative assessment.	*As the authors (Foundation for Critical Thinking) of this concept state, "Blind conformity to group restrictions is automatic and unreflective. Most conform without recognizing their conformity. They internalize group norms and beliefs, take on group identities, and act as 'expected'—without the least sense that what they are doing might reasonably be questioned." It is the hope that students grow in their identity as they see choices and reflect on the groups/dynamics to which they belong.*
Extension Activity	
Juvenile Justice Offenders Visit Have students prepare questions they wish to ask the youth visitors ahead of time. The majority of questions should reflect concepts from the sociocentrism unit.	*If there is an opportunity to have incarcerated juveniles come visit, it is a powerful experience. Our visitors came as part of their rehabilitation—going to schools to share their stories. What came from this were stories of pressures, expectations, group norms, and so on, on a very high level. What also was shared was the determination of the youths to withstand serious types of conformity in thought, emotion, and action in their lives after release and their goals for the future.*

ANTICIPATION GUIDE WORKSHEET

The Outsiders, by S. E. Hinton

Purpose of the Strategy

Anticipation guides are reading aids that allow the reader to make predictions. By making predictions about text, readers are able to eliminate unlikely possibilities. Also called *reaction* or *prediction guides*, the anticipation guide is a way to prepare readers prior to a reading assignment by asking them to react to a series of statements related to the content of the material. The three reasons for using anticipation guides include: (1) relating prior knowledge to new information enhances comprehension, (2) creating interest stimulates discussion on the topic, and (3) they create possibilities for integrating reading and writing instruction.

Directions

1. *Read passage or story.* Read and analyze the text to identify its major concepts (both explicit and implicit).

2. *Decide on major concepts.* Decide which concepts are most important. Use these to create student interest and to agitate or stimulate reflection on prior knowledge and beliefs.

3. *Write statements on major concepts.* Write a series of short, declarative statements about the major concepts in the passage or story. The statements should be thought-provoking and reflect the students' backgrounds. General statements are better than abstract or overly specific ones. Famous quotations and idioms work well. The statements should be written in a format that will allow students to predict and anticipate.

Retrieved and adapted from http://forpd.ucf.edu/strategies/stratAnt.html on May 20, 2009.

READING RESPONSE QUOTES WORKSHEET

Name: _____

Directions: From each page that you read, select one sentence that seems the most powerful to you. Tell why it was your choice—what was important about it or why it was important to the story, setting, characters, and so on.

Page	Quote	Response

Copyright © 2010 by Corwin. All rights reserved. Reprinted from *Parallel Curriculum Units for Social Studies, Grades 6–12*, edited by Jeanne H. Purcell and Jann H. Leppien. Thousand Oaks, CA: Corwin, www.corwinpress.com. Reproduction authorized only for the local school site or nonprofit organization that has purchased this book.

READER'S RESPONSES WORKSHEET

Things to Consider When You Read

- **What does the text have to do with you, personally**, and with your life (past, present, or future)? It is not acceptable to write that the text has *nothing* to do with you, since just about everything humans can write has to do, in some way, with every other human.

- **How much does the text agree or clash with your view of the world and what you consider right and wrong?** Use several quotes as examples of how the text agrees with and supports what you think about the world, about right and wrong, and about what you think it is to be human. Use quotes and examples to discuss how the text disagrees with what you think about the world and about right and wrong.

- **How did you learn, and how much were your views and opinions challenged or changed by this text, if at all?** Did the text communicate with you? Why or why not? Give examples of how your views might have changed or been strengthened (or perhaps, of why the text failed to convince you). Please do not write "I agree with everything the author wrote," since everybody disagrees about something, even if it is a tiny point. Use quotes to illustrate your points of challenge, or where you were persuaded, or where it left you cold.

QUESTIONING OUR SOCIOCENTRISM WORKSHEET

Living a human life entails membership in a variety of human groups. This typically includes groups such as nation, culture, profession, religion, family, and peer. We find ourselves participating in groups before we are even aware of ourselves as living beings. What is more, every group to which we belong has some social definition of itself and some (usually unspoken) rules guiding the behavior of all members. Each group to which we belong imposes some level of conformity on us as a condition of acceptance. This includes a set of beliefs, behaviors, and taboos.

For most people, conformity to group restrictions is automatic and unreflective. Most conform without recognizing their conformity. They internalize group norms and beliefs, take on group identities, and act as expected—without the least sense that what they are doing might reasonably be questioned. Most people function in social groups unreflectively, assuming the rightness of the system of beliefs, attitudes, and behaviors to which they conform.

This conformity of thought, emotion, and action is not restricted to the masses, or to the lowly, or to the poor. It is characteristic of people in general, independent of their role in society, independent of status and prestige, independent of their years of schooling. Conformity of thought and behavior is the rule in human life, independence and nonconformity are the rare exception.

Sociocentric thinking is egocentric thinking raised to the level of the group. It is as destructive as egocentric thinking, if not more so, as it carries with it the sanction of a social group. When sociocentric thinking is made explicit in the mind of the thinker, its unreasonableness is generally evident. However, just as individuals deceive themselves through egocentric thinking, groups deceive themselves through sociocentric thinking. Just as egocentric thinking functions to serve one's selfish interest, sociocentric thinking operates to validate the uncritical thinking of the group.

Questions to ask:

- What groups do I belong to and how do they influence my behavior when I am with them? How do these groups influence my behavior when I am away from them?
- Is it in my best interest to belong to these groups?
- What does this group require of its members (what are its demands)?
- What behaviors does this group forbid (what are its taboos)?
- What behaviors are allowed within the group (what is its range of free decision)?
- What would happen to me if I went against the taboos of the group or culture? Would I be ostracized? Would I be imprisoned? Would I be killed?
- How does my society influence my behavior?
- What is involved in thinking like an . . . American (a German, the Japanese, etc.)?
- Have I ever thought within the perspective of another culture?
- What beliefs and behaviors does my culture punish? Are these forbidden behaviors unethical, or are they culturally relative?
- What would happen to me if I violated any of the taboos of my culture?

Copyright © 2010 by Corwin. All rights reserved. Reprinted from *Parallel Curriculum Units for Social Studies, Grades 6–12*, edited by Jeanne H. Purcell and Jann H. Leppien. Thousand Oaks, CA: Corwin, www.corwinpress.com. Reproduction authorized only for the local school site or nonprofit organization that has purchased this book.

QUESTIONING OUR SOCIOCENTRISM

(The groups we belong to and the rules that bind us . . .)

Groups	How does this group influence my behaviors?	What are the demands this group places on its members?	What behaviors does this group forbid?	What would happen if I went against the rules of this group/culture?
Family				
School				
Religion				
Race				
Gender				
Adolescence (age)				
Other				

Copyright © 2010 by Corwin. All rights reserved. Reprinted from *Parallel Curriculum Units for Social Studies, Grades 6–12*, edited by Jeanne H. Purcell and Jann H. Leppien. Thousand Oaks, CA: Corwin, www.corwinpress.com. Reproduction authorized only for the local school site or nonprofit organization that has purchased this book.

LESSON 5: THE CITY (1–2 WEEKS)

Concepts

M1: Identity
M4: Voice

Discipline-Specific Concepts

- Community
- Environment

In this unit, students begin to deepen their views and perspectives about identity. They progress from inner observations about identity to the realization that identity is more than just who we are on the inside. They investigate the idea that identity is shaped and fashioned through a dimensional lens that allows many factors to be incorporated.

Principles

P4: Writers' voices reveal much about their identities and reflect their personality, time, culture, and so on.
P2: Our identities change and are shaped by our environment and experiences.
P13: Communities and cities can have very unique and individual identities that influence who we are.

Skills

S1b: Summarize and synthesize fiction and nonfiction
S1d: Infer, using information in a variety of texts and genres
S6a: Read and respond to a variety of literature that represents perspectives from places, people, and events that are familiar and unfamiliar
S5a, 5b: Use organizational features of printed and electronic text to locate information
S2c: Use language that supports and enriches the idea
S4d: Recognize an author's or speaker's point of view and purpose

Standards

SD1: Students read a wide range of print and nonprint texts to build an understanding of texts, of themselves, and of the cultures of the United States and the world; to acquire new information; to respond to the needs and demands of society and the workplace; and for personal fulfillment. Among these texts are fiction and nonfiction, classic and contemporary works.
SD2: Students read a wide range of literature from many periods in many genres to build an understanding of the many dimensions (e.g., philosophical, ethical, and aesthetic) of human experience.
SD3: Students apply a wide range of strategies to comprehend, interpret, evaluate, and appreciate texts. They draw on their prior experience, their interactions with other readers and writers, their knowledge of word meaning and of other texts, their word identification strategies, and their understanding of textual features (e.g., sound-letter correspondence, sentence structure, context, and graphics).
SD4: Students adjust their use of spoken, written, and visual language (e.g., conventions, style, and vocabulary) to communicate effectively with a variety of audiences and for different purposes.

(Continued)

(Continued)

SD5: Students employ a wide range of strategies as they write and use different writing process elements appropriately to communicate with different audiences for a variety of purposes.

SD6: Students apply knowledge of language structure, language conventions (e.g., spelling and punctuation), media techniques, figurative language, and genre to create, critique, and discuss print and nonprint texts.

SD12: Students use spoken, written, and visual language to accomplish their own purposes (e.g., for learning, enjoyment, persuasion, and the exchange of information).

Guiding Questions

- What are the unique traits and identities of different cities—what makes these identities?
- How does environment shape identity?
- How do different environments compare or contrast in identity creation?
- How has your environment shaped your identity?
- Will environment cease to affect identity?
- If environment changes, does identity change as well? Always? Is this always a positive change?

These questions are asked with the intent that students develop an understanding of the reciprocal relationship between environment and identity.

Unit Sequence—Curriculum of Connections	Teacher Reflections
Introduction	
Begin the unit with the picture book poem "Harlem" by Walter Dean Myers (1997). Add other poems related to cities that you find (e.g., "City" by Langston Hughes, "The City is so Big" by Richard Garcia, "In the Inner City" by Lucille Clifton, "Daybreak in Alabama" by Langston Hughes).	*Give the students an opportunity to listen to the words and the sentence fluency before they are asked to analyze the text.*
On the first read, the teacher should read the book aloud to the students while they listen. On the second read, the teacher should read aloud as listening students create a graffiti board. Students then share with the class what they wrote/drew on their graffiti board. Ask guiding (essential) questions as students share. • What do you know about Walter Dean Myers? • How has his environment shaped his identity? • How did the city of Harlem have a unique identity of its own? How do you know? • What evidence do you hear in the poem? • Did his environment have a positive or negative effect on his identity? • How was his environment similar/different from yours?	*Graffiti Board: A group of four students share one large piece of paper. Using markers, they write words and phrases or draw pictures or diagrams of what they hear in the poem—essentially putting graffiti on the paper.* *Students then share and discuss what they wrote/drew on their graffiti board, making connections with the text and essential questions.*

Unit Sequence—Curriculum of Connections	Teacher Reflections
Teaching Strategies and Learning Experiences	
Students begin their own book annotation of "Harlem." They begin by brainstorming ideas about the city they believe has shaped their own identity the most. Students use their brainstorming and voice techniques to write their own city poem, expressing the unique characteristics of their city and how their identity has been shaped by this environment. They use "Harlem" as a base text, borrowing formatting ideas from Myers. Students create a final draft of their city poem and read it to the class. Other students have an opportunity to ask the poet about the environment that shaped their identity and pose questions similar to those that were asked while reading "Harlem." (See Examples of Student Poems that are included at the end of Lesson 5.)	*Students brainstorm events, places, people, memories, and experiences of the city of their choice, using a circle map format. (See example posted at http://www.thinkingmaps.com/httmexam.php3)* *"Harlem" ends with the word Harlem and a single period. As a class, we discuss the importance of this simple yet meaningful ending and encourage students to end their poem the same way.*
Closure	
Students browse through many other poem books looking for poems about environment. They are invited to choose two poems: one with an environment similar to the one they have experienced and another in contrast to that. Both poems are recited to the class. Students discuss similarities and differences between the two poems' environments and their effects on identity.	*Struggling readers have a dire need to improve fluency. Rereading large passages, articles, and novels to strengthen fluency can be daunting and discouraging. However, rereading poetry is much more manageable and motivating. In order for students to be able to recite the poems, several readings must take place beforehand, thus improving fluency skills.*

EXAMPLES OF STUDENT POEMS

City Poem (6th grader)

The smoke in the air
Coughing and sneezing.
People walking on both
Sides of the street.
Bumping left and right
Trying to stay on a steady course.
Looking at the skyscrapers
Up and up they go
Looking like soldiers waiting for a command.
Going to shop and seeing what you can buy
Sitting on the bus watching
All kinds of people getting on and off,
Coming and going
Seeing cars zoom past the bus.
Rich people, poor people going to the 16th street mall.
Honking up and down the streets,
Jets fly in the sky
Booming like guns.
LODO

Lake Havasu City (6th grader)

Waves hitting the beach banks, seagulls flying above
Children swimming, fish in the water
Scorching sun on my face
Snakes in the desert, lizards under rocks
Big dead trees
Garage sales everywhere, families in every house
Children running around
Hot asphalt, Dairy Queens everywhere
Girls in bikinis
Carnivals every year, fireworks on the Fourth of July
Dogs barking, Dogs Walking, Dogs sleeping
Paint-balling in the desert

Walking on the London Bridge
Ice cream in the summer, baseball at every park
Children at every playground, tank tops and shorts, bathing suits
Ice cold water, 118 outside
Air conditioning in every house
Beach parties, knee boarding, tubing, wave boarding
Fishing everywhere, sunglasses on everyone's face
Sun block on everyone's back
Colorful beach balls, sandcastles on the beach
Towel on the hot sand, goggles on the children's faces
Slip 'n slide in every park
Camping out in the backyard, swap meet on every Sunday
Jet ski races
The one and only .... Lake Havasu City

City Poem (7th grader)

Through the streets of Lahore
People burning up
Bumpy roads
Sand and dirt—all over the place
Stores on every corner
Smell of bakeries
Pastries and cake
Crowds of people—
People walking through the rush of cars
Kids at the age of 10 driving
Gangs teaming up with police
All the same old white Hondas
Busted up Camrys
No street lights
Stop signs, or police officers saying,
"You are under arrest"
The smell of strong foods
Spicing up your mouth
People homeless—walking
Knocking on your car doors
Always stopping you—asking for money
People running around

Trying not to miss the bus

Everywhere you go

People on bull carts

Family reunions—all the time

People sitting—on the roofs of their houses

City fairs, festivals, carnivals

Agricultural fields

Full of fruit and vegetables

Trees full of oranges

Fields of sugar canes

Students walking to school

All dress up the same

Schools separated by gender

Students standing up

Giving respect to the teacher

Shops full of stuff—bangles, clothes, jewelry

Cows, buffalos, and sheep

In everyone's houses

People going to church—praying 5 times a day

Never losing hope—always having dreams

Someone always at your house

Walking over rooftops

Simple and shy people

Living in the small villages

Modern out-going people

Living in the cities

Lovable people

Girls putting on henna tattoos

Boys playing Cricket

Always happy

Full of life

Lahore!

Copyright © 2010 by Corwin. All rights reserved. Reprinted from *Parallel Curriculum Units for Social Studies, Grades 6–12*, edited by Jeanne H. Purcell and Jann H. Leppien. Thousand Oaks, CA: Corwin, www.corwinpress.com. Reproduction authorized only for the local school site or nonprofit organization that has purchased this book.

LESSON 6: THE GREAT DEPRESSION (4 WEEKS)

Concepts

M2: Change
M5: Perspective
M1: Identity

The unit progresses to the concept of the unique identity of countries, in this case the United States. Students will discover that the United States has undergone changes and that the domino effects and ramifications from the event continue to be felt long after it is over. As we look at similarities across time, we continue to explore the social and cultural outcomes of historic events.

Principles

P14: The Great Depression and the Dust Bowl altered the identity of America politically, economically, socially, and culturally.
P15: Hardships and catastrophic events lead to both positive and negative changes due to coping, making sacrifices, working cooperatively, and government programs.
P16: Relationships exist between "then" and "now."

Skills

S1b: Summarize and synthesize fiction and nonfiction
S1c: Locate and paraphrase main ideas and supporting details from fiction and nonfiction
S1d: Infer, using information in a variety of texts and genres
S5a, 5b: Use organizational features of printed and electronic text to locate information
S6a: Read and respond to a variety of literature that represents perspectives from places, people, and events that are familiar and unfamiliar
S2c: Use language that supports and enriches the idea
S4d: Recognize an author's or speaker's point of view and purpose

Standards

SD1: Students read a wide range of print and nonprint texts to build an understanding of texts, of themselves, and of the cultures of the United States and the world; to acquire new information; to respond to the needs and demands of society and the workplace; and for personal fulfillment. Among these texts are fiction and nonfiction, classic and contemporary works.
SD3: Students apply a wide range of strategies to comprehend, interpret, evaluate, and appreciate texts. They draw on their prior experience, their interactions with other readers and writers, their knowledge of word meaning and of other texts, their word identification strategies, and their understanding of textual features (e.g., sound-letter correspondence, sentence structure, context, and graphics).
SD7: Students conduct research on issues and interests by generating ideas and questions and by posing problems. They gather, evaluate, and synthesize data from a variety of sources (e.g., print and nonprint texts, artifacts, and people) to communicate their discoveries in ways that suit their purpose and audience.

(Continued)

(Continued)

SD8: Students use a variety of technological and information resources (e.g., libraries, databases, computer networks, and videos) to gather and synthesize information and to create and communicate knowledge.

SD12: Students use spoken, written, and visual language to accomplish their own purposes (e.g., for learning, enjoyment, persuasion, and the exchange of information).

Guiding Questions

- How did the Depression era change the identity of the individuals who lived during this time?
- How was the American identity changed?
- How did the Depression alter family roles and bonds?
- What are the processes in the formation of values/what is your social responsibility to your government?
- What is the possibility of and the factors that could impact another depression?
- Have we had one? What groups were impacted the most and why?

We want students to be aware of the difference between the Great Depression and recessions or smaller depression times (e.g., after 9/11).

Unit Sequence—Curriculum of Connections	Teacher Reflections
Introduction	
Students are presented with words that pertain to the Depression and the Dust Bowl of the 1930s: panhandling, hobo-jungles, dust bowl, stock market, Black Tuesday, Okies, lean-to, and so on. Students discuss what these terms may mean and are told they will be researching the terms in order to understand the identity of that specific era.	*It is vitally important to prepare students with vocabulary and background knowledge for this unit. It also requires them to pursue, investigate, and question as we set the stage for understanding the entire mini-lesson and reading the novel. This helps students deepen their thinking to uncover generalizations about people, time periods, and issues as they occur in the past, today, and over time.* *This list of Depression era words should remain visible in the classroom throughout the entire unit to allow for additions as students discover new terms relating to this period. This can be done in conjunction with a point/reward system as well if desired.* *This activity fulfills several needs: using research skills, text interpretation, summarizing, synthesizing, inferring, and using organizational features of electronic text to locate information. Students learn how to apply the skills of a practitioner and to draw conclusions about individuals, society, and American culture.*

Unit Sequence—Curriculum of Connections	Teacher Reflections
Web Activities Students are presented with a series of Web sites and a series of questions and required to formulate questions (see Web Activities to Explore the Great Depression [Mini-Examples] Worksheet included at the end of Lesson 6). Much of this would be Core information as they are finding and developing basic concepts of this time. Students should come to the conclusion that people of the time were faced with the unimaginable challenges of extraordinary times. Obtain a copy of the film *Riding the Rails* (see film transcription at http://www.pbs.org/wgbh/amex/rails/filmmore/description.html). *Riding the Rails* is a powerful documentary with real footage from the '30s that shows rampant poverty and the desperation that forced thousands of teens into a "refugee" life, traveling from town to town, begging for money and food, and sleeping in hobo camps. Students are directed to note information about why teens left home during the Depression era, what experiences they had, and to pose questions as they occur to them as they watch. *"Note at least 15 to 20 new pieces of information and at least 10 questions you have while you view the movie."* Debriefing: in groups or as an entire class: - How did the Great Depression change the identity of the individuals who experienced it? - In what ways was the U.S. identity changed? - How did the Depression alter family roles and bonds? - What actions did the government take to aid people of the times? - What questions did you have and can anyone propose possible answers?	*We started with a Web site (http://www.english.uiuc.edu/maps/depression/photoessay.htm) that was primarily photographs with captions.* *As students read to identify elements of an era's identity, they will learn to distinguish between meaningful versus less significant information.* *This fascinating saga is emotionally evocative. Particularly with connections made to today's homeless, it is a story of overwhelming importance. The film begs discussion of what immigrants, refugees, and homeless people face all over the world. This is a great way for students to examine the similarities of problems over time, cultures, and systems. In turn, students make connections between factors that create catastrophic events and factors that may help mitigate them.*

(Continued)

(Continued)

Unit Sequence—Curriculum of Connections	Teacher Reflections
Teaching Strategies and Learning Experiences	
Children of the Dust Topical Questions: • Where did the Dust Bowl occur and what were the causes? • How did the Dust Bowl affect Midwest farm families? • What were events specific to the Dust Bowl (dust pneumonia, grasshopper plague, etc.)? *Out of the Dust* Students read specific parts/chapters of the book *Out of the Dust* and discuss historical fiction as a genre as well as the connections they see to actual events.	*This is a wonderful photographic text for building background knowledge.* *A good Web site to use for photographs is http://www.weru.ksu.edu/new_weru/multimedia/dustbowl/dustbowlpics.html* *Some students are unfamiliar with the genre of historical fiction, but a parallel to the popular movie, The Titanic, helps bring the idea into focus. Various types of reading styles occur with this book: partner reading, class reading, and individual chapter reading for information where students read and share their information with the class. This makes them solely responsible (or with a partner) for reading and summarizing important main ideas and details.*
Closure	
Use the Great Depression Tic-Tac-Toe Worksheet, included at the end of this mini-unit, and the Jeopardy game described in the right-hand column to review information gathered about the Great Depression. **Culminating Activity—Depression Era Interviews** This is the culminating activity of this mini-unit. Students individually create questions prior to meeting adults who lived during the Depression and write up the interview using a true interview format.	*These two game formats are ideal for middle school students in intervention classes. Students work with teams or partners to discuss, review, and process information at a high level of thinking and with a high level of motivation. The Jeopardy link allows you to format the game with your own questions and answers specific to this unit and class/teacher individual characteristics.* *http://facstaff.uww.edu/jonesd/games/games_parade_jeopardy.html* *Develop a rubric to evaluate the thoughtfulness and effectiveness of questions and the depth and breadth of their interviews.* *This interview process can lead to thoughtful dialog that invites reflective and critical thinking. The activity puts the students into the role of true investigators on a very personal level. Students learn from the interview process and from*

Unit Sequence—Curriculum of Connections	Teacher Reflections
Examples of student questions include: • In what ways were you impacted by the Great Depression and/or Dust Bowl? • Did you or anyone you know leave home or get forced from home, and how did that impact the family? • What jobs were available to you/your parents during this time? • How did this time period alter the identity of America politically, economically, socially, and culturally? • How were you affected both positively and negatively by coping, making sacrifices, working cooperatively, and by any of the government programs of this time? • What relationships exist between "then" and "now" as you think about this time period? **Debriefing** Students are invited to share interesting anecdotes they gleaned during their interviews. Ask students to explain how the interview responses help to address the guiding questions posed at the beginning of this unit segment.	*integrating their research and information into thoughtfully posed questions. Assisted living facilities and nursing homes are often open to visits from schools for residents to share their personal stories. Students also had the option of interviewing known adults, such as grandparents.* *As they share their interview, students should also be asked how individual identities can be shaped by the times and how their lives are shaped by the events that take place during their lives.*

WEB ACTIVITIES TO EXPLORE THE GREAT DEPRESSION (MINI-EXAMPLES) WORKSHEET

Name: _____

Task 1: Go to http://www.english.illinois.edu/maps/depression/photoessay.htm and look through the pictures and read each caption. Select 20 photos that have an impact on you, and write a description or short reflection about that impact or about what you learned.

Example:

Picture 3: (Unemployed men vying for jobs at the American Legion Employment Bureau in Los Angeles during the Great Depression.) This picture . . .

Task 2: Go to http://www.pbs.org/wgbh/amex/dustbowl/index.html and view the information at this location to respond to the following questions:

- What were the Roaring Twenties?
- What was Black Tuesday?
- What period of time did the Great Depression encompass?
- How many Americans were out of work?
- Why did the depression hit men the hardest?
- Why did African Americans suffer more than whites?

Task 3: Go to http://www.michigan.gov/hal/0,1607,7-160-15481_19268_20778-52530-,00.html, which includes a chart for you to complete on the Then & Now Prices comparing the Great Depression with current times. Print the chart and fill it in with the costs of today. If you need to research more for prices, do so. Provide then and now prices for the items that follow and then and now wages for the jobs. Why was it so difficult for people to purchase even the basics when prices seem so cheap to us?

Winter coat	Sled that steers	Electric sewing machine
Leather bag	Ping-Pong table	Electric washing machine
Bathrobe	Mechanical toys	Gas stove (i.e., $19.95 then)
Men's shirt	Doll	
Wool sweater	Table lamp	

Wages

Production worker

Cook

Doctor

Accountant

Copyright © 2010 by Corwin. All rights reserved. Reprinted from *Parallel Curriculum Units for Social Studies, Grades 6–12*, edited by Jeanne H. Purcell and Jann H. Leppien. Thousand Oaks, CA: Corwin, www.corwinpress.com. Reproduction authorized only for the local school site or nonprofit organization that has purchased this book.

GREAT DEPRESSION TIC-TAC-TOE WORKSHEET

Out of the Dust Tic-Tac-Toe

Names: _____

Pages 90, 100, 102, 104, 109, 117, 119, 127, 136, 140, 142

After reading/reviewing these pages, get with a partner and play tic-tac-toe. Write both your partner's and your own answers on an answer sheet that will be turned in. You must agree with your partner's answer before they are allowed to put their name in the square.

List three important details of these pages.	What was the significance of this time period for specific people/characters?	What description/detail is the hardest to understand?
Think about something you know about that is similar to the Depression or Dust Bowl. List two ways it is similar and two ways it is different.	What two features of these pages do you find most interesting?	Identify a hidden detail that most people wouldn't notice from these pages.
List three questions that could come from these pages.	List three things that you know about the Dust Bowl or Depression that relate to this story.	Give three reasons why it is important to learn about this topic/unit.

Copyright © 2010 by Corwin. All rights reserved. Reprinted from *Parallel Curriculum Units for Social Studies, Grades 6–12*, edited by Jeanne H. Purcell and Jann H. Leppien. Thousand Oaks, CA: Corwin, www.corwinpress.com. Reproduction authorized only for the local school site or nonprofit organization that has purchased this book.

LESSON 7: A SIGN OF THE TIMES (2–3 WEEKS)

Concepts

M7: Conflict
M2: Change
M5: Perspective

Discipline-Specific Concepts

- Globalization
- Information age
- Technology

One of the driving reasons for this lesson and its accompanying concepts was the realization that students generally lack knowledge of historical events prior to the last five years of their lives. As we explore our country's identity, students need to be aware of the events that still affect us today, whether through political, social, economic, or cultural avenues.

Principles

P17: Cultural identities are developed, and they change over time.
P18: Time periods have trends and themes associated with them.
P19: Conclusions can be drawn about society and culture from these trends and themes.
P20: These identities are shaped by intentional acts and chance occurrences.
P21: Artists' voices reflect and can shape culture, personality, time, and opinions.

Skills

S1b: Summarize and synthesize fiction and nonfiction
S1c: Locate and paraphrase main ideas and supporting details from fiction and nonfiction
S5a, 5b: Use organizational features of printed and electronic text to locate information
S2a: Write in a variety of modes such as narrative, expository, descriptive, and persuasive, for various audiences and purposes
S2b: Organize writing using a logical arrangement of ideas
S2c: Use language that supports and enriches the idea
S2g: Develop ideas and content with relevant details, examples, and/or reasons

Standards

SD1: Students read a wide range of print and nonprint texts to build an understanding of texts, of themselves, and of the cultures of the United States and the world; to acquire new information; to respond to the needs and demands of society and the workplace; and for personal fulfillment. Among these texts are fiction and nonfiction, classic and contemporary works.
SD4: Students adjust their use of spoken, written, and visual language (e.g., conventions, style, and vocabulary) to communicate effectively with a variety of audiences and for different purposes.
SD5: Students employ a wide range of strategies as they write and use different writing process elements appropriately to communicate with different audiences for a variety of purposes.
SD7: Students conduct research on issues and interests by generating ideas and questions and by posing problems. They gather, evaluate, and synthesize data from a variety of sources (e.g., print and nonprint texts, artifacts, and people) to communicate their discoveries in ways that suit their purpose and audience.

> SD8: Students use a variety of technological and informational resources (e.g., libraries, databases, computer networks, and videos) to gather and synthesize information and to create and communicate knowledge.
>
> SD12: Students use spoken, written, and visual language to accomplish their own purposes (e.g., for learning, enjoyment, persuasion, and the exchange of information).
>
> ### Guiding Questions
>
> - How did these events impact the world as a whole?
> - What continuing ramifications are there from these events, if any?
> - What lasting or changing impact did these events have on the people of the time?
> - How do different countries or communities respond to events such as these?
> - How does America's identity change with events such as these?
> - How is America viewed today throughout the world?
>
> It is important for students to understand that historical events continue to have impacts long past the original event, sometimes creating a domino effect.
>
> Create questions for investigations related to core historical themes and specific time periods.

Unit Sequence—Curriculum of Connections	Teacher Reflections
Introduction	
Students listen to Billy Joel's song "We Didn't Start the Fire." Ask students to recall if they have ever heard this song before and consider why Billy Joel would have created this song. What was his voice trying to say to listeners?	*There are several sites that have photos in conjunction with the lyrics. This song chronicles the years from 1949 to 1989, with many important aspects highlighted during each year/decade, including political, economic, and cultural statements.* *Two sites are listed here, but many others are available.* • *http://www.teacheroz.com/fire.htm* • *http://www.ugcs.caltech.edu/~yeli23/Flash/Fire.html*
Teaching Strategies and Learning Experiences	
Students choose a specific year from the song to research. Set up several Web sites ahead of time for them to access. Student must not only investigate the specific events but must determine what impact the events of their chosen time period had, and continue to have, on our society and if applicable, on our world. From their research, students will compile their investigations into a product: (poster, PowerPoint, newspaper).	*Again, there are several sites with links to the specifics in the song that students can access. A page of specific sites was made for students to access (bms.westport.k12.ct.us/lmc/WDStF.htm).* *The worksheet that divides up the years is also listed for use if desired: www.rhinelander.k12.wi.us/.../Class%20links%20&%20TeacherWebs/Social%Studies/Fire/student_track.doc.*

(Continued)

(Continued)

Unit Sequence—Curriculum of Connections	Teacher Reflections
The projects are shared by the students with their peers and are open to peer questioning and critique. Again, the guiding questions are reviewed and pursued specifically: How did these recent events impact the American identity? How is the United States viewed (over time) by other countries?	*Use the rubric for project evaluation that is included at the end of this mini-unit, Research Report: We Didn't Start the Fire Rubric, for scoring the accuracy of information about specific events and the thoughtfulness of students' conclusions about the ramifications of events.*
Closure	

Creating Personal Newspapers As a class group, students discuss the specific parts of a newspaper and the placement of sections of the paper (actual examples available). Students will compose a personal newspaper with events and information from the decade of their birth. It is the job of a reporter to inform the reader about events and their impacts on community, nations, and the world. Students are instructed to go to Microsoft Office, to publications for print, newsletters, and pick a format of their choice. They were to include "hard news" and "soft news," keeping in mind the essential questions to guide their writing. World and national "hard" news was printed in the first two pages with "softer" news, such as costs of the times, movies, sports, and so on, on the last two pages. Students read excerpts/mini-articles from resources that include The Hubble Telescope, LA Riots, Hurricane Andrew, Waco, O.J. Trial, Oklahoma City bombing, Docking of Atlantis with Mir, Unabomber, Cloning controversy, Mission to Mars. In "1990s: The Way We Lived," we read excerpts of lighter news that also impacted the times: The Technological Revolution, Beanie Babies, cell phones, chat rooms and e-mail, coffee houses, and so on. This gave students examples of hard and soft news they could use in their own newspapers. **Extension Activities** Students can create new lyrics from 1990 to the present that would fit into the "We Didn't Start the Fire" format.	*The purpose of the project is to show the impact that the events of an era have on the lives of people in the entire world. Focus is placed on reading for the 5 Ws: Who, What, Where, When, and Why.* *We discussed how reading a newspaper is a different type of reading. If one wants basic information, it is most often in the beginning paragraphs. Also, there is not as much voice in news reporting, with the exception of editorials that include perspective/point of view and persuasion. We discussed tabloids, propaganda, and how to judge an author's credibility and attempts to persuade and influence a reader. (This provided a nice segue into our next mini-unit.) Students with disabilities often are characteristically literal and concrete thinkers and thus often view much that is in writing as truth.* *This was a tremendously motivating project, where students were often coming in at lunch to work on their own newspapers.* *This activity allowed many skills to be practiced: decoding, interpreting, analyzing, summarizing, paraphrasing, and categorizing.* *Students were asked to choose what articles were of interest to them. They were allowed time to silently read before being responsible for sharing their information with the class: What happened, and what effects do we still see from these events? Students truly started to see a connection between past events and their continuing effects on our society in different realms: political, social, technological, environmental, and economic.* *Books and sites include but are not limited to* • *"1990s: The Way We Lived"* • *America in the Twentieth Century (see references for full citation.)* • *www.digitalhistory.uh.edu/learning_history* • *http://dmarie.com/timecap/step1asp*

RESEARCH REPORT: WE DIDN'T START THE FIRE RUBRIC

Teacher name: _____

Student name: _____

Criteria	4	3	2	1
Quality of information	Information clearly relates to the main topic. Information is accurate.	Information clearly relates to the main topic. Only 1 to 2 inaccuracies/ missing pieces of info.	Information loosely relates to the main topic. Inaccurate or missing major pieces of info.	Information has little or nothing to do with the main topic.
Impact/ ramifications	Fully critiques events' impact on current US identity/situations.	Critiques most of events' impact on current US situations.	Makes loose connections from past events to the present day.	Makes no connections/ mention of impact of events.
Diagrams and illustrations	Diagrams and illustrations are neat, accurate, and add to the reader's understanding of the topic.	Diagrams and illustrations are accurate and add to the reader's understanding of the topic.	Diagrams and illustrations add little to the reader's understanding of the topic.	Diagrams and illustrations are not accurate *or* do not add to the reader's understanding of the topic.
Mechanics	No grammatical, spelling, or punctuation errors.	Almost no grammatical, spelling, or punctuation errors.	A few grammatical, spelling, or punctuation errors.	Many grammatical, spelling, or punctuation errors.
Paragraph construction	All paragraphs include an introductory sentence, explanations or details, and a concluding sentence.	Most paragraphs include an introductory sentence, explanations or details, and a concluding sentence.	Paragraphs include related information but were typically not well constructed.	Paragraph structure was not clear and sentences were not typically related within the paragraphs.
Notes:				
Totals:				

Copyright © 2010 by Corwin. All rights reserved. Reprinted from *Parallel Curriculum Units for Social Studies, Grades 6–12*, edited by Jeanne H. Purcell and Jann H. Leppien. Thousand Oaks, CA: Corwin, www.corwinpress.com. Reproduction authorized only for the local school site or nonprofit organization that has purchased this book.

LESSON 8: PERSUADE ME! (2 WEEKS)

Concepts

M5: Perspective
M7: Conflict

This unit focuses primarily on the speaking and writing genres of persuasion. Current events are used to help students understand the concepts of this unit and, in particular, to help them understand change in the world and the impact one person or group can have on those changes.

Principles

P19: Conclusions can be drawn about society and culture from trends and themes.
P22: Word and sentence choices influence people's thinking.
P23: Conflict leads or lends itself to change.
P24: Conflict influences individual decisions and actions.

Skills

S5a, 5b: Use organizational features of printed and electronic text to locate information
S2a: Write in a variety of modes, such as narrative, expository, descriptive, and persuasive, for various audiences and purposes
S2b: Organize writing using a logical arrangement of ideas
S2c: Use language that supports and enriches the idea
S2g: Develop ideas and content with relevant details, examples, and/or reasons
S4d: Recognize an author's or speaker's point of view and purpose

Standards

SD4: Students adjust their use of spoken, written, and visual language (e.g., conventions, style, and vocabulary) to communicate effectively with a variety of audiences and for different purposes.
SD5: Students employ a wide range of strategies as they write and use different writing process elements appropriately to communicate with different audiences for a variety of purposes.
SD6: Students apply knowledge of language structure, language conventions (e.g., spelling and punctuation), media techniques, figurative language, and genre to create, critique, and discuss print and nonprint texts.
SD7: Students conduct research on issues and interests by generating ideas and questions and by posing problems. They gather, evaluate, and synthesize data from a variety of sources (e.g., print and nonprint texts, artifacts, and people) to communicate their discoveries in ways that suit their purpose and audience.
SD12: Students use spoken, written, and visual language to accomplish their own purposes (e.g., for learning, enjoyment, persuasion, and the exchange of information).

Guiding Questions

- What is a debatable topic?
- How is an actual debate carried out (vs. just an argument)?
- How are current events or topics of today influencing the identity of our country?
- How can and do societal conflicts lead to change?

Middle school students love to argue, and it is enjoyable to harness this love into a well-developed skill where they can actually realize the power of debate to influence and change attitudes and ideas.

Students at Sky Vista are also familiar with Socratic-seminar types of discussions, where one can be influenced to change sides. It was interesting to watch students as they wrestled with the dynamics of defending a position as a team.

Unit Sequence—Core Curriculum and Curriculum of Identity	Teacher Reflections
Introductory Activity	
Have a male teacher, drama teacher, or you come to class in a white beard, large hat, and overalls and bring in a large tree stump (wilderness look). Deliver a speech in a car-salesman-like manner and pitch all the uses that the stump might be used for: scratching your back against it, burning it if your house is cold, sitting on it for furniture, cutting on it for a toothpick if you have food between your teeth, confiding in your stump if you have a problem, hanging laundry to dry on the stump, and so on.	*This is the type of hook that captivates reluctant students, generates student suspense and curiosity, and deepens learning. Being imaginative, creative, and weird can let students view you as a risk taker and invite them to be willing to do the same.*
Tell students that they can be chosen to be part of a top-notch marketing team *if* they can pitch their products. Divide students into teams and hand out a series of everyday objects (comb, cardboard box, etc.). Each team must do the following: • Choose a spokesperson to present their ideas. • Brainstorm ideas on why someone should buy their product, and write a list. • The spokesman pitches the product and decides which group or groups have met the criteria for earning a marketing job.	
Debrief with students about what a persuasive essay is and how they just outlined one for themselves (in style/format/ideas).	
Students are divided into two groups. A class discussion takes place as to what makes a debatable topic: it must be serious and with specific issues of opinions not just personal preference (e.g., What is better, a Ford or a Dodge?). Students are reminded that there is also no right or wrong answer. Several possible student-generated topics of debate are posted on the board, allowing for discussion.	*This activity is not meant to be a truly research-based debate. It is merely for the purpose of understanding a debating format and presenting relevant and supportive facts/arguments for a topic.* *A modified debating format was developed to demonstrate to students the concepts of presenting facts and rebutting arguments with evidence, facts, and/or statistics.*
Some examples of student generated ideas include the following: border/wall of Mexico, capital punishment, women in the military and should they be allowed in actual combat situations, driving age adjusted to 18 years, professional athletes' salaries being too high, war in Iraq, and so on.	• *1st speaker (Group 1) presents first argument/reason to support pro/con on a certain issue.* • *1st speaker of opposing side rebuts their first reason and presents their first pro/con argument/reason.* • *2nd speaker (Group 1) rebuts the previous argument and then states point two of their side.*

(Continued)

(Continued)

Unit Sequence—Core Curriculum and Curriculum of Identity	Teacher Reflections
Students are then introduced to a modified version of a debating format, following the structure outlined in the right-hand column. Students come up with a topic and take sides. They are then given time to get together in groups to discuss and develop three reasons for supporting their side of the argument. They are given the directive to select four speakers and make sure to save their strongest point for the end. Students are reminded of general rules during the actual debate: • No put downs • Points will be lost for interruptions • Points will be lost for whispering while a speaker is talking, whether on your team or the opposition • All guiding questions must be addressed in the debate	• 2nd speaker (opposing side) rebuts speaker 2's argument/reason and states 2nd point in defense of their opinion. • 3rd speakers state 3rd reasons, rebut previous speakers. • 4th speakers restate positions with all points made and why their argument is the strongest. *Step-Up-Writing presents "EITHER/OR" rules of persuasion that the students could memorize or have access to (Everyone is doing this, Intelligent people buy into this, This is good for you, Happiness will come to you, Every reasonable person would agree, Right – this is your right, Opinion of an expert, Responsibility).* *High-risk or high-need kids often do not understand or apply social-language skills to be able to effectively disagree or to accept opinions that differ from their own. This has been a highly effective way of developing these skills.* *The Read, Write, Think Web site has a debating rubric at www.readwritethink.org/lesson_images/lesson819/rubric2.pdf.* *(Categories evaluated are viewpoint, use of facts/examples, relevance of supporting agreements, strength of arguments, speaking voice, preparation.)*
Teaching Strategies and Learning Experiences	
Students are shown examples of five paragraph essays of persuasive writing. Either in groups or with partners, they identify the parts of writing that are comparable to the debating format. Students are given the task of choosing a topic for their persuasive essays. Students are reminded that their essays will need to include a rebuttal to the opposition.	*An example of some five paragraph essays are found in 100% Writing – Persuasion by LinguaSystems, Inc. (helmet law requirement, alien visitation, mall curfew times, etc.).* *Current persuasive topics can be found readily online to aid kids in finding a topic of passion.* *This is an excellent time to review the format of a five paragraph essay. We list topics and discuss different types/lengths of essays (i.e., What would a one paragraph piece look like, a three paragraph essay, a four and a five paragraph essay?).*

Unit Sequence—Core Curriculum and Curriculum of Identity	Teacher Reflections
Closure	
Students draft and complete their own persuasive essays with topics relevant to current events: stem cell research, the border between the United States and Mexico, war in Iraq, and so on. Remind students that the essay must address the guiding questions listed at the beginning of this section. Students are guided first through listing the pros/cons of their topic and the outlining phase, then the topic paragraph, body paragraphs, conclusion, and editing. Students are put with partners to read, give feedback, and edit their work before turning in a final draft.	*This activity is divided up into phases: outlining, topic paragraph, body paragraphs, conclusion paragraph, and editing. Students with writing deficits often need the modification of having assignments broken down into more manageable parts with more constant feedback and guidance.* *Rubrics for persuasive essays are readily available online or can be formatted for specific needs/classes at Rubistar.com. An excellent version of a 5 paragraph essay has been created by teachers in the Greece Central School District in New York. Use this site and then click on persuasive rubric (http://www.greece .k12.ny.us/instruction/ELA/6-12/ Rubrics/Index.htm).*

LESSON 9: PLANET EARTH (2 WEEKS)

Concepts

M9: System
M10: Transcendence
M11: Altruism

Discipline-Specific Concepts

- Global warming
- Ecological responsibility
- Stewardship
- Sustainable development

Through this culminating unit, students develop a sense that we are all part of something much larger than ourselves—a larger system that is not just about our own needs and concerns. It is up to us to help protect and manage resources, not only for now but for the future.

(Continued)

(Continued)

Principles

P25: Preserving our environment and resources is integral to human, plant, and animal survival.

P26: People, communities, and countries have certain responsibilities to ensure a continued, viable environment.

P27: Political and economic conflicts occur in the balancing of human development and wilderness/environmental preservation.

Skills

S1b: Summarize and synthesize fiction and nonfiction
S2b: Organize writing using a logical arrangement of ideas
S2c: Use language that supports and enriches the idea
S2g: Develop ideas and content with relevant details, examples, and/or reasons

Standards

SD4: Students adjust their use of spoken, written, and visual language (e.g., conventions, style, and vocabulary) to communicate effectively with a variety of audiences and for different purposes.

SD5: Students employ a wide range of strategies as they write and use different writing process elements appropriately to communicate with different audiences for a variety of purposes.

SD8: Students use a variety of technological and information resources (e.g., libraries, databases, computer networks, and videos) to gather and synthesize information and to create and communicate knowledge.

SD12: Students use spoken, written, and visual language to accomplish their own purposes (e.g., for learning, enjoyment, persuasion, and the exchange of information).

Guiding Questions

- Why does Al Gore choose this as a title?
- Why would government leaders want to ignore this problem?
- What groups are discrediting global warming? Technology is largely seen as something that improves a civilization and the people in it—why then could this be ironic?
- What can the nations of the world do to act against the threat of global warming?
- How have countries come together in the past to combat worldwide problems or issues?
- What are our ecological responsibilities to the environment?
- When do environmental, political, and/or economic issues conflict?
- How do we balance human development with wilderness preservation?
- What are the consequences or repercussions, and what is the significance of, losing a vast number of species and ecosystems?

Some of the world issues that were addressed in the past included movements such as Save the Whales, the push toward the elimination of pesticides, Save the Rainforests, and the efforts to protect the ozone layer.

Students understand that there is a need for strategies, passion, and campaigning for the quality of lives—our own, people from other cultures', our children's.

Threats to ecosystems come from population (human development), economics (need or use of resources), politics, and climatological concerns (as only about one-fourth of the land surface is still wilderness on the planet).

Unit Sequence—Connections, Practice, Identity Parallels	Teacher Reflections
Introduction	
Students will watch Al Gore's *An Inconvenient Truth*. While watching, students will be required to write a minimum of ten quotes from the movie using a two-column note format. After the movie, students will write a reflection for each quote on the other side of the notes. Reflections will be shared and discussed with the class. Two-column notes will be repeated while students watch *Planet Earth—The Future* (Disc 5). However, as opposed to writing quotes on the left hand side, students will be asked to write questions posed in the video and are encouraged to create questions of their own. Again, after the video, students are given time to reflect and answer their questions.	*Many times, students are asked to reflect but are not taught how to reflect. This is a teachable moment to instruct students on how to reflect and distinguish the difference between reflection and summary. Summary is a regurgitation of someone else's views and thoughts, where reflection requires personal critical-thinking skills and the ability to develop individual opinions. Students will need to practice this writing genre because they tend to be familiar with summaries and unfamiliar with reflections.*
Teaching Strategies and Learning Experiences	
Students use their questions to contribute to the fish bowl for a class discussion. Some example questions include the following: • Why should we care what happens to these wilderness ecosystems? • What benefits do we get now from preservation and what benefits will we get in the future? • What have been the plans to preserve in the past and what are the thoughts for now or the future? • What are the differing views of "development"—Western materialism versus nonmaterialistic cultures? • How is preserving our environment and resources integral to human, plant, and animal survival? • What responsibilities do people, communities, and countries have to ensure a continued, viable environment? • What political and economic conflicts could occur in the balancing of human development and wilderness/environmental preservation?	*In a fish bowl discussion, questions are written on individual pieces of paper and placed in a "fish bowl." Students are placed in heterogeneous groups and asked to pull one question from the bowl. They have time to discuss and reflect on an answer with other group members. The group then shares with other groups.* *Some of the points made in the film include:* • *Benefits: aesthetic, medicine, tourism, and unknown, which needs protected as well.* • *Earlier attempts at species preservation: establishment of parks/preserves, information campaigns, armies to fight poaching.* • *"Sustainable development" is one new idea that balances human needs/development with ecological preservation. Who should make/be involved in those judgments (local communities vs. westernized ways)?* *The last three questions return back to the questions posed earlier in the unit. Students should be asked to back their responses with film references when noted.*

(Continued)

(Continued)

Unit Sequence—Connections, Practice, Identity Parallels	Teacher Reflections
Culminating Activity Read the article in *Time* "Global Warming Issue: The Actions" (April 9, 2007). (The article is available at the following Web site: http://www.time.com/time/specials/2007/environment/article/0,28804,1602354_1603074,00.html) Students are placed in groups and jigsaw the 50 actions people can take to mitigate the effects of global warming. Each group will read 10 actions and report to the class a brief summary of each action.	*The jigsaw method allows students to break up a lengthy piece of reading by assigning different parts to different groups and reporting out to the entire class on each individual section.* *Once again, the reiteration of the difference between summarizing and reflecting is a beneficial instructional moment.* *Aligning with the parallel of Practice ideals, this piece encourages students to take on the role of an environmentalist who both practices and informs others about the importance of their work. It also asks students to work in a team approach, just as real scientists work together.*
Going Green Project Students will participate in the Sieman's "We Can Change the World Challenge." The challenge offers a unique way for middle school student teams to create sustainable local solutions that can have global impact. It's the first and only national sustainability education initiative aligned to national standards and classroom objectives. The challenge is found at this Web site and includes a planning guide to direct student learning (http://wecanchange.com).	*The contest is not limited to typical environmental problems. Any urban, rural, or suburban environmental issue can be selected. In doing so, students are encouraged to explore a wide range of environmental issues, perspectives, and positions in their research.* *Teams are encouraged to select and study an issue that they truly care about, not one that is assigned. In doing so, they will practice civic skills and learn to become leaders in understanding and addressing relevant environmental issues.* *Teams are challenged to use measurable data, including evidence that their issue is a problem in the community and proof that their solution worked.* *Teams will learn from real scientists and authentic experiments and then apply that knowledge to their own solutions. Collaborations within the community are encouraged.* *Students will share what they learn with others in an online repository, thereby continuing the important scientific process of new ideas building on old ones.*

Unit Sequence—Connections, Practice, Identity Parallels	Teacher Reflections
Closure	
These unit modules have explored how identities are shaped by multiple forces and influences, including those that we experience on a personal, national, and world level, and how our lives are in a reciprocal relationship to these environments.

An interesting approach to the final assessment is to list all the principles on a large chart-sized web that can be posted on a classroom wall. Individually, have students orally explain to you what they have now come to understand about these ideas and if they agree or disagree with them, and why or why not? If students have iPods or MP3 players with recorders, they can respond to these principles with their ideas by recording their responses. | At the closure of this unit, you will want to return to the principles that have served as targeted achievement goals for the unit. By now, students should have a broader view of how identities are shaped and should understand that who we are can be influenced by many factors and that the same holds true for a nation and world.

The idea for the assessment is to return to these big ideas to see what students have come to understand as result of engaging in the teaching and learning experiences. You can format this assessment in any way that you choose, as long as you are able to have students reflect on the ideas and what they have now come to mean for them personally. |

REFERENCES AND RESOURCES

Aumman, M. (2003). *Step up to writing* (2nd ed.). Frederick, CO: Sopris West.
Coppola, F. F. (1983). *The outsiders*. Warner Home Video.
Fothergill, A. (2007). *Planet earth: The future*. BBC.
Guggenheim, D. (2006). *An inconvenient truth*. Paramount Home Entertainment.
Knauer, K. (Ed.) (2007). *Time: Global warming*. New York: Time Books.
Leish, K. W. (1999). *The American scene, volume 9*. Danbury, CT: Grolier.
Martin, J. B. (1998). *Snowflake Bentley*. Boston: Houghton Mifflin.
McGraw-Hill, Glen-Jamestown Publishers. (2007). *Critical reading series: Eccentrics*. Lincolnwood, IL: Glencoe McGraw-Hill.
Myers. W. D. (1997). *Harlem*. New York: Scholastic.
Murray, R. (2006). *Unknown white male*. Genius Entertainment.
Patterson, J. T. (1999). *America in the twentieth century: A history* (5th ed.). Fort Worth, TX: Harcourt College Publishers.
Pendergast, S., & Pendergast, T. (Eds). (2002). *Bowling, beatniks, and bell-bottoms*. Detroit, MI: Thomson Gale.
Silverstein, S. (1994). *Where the sidewalk ends*. New York: Harper and Row.
Stepanek, M. (2002). *Loving through heartsongs*. New York: Hyperion Books, HarperCollins.
Stepanek, M. (2005). *Heartsongs*. New York: Hyperion Books, HarperCollins.
Uys, M., & Lovell, L. (2005). *Riding the rails*. PBS: American Experience Videos.

3

Subversion and Controversy

Sociological Considerations of Humor, a Cross-Curricular Unit in Sociology and Literature

Grades 7 and 8

Kelly M. Dausel

BACKGROUND INFORMATION

Although philosophers have examined humor since Plato, there are few definitive answers about what humor is or what causes something to be funny. However, many people recognize that humor is important to humanity. One of the goals of middle school English is to assist students in knowing the forms and functions of literature and communication in society in order to develop critical reading and thinking skills that will transfer to other learning situations. Specifically, this unit focuses on how a speaker's or writer's attempt to communicate with a given audience through humor can reveal psychological and societal themes as the reader or listener interprets conflict, language, character, and symbolism as shaped by cultural and historical influences. These are literature and communication concepts commonly studied in middle school (see the Grade 7 concept map created by my teaching partner, Eric Bone, and me in 2005). This study of humor is half of a larger unit that focuses on variations of literature that tend to arise from conflicts within and discontent linked to societal and political conditions; following this unit, students also study science fiction, making connections through the social sciences once again.

CONTENT FRAMEWORK

Organizing Concepts

Macroconcepts	Principles
M1: Society	P1: Society is a process of interactions among individuals and groups.
M2: Interaction	P2: Every society develops a system of rules, norms, values, and sanctions that guides the behavior of individuals within society.
M3: Conflict	P3: Individuals are shaped by social factors.
M4: Power	P4: Conflicts between the individual and society often reflect beliefs about balance of power and the value of freedom.
M5: Freedom	P5: People use various means of communication in order to make sense of conflict and promote change.
M6: Change	P6: A speaker or writer's attempt to communicate with a given audience through humor can reveal genuine themes as the reader or listener interprets conflict, language, character, and symbolism as shaped by cultural and historical influence.

GUIDING QUESTIONS FOR EACH PARALLEL

Curriculum of Practice

1. What are the theories that govern the knowledge of the field of sociology?
2. How do sociologists organize their knowledge and skills in the discipline?
3. How do sociologists apply the principles of sociology to inform their understanding of society?
4. What issues related to humor concern sociologists?
5. What methodologies do sociologists use to study society?
6. How might a sociologist decide which methodology to use in a given instance?
7. How do sociologists gather data, and how might they use the data to draw conclusions? What do sociologists do with the knowledge they gain from studying society?

Curriculum of Identity

1. What do sociologists think about?
2. To what degree are these ideas familiar, surprising, and/or intriguing to me?
3. How do sociologists think and work?
4. How do I relate to these processes?
5. What are the problems and issues that sociologists spend their lives studying?
6. To what degree do these intrigue me?
7. What are the ethical principles at the core of the discipline?
8. What wisdom can sociology contribute to the world?
9. How might that wisdom affect me?

Skills: (GB) Benchmarks for Gifted Students (Virginia Beach)

GB1 Grade 8 Goal: To develop an understanding of systems of knowledge, themes, issues, and problems that frame the external world, gifted students will

- reflect on issues that impact society, noting personal biases and prejudices;
- justify personal perspectives on a given concept, theme, or issue;
- analyze and interpret appropriate solutions to real-world problems;
- recognize their role in the systems of issues and problems occurring in the external world; and
- develop generalizations related to major systems, themes, issues, and problems.

GB2 Grade 8 Goal: To develop critical thinking, creative abilities, and problem-solving skills, gifted students will

- apply various problem-solving techniques to problem situations (e.g., mathematical, scientific, literary, technological);
- construct generalizations and synthesize across data, concepts, and perspectives; and
- apply the cognitive processes of application, synthesis, analysis, and evaluation to the research process.

GB3 Grade 8 Goal: To develop metacognitive skills that foster independent and self-directed learning in order to develop self-understanding, gifted students will

- plan, conduct, and complete complex assignments independently;
- exhibit scholarly skills and behaviors; and
- demonstrate openness and respect for diverse viewpoints.

Standards: Virginia English Grade 7 Standards of Learning (SOL)

SD7.1: The student will give and seek information in conversations and group discussions.

SD7.2: The student will identify the relationship between a speaker's verbal and nonverbal messages.

SD7.5: The student will read, write, respond to, and demonstrate comprehension of a variety of fiction, narrative nonfiction, and poetry.
- c. Describe the impact of word choice, imagery, and poetic devices.
- f. Make inferences based on explicit and implied information.

SD7.6: The student will read and demonstrate comprehension of a variety of informational texts.
- d. Identify the source, viewpoint, and purpose of texts.
- e. Describe how word choice and language structure convey an author's viewpoint.

SD7.7: The student will apply knowledge of appropriate reference materials.
- b. Use graphic organizers to organize information.
- c. Synthesize information from multiple sources.

SD7.8: The student will develop narrative, expository, and persuasive writing.
- b. Elaborate the central idea in an organized manner.
- e. Revise for clarity and effect.

Making Sure That the Curriculum of Practice and Identity Remain Central in Teaching and Learning

Curriculum Component	To Ensure Focus on Key Concepts for Each Parallel
Content	Students will use general methodologies, such as making observations, recognizing cause and effect, drawing inferences, and making deductions, as they examine examples of humor to explore the sociological concepts of society, interaction, conflict, power, freedom, and change.
	Curriculum of Practice: Students develop skills to analyze and interpret situations in the role of sociologist in order to understand methods of gathering relevant information and analyzing its implications. They will apply the advanced thinking skills mentioned above as they identify a personally interesting research question, develop a research study using one of the major sociological research methodologies, and produce a report of their findings.
	Curriculum of Identity: Students understand the role of the individual in society, as well as the societal rules, norms, and sanctions that govern the behavior of individuals. They will question their own behavior and that of society at large while considering the wider implications of various choices.
Assessments	A variety of assessments are embedded throughout the unit to allow the teacher to assess students' development of thinking skills needed to eventually conduct their own sociological research. These assessments also focus on developing sociological frames of understanding that will allow for developing

Curriculum Component	To Ensure Focus on Key Concepts for Each Parallel
	independent research questions. The assessment techniques will vary in each of the parallels and move students toward self-assessment as they approach the Curriculum of Identity.
Introductory activities	Introductory activities focus on a series of question prompts that build an understanding of the principles and key concepts. *Curriculum of Practice:* The introductory activity invites students to consider an environment with which they are familiar—the school cafeteria—and view it through a sociological lens. *Curriculum of Identity:* The introduction asks students to recognize their own place in the school cafeteria as a member of that society.
Teaching strategies	Strategies in the unit focus on skill development—especially thinking skills related to analysis and synthesis. Working as a practicing sociologist by conducting research gives students an authentic taste of the Curriculum of Practice, and with the use of the Curriculum of Identity, they can reflect on the meaning of the unit concepts and principles in their own lives.
Learning activities	Learning activities in this unit draw attention to interactions in society and how they reflect balance of power and the interpretation of personal freedom. The ultimate goal for students is to conduct research as a sociologist, so the tasks are scaffolded to promote the thinking skills needed for authentic practice. A variety of resources are used to provide for multiple perspectives on and repeated exposure to the unit's principles.
Grouping strategies	Various grouping strategies insure that all students have access to the concepts and principles of the unit. During the earliest stages of the unit, students work in small groups to allow them to share a variety of perspectives, increasing the understanding of individuals. Whenever literature or other reading texts are used, there are a variety of choices given, which can either be assigned based on reading or analytical readiness or selected by students based on interest in topic or format. At a few junctures, students are given a choice to work on self-selected tasks as individuals, in partnerships, or in small groups, depending on their preferences. Finally, as students conduct research, they again may choose the size of their research team depending on the needs of their study.
Products	Ongoing products and planned student reflections are organized around students demonstrating and providing evidence of understanding the key principles and concepts.

(Continued)

(Continued)

Curriculum Component	To Ensure Focus on Key Concepts for Each Parallel
Resources	Suggested resources guide the students' focus on the work of a sociologist and provide guidance in bringing the products of their research in close alignment with the actual work of a sociologist. Online video clips, supplementary resource suggestions, and Internet Web addresses have been written into the unit to ensure that students and teachers have the resources available to complete the unit. **Background References** - United Feature Syndicate, Inc. (2005). Comics.com. Retrieved July 9, 2008, from http://www.comics.com - Koller, M. R. (1988). *Humor and society: Explorations in the sociology of humor*. Houston, TX: Cap and Gown Press. **Video References** - Discovery Education. (1999). Coping with differences. Retrieved July 9, 2008, from http://streaming.discoveryeducation.com - Discovery Education. (2005). The lighter side of writing. Retrieved July 9, 2008, from http://streaming.discoveryeducation.com
Extension activities	Extension activities, included in the teacher's reflections, are included in the final module. These allow students to explore the unit's big ideas in areas of particular interest to them and to work at appropriate challenge levels while doing so.
Modifications for learner need (Including Ascending Intellectual Demand)	Throughout the unit, instruction, materials, tasks, and criteria for success are modified in response to learner readiness and interest. All students are asked to engage in the work of a sociologist, and Ascending Intellectual Demand for advanced students can be expected to explore advanced resources and approach expert-like production. All students can approach the concepts and principles at some level, with advanced learners seeing deeper connections and drawing less obvious conclusions. Scaffolds are provided in the unit for tasks requiring advanced analysis and for scholarly skills such as note taking. In addition, each lesson includes access to the content in nonwritten formats and choice in styles of expression, which will allow all students to demonstrate their learning in ways that maximize their strengths. These modifications are included within the individual lessons.

UNIT ASSESSMENTS

The preassessment asks students to share their preliminary thoughts on the topic of humor in society. These questions are linked to the key principles of the unit to determine the level at which students are currently thinking about these topics.

The information gathered may help the teacher make instructional decisions about the pacing, resources, and scaffolding students may require; it will certainly provide a baseline for assessing student growth in their sociological thinking as the unit progresses.

There are periodic assignments and research tasks given to students throughout the unit to check for student understanding. Conceptual understanding—assessed through the use of rubrics, conferencing, and discussion—documents student growth. Proficiency of skills and evidence of personal growth are demonstrated as students are asked to work as practicing sociologists by conducting research and presenting their findings.

OVERVIEW OF THIS UNIT

This unit incorporates a variety of learning strategies to help students to first understand the interests and role of a sociologist. The Curriculum of Practice parallel was used to construct learning activities whereby students learn common forms of humor and examine literature and video samples through the lens of a sociologist, considering the function, scope, and limitations of humor used in society. The lessons within this portion of the unit extend the students' use of the skills of inference-making and drawing conclusions about how literature reflects the role of humor in society, as well as the ways it, in turn, can influence its audience. In the research module of this unit, students study an aspect of humor in society by applying the methodologies used by sociologists to carry out their own studies. This unit focuses especially on the role of humor in society, moving toward studying humor as a sociologist would. As a result of this unit, students will know that tone and theme are closely linked and must both be considered if the fullness of a speaker or writer's message is to be understood. In addition, students will develop a broader repertoire of research skills and a keener awareness of subtleties in communication that will assist them as scholars and citizens.

The Curriculum of Identity is also addressed in this unit since humor in middle school can cause discomfort and uncertainty for students; early adolescents must determine and decide where the line is for joking behaviors, especially since teasing, bullying, and race- and gender-based jokes can get out of hand. The hope is that by examining these issues as sociologists, students will understand their own role in maintaining an emotionally and psychologically safe environment for others and will be forced to consider the effects of their behavior on others. Addressing these issues foremost through the disciplinary lens of sociology provides some distance from which students can discuss difficult, even controversial, topics in a more impersonal way. Through reflection, the aim is that students will consider and internalize their responsibilities as members of society.

Preparing to Teach This Unit

Before undertaking the unit, check the materials and resources needed for each lesson and module. With much of the learning placed firmly into the hands of the students, many of the lessons require production or collection of resources in advance. The good news is that, with explicit classroom structures in place, the teacher will find him or herself in the role of a guide and coach. This unit assumes that students have background knowledge in literary analysis.

To enhance Ascending Intellectual Demand (AID) in the Curriculum of Practice, invite a sociologist to speak to the students early in the unit and to, perhaps, participate in a symposium at its conclusion. Search the nearest university or college for a sociology department; in addition, some businesses hire sociologists, especially if they are hoping to track consumer behavior or perform product research. Having a professional speak increases student interest and validates their educational pursuits in this unit. In addition, when students know that professionals will serve as audiences for their research, they work more diligently to increase the quality of their products and performances.

Figure 3.1 Grade 7 Content Map

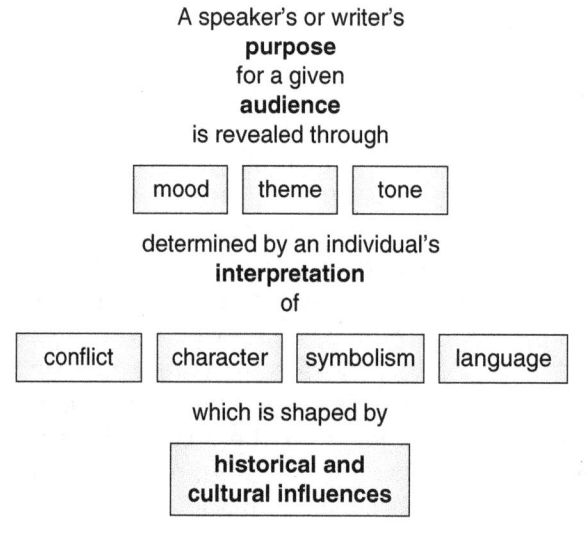

UNIT SEQUENCE, DESCRIPTION, AND TEACHER REFLECTIONS

LESSON 1: INTRODUCTION TO SOCIOLOGY AND HOW SOCIOLOGISTS THINK (2–3 CLASS PERIODS)

Concepts

M1: Society
M2: Interaction
M3: Conflict

Principles

P1: Society is a process of interactions among individuals and groups.
P2: Every society develops a system of rules, norms, values, and sanctions that guides the behavior of individuals within society.

Skills

GB1 Grade 8 Goal: To develop an understanding of systems of knowledge, themes, issues, and problems that frame the external world, gifted students will
- reflect on issues that impact society, noting personal biases and prejudices;
- justify personal perspectives on a given concept, theme, or issue;
- analyze and interpret appropriate solutions to real-world problems;
- recognize their role in the systems of issues and problems occurring in the external world; and
- develop generalizations related to major systems, themes, issues, and problems.

Standards

SD7.2: The student will identify the relationship between a speaker's verbal and nonverbal messages.

Unit Sequence—Curriculum of Practice	*Teacher Reflections*
Introduction	
Preassessment Learning Task Post or provide students with the following diagram. | What causes people to laugh at something?	What might cause people not to laugh at something?
Do people laugh when things aren't funny? Why or why not?	What role does humor play in society? | Tell students that they are about to begin a unit looking at the role of humor in society and how society affects individuals' responses to humor. Allow students time to jot down their ideas in each of the boxes as a preassessment to gauge their level of current understanding of the unit's principles and concepts. Provide enough time for students to record their ideas in each box. Students can place their completed preassessments on their desks, and the teacher can collect them during the visualization activity that follows.	*Required resources for this lesson:* • *Overhead transparencies with markers, chalk, or whiteboard for recording ideas* • *Copies of Graphic Organizer to analyze causes and effects, one for each group of three to four students* • *Overhead of Journal prompts for closure* *Suggested resources for this lesson:* • *A large piece of paper or board space upon which a list of vocabulary related to sociology and humor can be posted for reference throughout the unit.* *The preassessment asks students to share their preliminary thoughts on the topic of humor in society. These questions are linked to the key principles of the unit to determine the level at which students are currently thinking about these topics. The information gathered may help the teacher make instructional decisions about pacing, resources, and the scaffolding students may require; it will certainly provide a baseline for assessing student growth in their sociological thinking as the unit progresses.*

(Continued)

(Continued)

Unit Sequence—Curriculum of Practice	Teacher Reflections
	Modification for Learner Need *For the preassessment, a Frayer-like diagram was chosen because the informal format minimizes the anxiety or lack of ability students may have about communicating in well-composed sentences. Students may respond with complete thoughts, but they may also choose to create a bulleted list, jot down words or phrases, create a small graphic organizer, or even illustrate their responses. The focus can then be on conceptual ideas, rather than written expression.* *Read the narration, pausing at least 15 seconds after each prompt to allow students to visualize details. A visualization exercise allows students to access the ideas without reading anything, draws on their past experiences, and strengthens visualization skills for reading and problem-solving tasks.*
Teaching Strategies and Learning Activities	
Guided Visualization and Follow-Up Discussion Lead students through this guided visualization: *Close your eyes. Visualize the cafeteria during a typical lunch period. In your mind's eye, look around at the people you sit with. What is each of them doing?* *Look around and notice how students are grouped at tables. How does what they are doing compare to your group?* *Look around and find where the adults are standing. What are they doing?* *Suddenly, a student drops a tray full of food. How does the group react? How do you react? Does anyone react differently from the majority of the group? How do the adults react?* Have students open their eyes. Ask students about what they noticed. Some questions to help lead this discussion might include the following: • What are the "rules" that affect where people sit in the lunchroom? • What behaviors do and do not seem acceptable for individuals and groups in the lunchroom? • What forces influence the behaviors of the group, other individuals, and you?	*These questions are related to the guiding principles of the unit, especially through the Curriculum of Practice. During this discussion and the one that follows, any answers that are relevant and can be explained by the students are permissible. The goal during this discussion is to introduce students to the types of questions sociologists are interested in. They represent the types of unanswered questions that sociologists study.* *The continuing discussion begins to connect students to the field of sociology through the Curriculum of Identity question: To what extent am I interested in these things?*

Unit Sequence—Curriculum of Practice	Teacher Reflections
Conduct a guided discussion about the visualization exercise to introduce the field of sociology. Ask students: • Have you ever thought about these types of questions? • Do you know what professionals who study the behavior of individuals and groups in society are called? On the board, write "Sociology is the study of processes of interactions among individuals and groups in society." • Who might the study of sociology benefit? Why? • What are other things that impact society? • How is sociology connected with literature and communication? **How Sociologists Study Society—An Interactive Video, Small Group Activity, Follow-Up Discussion** Explain to students that they are going to view a social situation as a sociologist would: *One method sociologists use to study human behavior is observation. We are going to watch a video and make some observations about human behavior. Specifically, we are concerned with the humor in this scene. What do people laugh at and why? How is humor created? Because this is a scene from a film, it is going to be contrived (What does contrived mean?). We are also going to want to consider whether this imaginary situation is realistic and explain why it may or may not be. So look at the behaviors of the individuals in this clip and think about the forces that shape their behaviors in the group, especially as it relates to humor.* **Viewing the Video Clip** After the video, have students form groups of three or four members, based simply on whoever is sitting around them. Each group will need a copy of the graphic organizer titled "Causes and Effects of Individual and Group Behaviors" found at the end of this lesson. Ask students to describe the behavior we witnessed. Guide	*Locate a video clip that presents a social situation that involves humor within a group context. Especially effective clips would involve those that present an ethical issue connected with the humor that middle or high school students would relate to—when the social situation directs individual behavior. A video clip, "Dealing With Differences," published by Sunburst in 1999, is available from UnitedStreaming (http://streaming.discoveryeducation.com) if your school has access to this support resource. Other clips may be found from popular movies that show a bullying, teasing, or other "in group/out group" interaction where a group of people may be laughing at an individual or smaller group of people. The clip will need to be short, maybe five minutes or less, with the purpose being to engage students in thinking about the sociological issues involved in daily interactions.* *The trick with writing the descriptors is to make sure that they describe the behavior without judging it. For instance, "Jenna thinks she has a right to make jokes about people" or "Roger laughs because he wants to be friends with Jenna" would not fit the purposes of this exercise. For some groups of students, this may be difficult to do at*

(Continued)

(Continued)

Unit Sequence—Curriculum of Practice	Teacher Reflections
students toward writing a statement to be written in the Behavior box on the graphic organizer. For the "Dealing with Differences" video clip, some behavior descriptors might include the following: • Jenna makes jokes about people. • Roger laughs at Jenna's jokes and even adds to them. • Roger suggests that they stop making fun of the girl in the leg brace. • The other girl doesn't speak up in front of Jenna. To allow some differentiation by interest, a few (three to five) behavior descriptors could be written on the board and each group could choose one to discuss. Otherwise, the class or teacher could identify just one behavior to examine. If students are not aware of the meaning of internal and external as relating to causes and effects, explain that internal causes would be the things inside a person—their thoughts, beliefs, fears, and so on—whereas external causes would be things outside a person, like peer pressure or environment. Allow the groups five to eight minutes to discuss possible causes and effects of the behavior. While circulating around the room, ask questions to encourage students to be as specific as they can; for instance, what might Roger believe that affects his actions? Show the video clip again and direct students to examine specifically the effects of the behaviors, paying attention to visual and verbal clues as to what characters are thinking or feeling. Afterward, provide five to eight more minutes to write down specific effects related to causes and effects, as well as generalizations, implications, and questions that arise from the observations they have made. As groups work, circulate around the room to listen in on discussions and encourage specific descriptions.	*first. It may be helpful to explain to students that the statement must be purely descriptive and give examples based on students themselves first. ("Sandeep is wearing a blue shirt" vs. "Sandeep likes the color blue.")* **Modifications for Learner Need** *Groups for this activity may be heterogeneously or homogeneously grouped based on ability. If grouping homogeneously, adapt the task for struggling learners by narrowing their choices and directing them toward a more obvious behavior (ask them to share their ideas orally about a couple of the ideas and then direct them to choose the one they can speak about most fluently). For advanced learners, challenge them to focus more on internal causes and effects, as well as broader causes and effects (school, community, society) not readily apparent.* *Showing the video again allows students a chance to catch what they may have missed. As students are learning to think like sociologists, they are likely to notice things they were not looking for the first time.*

Unit Sequence—Curriculum of Practice	Teacher Reflections
After groups have had time for the second round of discussion, call on members of the groups to explain their responses to the following questions related to the information groups have recorded on the graphic organizers: • What types of things did your group find especially noteworthy? • What seemed to be the driving factors behind the characters' behaviors? • What were some positive results of the behavior? What were some negative results? • What have these observations taught us about human behavior in society? • What are the implications of what we have learned? • What are some other questions that arise because of what we have seen?	*During the class discussion, point out when students introduce examples or generalizations that connect to these important sociological concepts:* • *Norm: an expected form of behavior in a given situation* • *Rule: a principle or regulation governing conduct, action, procedure, arrangement* • *Values: the ideals, customs, institutions, and so on, of a society toward which the people of the group have an affective regard. These values may be positive, such as cleanliness, freedom, or education, or negative, such as cruelty, crime, or blasphemy.* • *Sanction: a penalty for disobedience or a reward for obedience* *Write the words on the board or on a vocabulary retrieval chart for the unit (basically, a large sheet of paper that will contain an ever-growing list of vocabulary related to talking like a sociologist as students analyze humor).* *Be sure to explicitly encourage use of these words whenever appropriate by cuing with a question such as, What word would a sociologist use to label what you are describing?*
<div align="center">**Closure**</div>	
To close this lesson, have students respond to one of the following prompts in their learning journal or on loose-leaf paper: *Practical Task:* How do issues in the field of sociology impact your own life? Give an example of a situation in which the norms, rules, values, and/or sanctions of society have significantly impacted your behavior. *Creative Task:* Identify a norm, rule, value, and/or sanction that affects your own life on a regular basis and briefly describe how it affects you and the people with whom you interact. Then, substitute the norm, rule, value, and/or sanction with another, and describe or illustrate how society would be different with the substitution. *Analytical Task:* Clarify the differences and relationships between norms, rules, values, and sanctions by providing either a written analysis in prose or a graphic organizer.	*The closure activity is an assessment of the students' level of understanding of the concepts of society, norms, rules, values, and sanctions. The teacher will be able to determine whether students understand these concepts.*

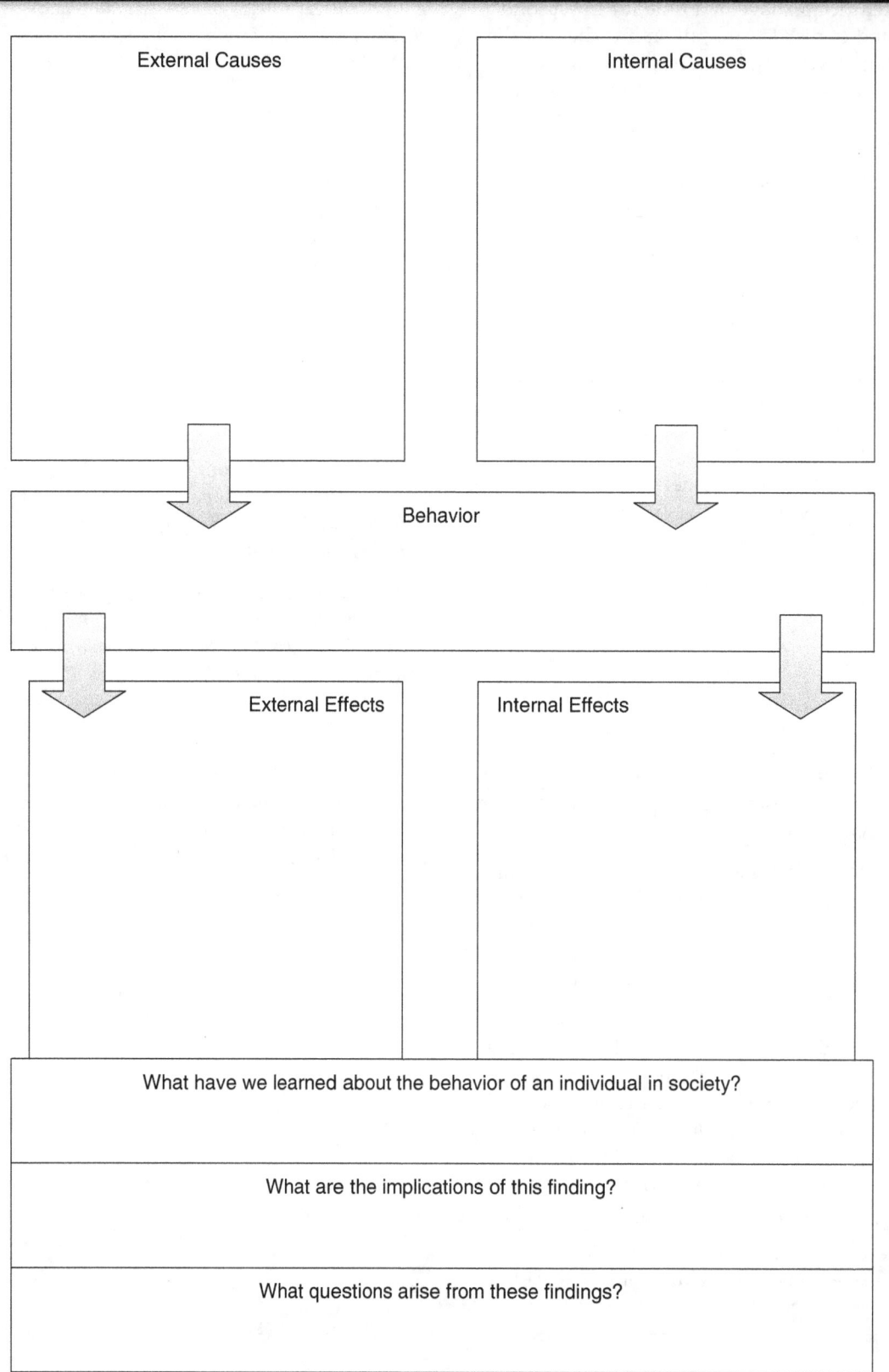

LESSON 2: HUMOR IN SOCIETY (2 CLASS PERIODS)

Concepts

M1: Society	M3: Conflict
M2: Interaction	M4: Power
M5: Freedom	M6: Change

Principles

P1: Society is a process of interactions among individuals and groups.
P2: Every society develops a system of rules, norms, values, and sanctions that guides the behavior of individuals within society.
P3: Individuals are shaped by social factors.
P4: Conflicts between the individual and society often reflect beliefs about balance of power and the value of freedom.
P5: People use various means of communication in order to make sense of conflict and promote change.
P6: A speaker or writer's attempt to communicate with a given audience through humor can reveal genuine themes as the reader or listener interprets conflict, language, character, and symbolism as shaped by cultural and historical influence.

Skills

GB1 Grade 8 Goal: To develop an understanding of systems of knowledge, themes, issues, and problems that frame the external world, gifted students will

- reflect on issues that impact society, noting personal biases and prejudices;
- justify personal perspectives on a given concept, theme, or issue;
- analyze and interpret appropriate solutions to real-world problems;
- recognize their role in the systems of issues and problems occurring in the external world; and
- develop generalizations related to major systems, themes, issues, and problems.

GB2 Grade 8 Goal: To develop critical thinking, creative abilities, and problem-solving skills, gifted students will

- apply various problem-solving techniques to problem situations (e.g., mathematical, scientific, literary, technological);
- construct generalizations and synthesize across data, concepts, and perspectives; and
- apply the cognitive processes of application, synthesis, analysis, and evaluation to the research process.

Standards

SD7.2: The student will identify the relationship between a speaker's verbal and nonverbal messages.
SD7.6: The student will read and demonstrate comprehension of a variety of informational texts.
   d. Identify the source, viewpoint, and purpose of texts.
   e. Describe how word choice and language structure convey an author's viewpoint.

Guiding Questions

To guide the discussion with students, ask the following questions, and post them so students can view them throughout these lessons.

(Continued)

(Continued)

- What purposes does humor serve?
- How do language, tone, audience, speaker, and context interact to cause something to be funny? In other words, why do people find some things humorous and others not?
- How do rules, norms, and sanctions guide behavior?
- How do people cope with the challenges of living within a society?
- What can literature, popular media, and other modes of communication reveal about the status and structure of groups within society?
- To what extent is written text conservative, and to what extent is it dangerous?
- How can various modes of communication serve as a catalyst for change?

Unit Sequence—Curriculum of Practice	Teacher Reflections
Introduction and Teaching and Learning Activities	
Terminology The following words should be placed within a student notebook or posted in the classroom: farce, irony, parody, satire, slapstick, pun. **Reviewing and Sharing of Work** Review with students the sociological concepts and essential questions discussed in the previous lesson, which included the concepts of roles, norms, values, and sanctions. Ask students to define and/or give examples as well as explain how these forces affect social interaction and to elaborate on these ideas by sharing their writing log responses. After students share some of their learning log responses, direct students' attention to the list of essential questions for the unit and ask students to identify the questions that were the focus of the last lesson: - What purposes does humor serve? - How do language, tone, audience, speaker, and context interact to cause something to be funny? In other words, why do we find some things humorous and others not? - How do rules, norms, and sanctions guide behavior? - How do people cope with the challenges of living within a society? *During the last lesson, we viewed a video clip and analyzed the causes and effects of humor, as well as reflected on the rules, norms, and sanctions that*	*This lesson is designed to provide students with the knowledge and language to describe common types of humor and their purposes. It begins by connecting to the first lesson through students' learning log responses. During the lesson, students will be exposed to a number of ways of thinking about humor from various practicing disciplines; doing so promotes flexibility of thought and increases available schema for developing the sociological study of humor.* *It is necessary to gather resources with which students can conduct their own explorations into the variety of practitioners who are interested in humor—what it is, how it works, and why it matters. There are other pieces of the lesson that require preparation.* **Suggested Resources:** - *A large piece of paper or board space upon which a list of vocabulary related to sociology and humor is posted for reference throughout the unit.* - *A list of the unit's essential questions and terminology posted or easily accessible to all students. If it is not possible to create a poster or write the words somewhere that they may remain for the remainder of the unit, they may also be printed for students to keep in their binder or folder to access during activities of this unit. The handout Subversion and Controversy: Sociological Considerations of Humor (included at the end of this lesson) consists of a single-page reference that can be distributed to students.*

Unit Sequence—Curriculum of Practice	Teacher Reflections
affect people's actions in society. Today we are going to look at some forms humor can take and continue considering the sociological implications of what we discover.	The introductory discussion will provide the opportunity to clear up any misunderstandings and provide a basis for further developing a critical eye towards humor.
Vocabulary Development Tell students the following: *We are going to start with a little vocabulary fun to give us some vocabulary to describe the types of humor we will encounter.* Pairs of students receive a plastic ziplock bag or envelope, within which are cards containing examples and definitions of the following six types of humor:	*Provide enough sets of vocabulary cards for half of the students in one class. Each card will have either a definition of one of the types of humor or an example along with the word describing the type of humor used in that sample. These cards can then be used as simple matching or as a memory game. It is suggested that these cards be made by mounting copies of the vocabulary cards on colored or wrapping paper, laminated and cut apart, especially if they will be used by more than one class. They can be stored by placing sets in envelopes or plastic ziplock bags.*

Farce	A comedy characterized by broad satire and improbable situations.
Irony	Incongruity between what might be expected and what actually occurs.
Parody	Humorous or satirical mimicry.
Satire	Witty language used to convey insults or scorn.
Slapstick	A boisterous comedy with chases, collisions, and practical jokes.
Pun	A humorous play on words.

Once students think they have matched the words with their definitions, they should raise their hands and have them checked; afterward, they can record the words that are new to them on their unit Vocabulary Chart (included at the end of this lesson). In addition, remind them of the words, values, norms, and sanctions from the last lesson, and have students add these words, as needed, using a dictionary to assist them in completing the chart. The root etymology column should contain a country of origin and the basic root with its meaning related to the word, and the memory cue column is for individual students to include a meaningful clue to help them store the word in their memories. For instance:

(Continued)

(Continued)

Unit Sequence—Curriculum of Practice	Teacher Reflections
<table><tr><th>Word</th><th>Root Etymology</th><th>Definition</th><th>Memory Cue</th></tr><tr><td>Satire</td><td>L satur = well-fitted</td><td>Witty language used to convey insults or scorn.</td><td>The satire was mean, but perfectly "fitting." (Could also be a rhyming couplet, a symbol, picture, joke, etc.)</td></tr></table> **Learning Choices and Follow-Up Discussions** As groups of students finish their vocabulary charts, collect the vocabulary cards and hand them the instructions for the next task, using the Experts Analyze Humor worksheet that is included at the end of this lesson. From the list below, select questions that seem interesting to you. The letter of each question refers to an article you may choose to read. A. How has the study of humor changed over time? How do people develop a sense of humor? B. What does research say about humor at work? C. What does research have to say about humor in education? D. How can humor be used in advertising? E. What are the medical benefits of humor? F. How does humor contribute to brain development? G. How and why might someone become a professional comedian? H. Have another question related to humor? Google it! Find an article or Web site that deals with your question.	*Copies of articles related to the study and uses of humor need to be gathered. These can be found by searching online for topics such as "humor and medicine," "study of humor," "humor in society," and "uses of humor." A visit to the library may yield books in psychology or sociology containing useful chapters or other excerpts. To allow students to read multiple articles, try to keep them relatively short based on your students' reading speed and readiness. Identify the main question that seems to be answered in this article, phrase it in a way to be intriguing to your students and alter the form included to match the articles you found. Before making multiple copies of each article (enough for about one-fifth of your class), prominently label each with the letter matching the question on the instructions. Make the articles available at a variety of places around the room, with signs posted above prominently to indicate which letter corresponds with the articles (use signs on the wall or table tents on the table).* *The directions for this task will need to be altered according to the articles you were able to locate, as well as the class management situation in your classroom.* **Modifications for Learner Needs** *The method for recording information for the questions is nonspecific. This ambiguity helps to*

Unit Sequence—Curriculum of Practice	Teacher Reflections
Around the room, you are provided articles connected to the questions. Start with the most interesting question you identified, and quietly walk to pick up one copy of the related article and return to your seat to read it. Read as many articles as you can in the next 40 minutes, returning each to its original location before picking up the next article. While you read, jot down information that will help you discuss the answers to the following essential questions: • What fields of study are concerned with humor? • How do language, tone, audience, speaker, and context interact to cause something to be funny (Details, Images, Diction, Language, and Sentence structure [DIDLS], see Lesson 3, page 128)? In other words, why do we find some things humorous and others not? • What purposes does humor serve? In other words, what effect does it have? **Closure** Have students share their responses as a whole class to discuss their findings. **Guided Viewing and Discussion** *Now that we have read about humor from a variety of other perspectives, we are going to come back specifically to humor as a sociologist might view it. As we watch this highly educational video clip, consider what causes something to be funny and what the effects of that type of humor might be. Look also for examples of the six types of humor you defined in your notes.* Show a cartoon video (see suggestions listed in the right hand column). After viewing an episode, stop the video and ask students some of the following questions (this could also be done as a silent response, with students writing down answers on a worksheet for a few episodes before having a whole class discussion):	*develop independent scholarly behaviors. If students are not quite ready for this level of independence, the following scaffolding options might be useful.* • *To promote reading for a purpose and preserving flow of reading, provide students with three small Post-it notes and have them write the following words: field of study, cause of humor, purpose of humor. These may be placed in the article as markers when students find the answer to each question. After students finish reading, they can record their answers on another page or in the chart provided as another scaffolding option.* • *Students may create the following chart to provide structure for their notes:* | Article letter	Who studies humor? (fields of study, –ologists)	What causes humor?	What is the purpose of humor? What are its effects?
---	---	---	---
				  • *Struggling learners may benefit from larger group exploration of these articles. With a whole group, students can vote on the article they want to read. Even if one article is analyzed together, students should be able to read at least one other article on their own, with a partner or small group of three. The elements of interest-based choice, learning independence, and gaining more than one perspective are important. The teacher may even identify a group of students to work together under close teacher supervision and support while the rest of the class works independently.* *Locate a collection of Saturday-morning-cartoon-type videos. Looney Tunes work well because they are innocently funny (for the most part) while still presenting some ethical issues. I have found success with the collection,* Looney Tunes—The Spotlight Collection, *Vol. 1 (Premiere Edition) (1955); however, many other collections or other favorite children's cartoons may be used. Be sure that the*

(Continued)

(Continued)

Unit Sequence—Curriculum of Practice	Teacher Reflections
• What in the video was funny (or supposed to be funny)? (For each example: What type of humor would you classify it as? Why was it funny—or not?) • What is the audience for this humor? Is there just one? What elements might appeal to different audiences and why? • Are there any problems with this humor? Would it be considered inappropriate or dangerous?	*videos will draw attention to the issues addressed in the follow-up questions. The suggested Looney Tunes collection begins with a Bugs Bunny Episode, which parodies "Goldilocks and the Three Bears," and has been proven to give students a lot to think about related to the sociological implications of humor.* *Student's activities in this lesson have focused on a number of disciplines that are concerned about or work with humor. Asking students to reflect on these fields allows them to connect to the learning—especially as they reflect on the types of thinking and problem solving in which these practitioners engage.*
Closure: Reflection Through the Curriculum of Identity	
Students will respond to one or more of the following questions in their learning log: • What do practitioners and contributors to this discipline think about? To what degree are these ideas familiar, surprising, and/or intriguing to me? • What are the problems and issues on which practitioners and contributors in this field spend their lives? To what degree do these intrigue me? • What is the wisdom this discipline has contributed to the world? How has that affected me? To what degree can I see myself contributing to that wisdom?	*These questions prompt students to reflect on how a discipline's skills, methods, and concepts might have meaning in their lives.*

SUBVERSION AND CONTROVERSY: SOCIOLOGICAL CONSIDERATIONS OF HUMOR: ESSENTIAL QUESTIONS

What purposes does humor serve?

How do language, tone, audience, speaker, and context interact to cause something to be funny? (DIDLS [Details, Images, Diction, Language, and Sentence structure] refers to a protocol for analyzing tone in piece of poetry or prose. Please see Lesson 3 for further information.) In other words, why do we find some things humorous and others not?

How do rules, norms, and sanctions guide behavior?

Does literature primarily shape culture or reflect it?

How do people cope with the challenges of living within a society?

What can literature, popular media, and other modes of communication reveal about the status of the structure of and groups within society?

To what extent is written text conservative, and to what extent is it dangerous?

How can various modes of communication serve as a catalyst for change?

Some types of humor: farce, irony, parody, satire, slapstick, and pun

---

Copyright © 2010 by Corwin. All rights reserved. Reprinted from *Parallel Curriculum Units for Social Studies, Grades 6–12*, edited by Jeanne H. Purcell and Jann H. Leppien. Thousand Oaks, CA: Corwin, www.corwinpress.com. Reproduction authorized only for the local school site or nonprofit organization that has purchased this book.

VOCABULARY CHART

Word	Root Etymology	Definition	Memory Cue

Copyright © 2010 by Corwin. All rights reserved. Reprinted from *Parallel Curriculum Units for Social Studies, Grades 6–12*, edited by Jeanne H. Purcell and Jann H. Leppien. Thousand Oaks, CA: Corwin, www.corwinpress.com. Reproduction authorized only for the local school site or nonprofit organization that has purchased this book.

EXPERTS ANALYZE HUMOR

From the list below, select questions that seem interesting to you. The letter of each question refers to an article you may choose to read.

A. How has the study of humor changed over time? How do people develop a sense of humor?

B. What does research say about humor at work?

C. What does research have to say about humor in education?

D. How can humor be used in advertising?

E. What are the medical benefits of humor?

F. How does humor contribute to brain development?

G. How and why might someone become a professional comedian?

H. Have another question related to humor? Google it! Find an article or Web site that deals with your question.

Around the room, articles are provided that are connected to the questions. Start with the most interesting question you identified, and quietly walk to pick up one copy of the related article and return to your seat to read it. Read as many articles as you can in the next 40 minutes, returning each to its original location before picking up the next article. While you read, jot down information that will help you discuss the answers to the following essential questions:

1. What fields of study are concerned with humor?

2. How do language, tone, audience, speaker, and context interact to cause something to be funny (DIDLS)? In other words, why do we find some things humorous and others not?

3. What purposes does humor serve? In other words, what effect does it have?

Copyright © 2010 by Corwin. All rights reserved. Reprinted from *Parallel Curriculum Units for Social Studies, Grades 6–12*, edited by Jeanne H. Purcell and Jann H. Leppien. Thousand Oaks, CA: Corwin, www.corwinpress.com. Reproduction authorized only for the local school site or nonprofit organization that has purchased this book.

LESSON 3: HUMOR IN COMMUNICATION
(2 CLASS PERIODS)

Concepts

M1: Society
M2: Interaction
M5: Freedom

M3: Conflict
M4: Power
M6: Change

Principles

P2: Every society develops a system of rules, norms, values, and sanctions that guides the behavior of individuals within society.
P3: Individuals are shaped by social factors.
P4: Conflicts between the individual and society often reflect beliefs about balance of power and the value of freedom.
P5: People use various means of communication in order to make sense of conflict and promote change.
P6: A speaker or writer's attempt to communicate with a given audience through humor can reveal genuine themes as the reader or listener interprets conflict, language, character, and symbolism as shaped by cultural and historical influence.

Skills

GB1 Grade 8 Goal: To develop an understanding of systems of knowledge, themes, issues, and problems that frame the external world, gifted students will

- reflect on issues that impact society, noting personal biases and prejudices;
- justify personal perspectives on a given concept, theme, or issue;
- analyze and interpret appropriate solutions to real-world problems;
- recognize their role in the systems of issues and problems occurring in the external world; and
- develop generalizations related to major systems, themes, issues, and problems.

GB2 Grade 8 Goal: To develop critical thinking, creative abilities, and problem-solving skills, gifted students will

- apply various problem-solving techniques to problem situations (e.g., mathematical, scientific, literary, technological);
- construct generalizations and synthesize across data, concepts, and perspectives; and
- apply the cognitive processes of application, synthesis, analysis, and evaluation to the research process.

GB3 Grade 8 Goal: To develop metacognitive skills that foster independent and self-directed learning in order to develop self-understanding, gifted students will

- plan, conduct, and complete complex assignments independently;
- exhibit scholarly skills and behaviors; and
- demonstrate openness and respect for diverse viewpoints.

Standards

SD7.5: The student will read, write, respond to, and demonstrate comprehension of a variety of fiction, narrative nonfiction, and poetry.
  c. Describe the impact of word choice, imagery, and poetic devices.
  f. Make inferences based on explicit and implied information.

SD7.8: The student will develop narrative, expository, and persuasive writing.
  b. Elaborate the central idea in an organized manner.
  e. Revise for clarity and effect.

Guiding Questions

- What purposes does humor serve?
- How do language, tone, audience, speaker, and context interact to cause something to be funny? In other words, why do we find some things humorous and others not?
- How do rules, norms, and sanctions guide behavior?
- How do people cope with the challenges of living within a society?
- To what extent is written text conservative, and to what extent is it dangerous?
- How can various modes of communication serve as a catalyst for change?

This lesson requires students to analyze written and verbal communication that uses humor in order to find evidence of the principles and answers to the sociological inquiry questions of this unit. These questions serve as a mechanism to discuss the major concepts of interaction, freedom, conflict, power, and change through ongoing questioning and probing.

Unit Sequence—Curriculum of Practice	Teacher Reflections
Introduction and Teaching and Learning Activities	
Introduction/Transition: Quotations Before students enter the room, post some or all of the following quotations around the room: - Humor is but another weapon against the universe. (Mel Brooks) - You grow up the day you have your first real laugh at yourself. (Ethel Barrymore) - Comedy is tragedy plus time. (Carol Burnett) - In the end, everything is a gag. (Charlie Chaplin) - Where humor is concerned there are no standards – no one can say what is good or bad, although you can be sure that everyone will. (John Kenneth Galbraith) - Humor is an affirmation of dignity, a declaration of man's superiority to all that befalls him. (Romain Gary) - What I want to do is to make people laugh so that they'll see things seriously. (William K. Zinsser) - Humor brings insight and tolerance. Irony brings a deeper and less friendly understanding. (Agnes Repplier) When class begins, instruct students to walk around the room in silent contemplation and read each of the quotations, considering each one carefully and deciding which one seems most right to them in regard to humor and	*The introductory task is intended to ease students back into critical thinking about humor. Allowing time to think about all of the quotes and then discuss their chosen quotation allows students of varying abilities to begin class in an area of interest and relative comfort. By having them regroup with a quotation that is a confusing one that seems not-quite-true to them, students will find a group of people who may be struggling as they are with some of the ideas. The discussions, because they cause students to explain their personal understandings of and interests in ideas about humor, link to the Curriculum of Identity.* *There are more quotations than would be necessary for this task, so the teacher may want to narrow them down or even find others according to what the students might find most engaging.* **Modification of Learner Need** *A possible extension or modification of the introductory task would be to provide small groups of students with the quotations (make them small enough for one page with enough space between them to have students cut them apart), along with the essential questions (on a different colored paper, arrange them like the quotations—able to be cut apart). Students could then use the questions as categories and classify the quotations beneath the questions, being prepared to justify their choices.*

(Continued)

(Continued)

Unit Sequence—Curriculum of Practice	Teacher Reflections
standing near it. Let them know they have three minutes to choose a spot. After three minutes, direct students to allow each person at the quotation to share something about why they selected that quotation. Repeat this procedure again, this time having students choose the quotation that doesn't seem quite right to them or maybe confuses them. They may need less (maybe two minutes) time; again, each person should have time to share why they selected that particular quotation. Students return to their seats. As a class, discuss the following sociological inquiry questions: • What did these quotations have to say about the purpose of humor? • In what ways did these quotations connect to the rules, norms, and sanctions that guide behavior? **Examining Essential Questions in Literature** Tell students the following: *Today, we are going to continue to examine essential questions related to humor, but whereas yesterday we looked at comics and cartoons, today we are looking at literature. You are going to have some choices to make about how you want to express your answers.* Distribute the Options for Considering Literature Through Sociological Inquiry Questions handouts to students (included at the end of this lesson). Point out that the first decision they have to make is which of the literature selections they will read. Students must have adequate time to read the stories and select and complete the activities. At least two class periods will be needed, but the actual time will be determined by the needs of the students. *DIDLS (as referred to on the Options for Considering Literature Through Sociological Inquiry Questions worksheet) is an AP Vertical Team strategy for helping students remember the elements of tone that they should consider when evaluating prose or poetry.	*There are no right or wrong answers for this task; the goal is to have students consider the essential questions carefully in terms of what they are asking and then make and justify connections through inferences.* *The culminating class discussion or the classification modification that follows links the Curriculum of Identity-based discussions back to the Curriculum of Practice through the use of sociological inquiry questions.* **Modifications for Learner Need** *It is important to realize that the suggested literature comes from an anthology from a text called,* What's So Funny, *published by Perfection Learning (www.perfectionlearning.com), but examples may be found in multiple places. Students could even be asked to locate and bring in short literature examples to be used for the activities during this lesson. Having students do this before the lesson is taught will allow time to screen and make copies of various examples. Although the literature samples for this series of activities are focused on the use of written texts, some of them are transcribed from verbal performances. To provide differentiation for learners who struggle with text, video or audio recordings of these or other examples can be located. It is also important to note that because of the broad nature of the questions, not all questions will work with every piece of literature equally well, but there should be adequate questions for each selection.* **AID and Modification for Learner Need** *There are a number of ways to differentiate this task for readiness. The teacher could assign literature selections to read (or view or listen to) based on reading levels. In addition, although this*

Unit Sequence—Curriculum of Practice	Teacher Reflections
Details: facts that are included or those omitted Images: vivid appeals to understanding through the senses Diction: the connotation of the word choice Language: the overall use of language, such as formal, clinical, or jargon Sentence Structure: how structure affects the reader's attitude A scoring guide for the Options for Considering Literature Through Sociological Inquiry Questions is located at the bottom of the handout. To promote quality of products, students may find it useful to have a few exemplars of some of the less-standard products, such as billboards and wanted posters, available.	*task is currently designed for each student to read one piece and answer three questions, some eager readers may elect to read more than one story, still being required to complete three tasks.* *Another strategy for differentiation would be to change the choice board menu into task cards; the teacher could distribute different task cards to students based on the student's readiness and challenge needs.*
Closure	
Have students share their work (see options listed in the right-hand column) and discuss their responses to the essential questions.	*A variety of approaches can be used to have students share their work and focus on the essential questions. One is a "fishbowl" approach, where the students who completed the activity for each section sit in the middle of a circle of desks or chairs and share what they did and how it answered the questions while the rest of the class sits on the outside of the circle.* *Another strategy is the use of the "gallery" approach. For this option, students can select their best work and display it on their desks, or even hang it around the room on the wall. Each of the students is then given two Post-it notes on which to write encouraging comments for their peers.* *Finally, students may share with each other in groups. To add some accountability to this conversation, hand out a copy of the essential questions and have a secretary for each group record the main points of the conversation about the essential questions.*

OPTIONS FOR CONSIDERING LITERATURE THROUGH SOCIOLOGICAL INQUIRY QUESTIONS

- **"Fish Eyes" by David Brenner.** Stand-up comedian David Brenner recalls his childhood growing up in a poor section of Philadelphia.
- **"Pancakes" by Joan Bauer.** Jill thinks that perfectionism can be a good thing. It helped her adjust through many changes of schools and got her a good job in a pancake house. However, a particularly bad morning at Ye Olde Pancake House teaches Jill that there are other priorities in life besides being in control.
- **"Money: Too Tight to Mention" by Sinbad.** In this stand-up routine, comedian Sinbad talks about the sometimes preposterous lengths to which his parents went to save money during his childhood.
- **"Duffy's Jacket" by Bruce Colville.** This short story uses expectation to surprise the reader as he describes the results of his cousin Duffy's scatterbrained brilliance.

Select one of the stories above to read for this task. Before you read the story, look over the following task options. As you read, consider which seem to be the best fit and which are interesting for you to think about. After reading, select three tasks (each answering a different question) to complete.

What purpose does the humor in this story serve? Consider each of the sociological concepts we are exploring in this unit and determine which one the author seems most concerned about. Write a sentence stating the purpose related to the concept and explain your answer either by writing a paragraph or completing a main idea chart. Be sure to use *specific* examples from the story.	How does the author use details, imagery, diction, language, and/or sentence structure to create humor? Complete a DIDLS* chart of the elements of writing that help create a humorous tone. Find at least five examples total. 	Pg.	Passage	Significance to Tone	DIDLS
					How can various modes of communication serve as a catalyst for change? Identify a theme of the story that suggests a need for something (a behavior, belief, or condition) to change. Then, either (a) Design a billboard providing evidence related to the story that would argue for change, or (b) Write a reflective paragraph where you express how the theme of this story affects your own personal development.
---	---	---
How do society's rules, norms, and sanctions guide behavior? Identify three to five rules, norms, or sanctions that affect the characters or plot in the story and the positive or negative consequences related to each. Then, either (a) Create a catchy musical jingle or slogan that promotes that rule, norm, or sanction, or (b) Write a paragraph arguing for or against one of the rules, norms, or sanctions.	How do people cope with the challenges of living within a society? Identify three to five external conflicts involving the characters in the story and describe the resolution of each (or lack thereof). Then, either (a) Create an editorial cartoon addressing the balance of power between society and individuals, or (b) Write a list of the top five issues related to an individual's ability to cope with conflict in society.	To what extent is written text conservative, and to what extent is it dangerous? Identify the ideas in the story that might be considered dangerous. Then, either (a) Create a "Wanted" or "Warning" poster related to this dangerous idea, or (b) Write a short editorial expressing your opinion on this dangerous idea.

Assessment Standards: For each of three activities, ask yourself, To what extent have I:

- clearly answered the question?
- linked the answer explicitly to the literature?
- produced a quality product?

Activity One:

	To a great extent	Generally	Not at all
Answer	2	1	0
Literature	2	1	0
Quality	2	1	0

Activity Two:

	To a great extent	Generally	Not at all
Answer	2	1	0
Literature	2	1	0
Quality	2	1	0

Activity Three:

	To a great extent	Generally	Not at all
Answer	2	1	0
Literature	2	1	0
Quality	2	1	0

Copyright © 2010 by Corwin. All rights reserved. Reprinted from *Parallel Curriculum Units for Social Studies, Grades 6–12*, edited by Jeanne H. Purcell and Jann H. Leppien. Thousand Oaks, CA: Corwin, www.corwinpress.com. Reproduction authorized only for the local school site or nonprofit organization that has purchased this book.

LESSON 4: SOCIOLOGICAL RESEARCH
(5+ CLASS PERIODS)

Concepts

M1: Society
M2: Interaction
M5: Freedom
M3: Conflict
M4: Power
M6: Change

Principles

P1: Society is a process of interactions among individuals and groups.

P2: Every society develops a system of rules, norms, values, and sanctions that guides the behavior of individuals within society.

P3: Individuals are shaped by social factors.

P4: Conflicts between the individual and society often reflect beliefs about balance of power and the value of freedom.

P5: People use various means of communication in order to make sense of conflict and promote change.

Skills

GB1 Grade 8 Goal: To develop an understanding of systems of knowledge, themes, issues, and problems that frame the external world, gifted students will

- reflect on issues that impact society, noting personal biases and prejudices;
- justify personal perspectives of a given concept, theme, or issue;
- analyze and interpret appropriate solutions to real-world problems;
- recognize their role in the systems of issues and problems occurring in the external world; and
- develop generalizations related to major systems, themes, issues, and problems.

GB2 Grade 8 Goal: To develop critical thinking, creative abilities, and problem-solving skills, gifted students will

- apply various problem-solving techniques to problem situations (e.g., mathematical, scientific, literary, technological);
- construct generalizations and synthesize across data, concepts, and perspectives; and
- apply the cognitive processes of application, synthesis, analysis, and evaluation to the research process.

GB3 Grade 8 Goal: To develop metacognitive skills that foster independent and self-directed learning in order to develop self-understanding, gifted students will

- plan, conduct, and complete complex assignments independently;
- exhibit scholarly skills and behaviors; and
- demonstrate openness and respect for diverse viewpoints.

Standards

SD7.1: The student will give and seek information in conversations and group discussions.
SD7.6: The student will read and demonstrate comprehension of a variety of informational texts.

   d. Identify the source, viewpoint, and purpose of texts.
   e. Describe how word choice and language structure convey an author's viewpoint.

SD7.7: The student will apply knowledge of appropriate reference materials.
  b. Use graphic organizers to organize information.
  c. Synthesize information from multiple sources.

SD7.8: The student will develop narrative, expository, and persuasive writing.
  b. Elaborate the central idea in an organized manner.
  e. Revise for clarity and effect.

Guiding Questions

- What purposes does humor serve?
- How do language, tone, audience, speaker, and context interact to cause something to be funny? In other words, why do we find some things humorous and others not?
- How do rules, norms, and sanctions guide behavior?
- How do people cope with the challenges of living within a society?
- To what extent is written text conservative, and to what extent is it dangerous?
- How can various modes of communication serve as a catalyst for change?

Unit Sequence—Curriculum of Practice	Teacher Reflections
Introduction and Teaching and Learning Activities	
Terminology to Add to Notebooks: Sociological Research Methodologies Content Analysis, Survey, Experimental/Quasi-Experimental, and Observation **Developing a Research Question: 4-Square Scaffold** Tell students: *Now, the real fun begins; we are going to add our own research to the body of knowledge in sociology. I have given you a Developing a Research Question worksheet for developing research questions (included at the end of this lesson). We are going to work through most of this together, but at the end, you will have to develop a question you want to explore. On this page, ignore the Types of Research column for now and don't worry about everything after the chart just yet. To begin, find the square that says "Concepts related to humor." There are a few there already. Think about the learning we've done so far—examining sociology, looking at different types of humor, and examining literature—and identify where we have touched on each of these concepts.*	*This section of the unit is called a module, rather than a lesson, because it represents a structure through which students can engage in research as a practicing sociologist would. The previous three lessons were designed to teach students to think like sociologists so that they will be able to identify a research question related to humor and conduct the research to answer that question using one of the methods of a sociologist: Content Analysis, Survey Research, Experimental and Quasi-Experimental Research, or Observational Research.* *The stages of the module take students through the steps of the research process. Students certainly use the research process in science class, so it may be useful to talk to the science teacher about the methods she or he uses and help students see similarities and differences in the approaches. This conversation may also allow for collaboration, as the science teacher may have taught the students to use other scaffolds and processes that are equally as effective in helping to design, conduct, analyze, evaluate, and share the results of an experiment.*

(Continued)

(Continued)

Unit Sequence—Curriculum of Practice	Teacher Reflections
(Provide 30–60 sec. of silent thinking time.) Ask students to share examples of activities related to the concepts listed: Society, Interaction, Freedom, Conflict, Power, and Change. Then, ask for other concepts that may be added to the list; these will be added if students can give specific examples and explain how these connect to one of the already listed concepts. On your own paper, record those concepts that you find most interesting…you don't have to add every one. Next, ask for a student to explain what "sociological issues related to humor" means. Ask students to volunteer examples of what they consider sociological issues. When they give an example, ask how that sociological issue might link to humor. These ideas can be added to the chart as they seem applicable. Then say, "Again, identify those that are interesting to you and add those to your 4-square." Finally, give students a few minutes to list places where humor can be found, and then move on to composing some research questions in a "just think about it mode" . . . not to *decide* what to research, yet. Pair up students and have them share their questions. Between the two of them, they can select the most interesting question to share (or create one together to share). After a few minutes, call on each pair to share their favorite question with the group. As each pair shares, listen for things that you didn't think of, but that you might be interested in pulling in to your research, and add these things to your 4-square or add to your questions as they change. After the pairs have shared their questions, ask students to share examples of things that were said that added to their own thinking. **Research Methodologies PowerPoint** Tell students: *At this point, we have a lot of good ideas for interesting research questions. What I'd like to do now, before you make a definite decision, is to introduce the methodologies that we have available to us to approach these topics. We are going to view this PowerPoint on research methods in the social sciences;*	*In this phase, encourage students to hold off on becoming too attached to any one idea too soon. This is difficult for middle school students—to focus on the process—but very necessary to help them learn the thinking skills that will serve them well on other tasks in the future. On the other hand, if there is a student who has a passion for a particular topic, it isn't necessary to dissuade their enthusiasm, but do encourage them to humor you by taking time with this process—it may lead to an even stronger question that they hadn't thought of yet; there will be plenty of opportunity to take off at one's own speed later.* *The research question-finding phase focuses on the concepts important to the discipline as well as how those concepts translate into practice. Questions related to the Curriculum of Practice include: What are the big ideas that govern sociology? How do sociologists organize their knowledge and skills? How do the concepts and principles that form the framework of the sociology relate to research questions sociologists might seek to answer?* *To connect to the Curriculum of Identity during this phase, and throughout the module, the teacher may ask students to voice their opinions on the processes sociologists use in their work: Do they find these processes useful? Would they want to work in this way for a living? When students face frustration, teachers may ask: How do you suppose a sociologist would handle this situation? What motivation might the sociologist have to persist? What strategies do you know that you can apply to solving the problems of working as a sociologist?* *Use the Internet Web site information to create a PowerPoint presentation for the students. The four sociological methods include:* • *Content Analysis: http://writing.colostate .edu/guides/research/content/index.cfm*

Unit Sequence—Curriculum of Practice	Teacher Reflections
it will give us four of the many ways social scientists, which include sociologists, conduct research.	• *Survey Research: http://writing.colostate.edu/guides/research/survey* • *Experimental Research: http://writing.colostate.edu/guides/research/experiment/index.cfm* • *Observational Research: http://writing.colostate.edu/guides/research/observe*
Before beginning to discuss how to take notes from the PowerPoint, hand each student a notecard or piece of paper and have him or her write on it the sociological issue that they find most interesting right now. This is not a final decision, but do encourage the students to choose something that just seems kind of interesting at this point. During the upcoming PowerPoint, many students will benefit from having a partner with whom to work out ideas.	*In this second phase of the module, students move onto other questions in the Curriculum of Practice, including the following: What are the methodologies and strategies a sociologist uses to conduct research? How does the sociologist know which methods to use under given circumstances? How might a sociologist know whether the methods used are or will be effective?*
Have students clear their desks of everything except their notecard, 4-square scaffold, a piece of notebook paper, and a writing utensil. Once everyone has complied, tell them that they are going to be able to seek out a partner with whom to discuss the items in the PowerPoint and that it will be helpful to have someone who is interested in the same issue. Each student also has the option to work alone, but point out that some of the new and abstract ideas might benefit from having a buddy to struggle with, and also assure them that this partner is just for the discussion phase, they do not have to work with the same person, or anyone, to conduct their research.	*Writing a topic of interest on a notecard will allow students to partner themselves with someone interested in the same topic. To prevent students from manipulating their answers in order to work with their friends, the teacher may choose not to mention the reason for writing this topic down on the card.*
Tell students: *Stand up and pick up your supplies. Hold your card in front of you. Without talking, walk around and look at what other people have written. Find someone who has the same or very similar idea and find a place to sit down next to that person. You have 45 seconds to find your partner and a place to sit. Go.* *As we view and discuss this PowerPoint, I want you to be thinking about the direction in which you may want to head for your research and how one of these methods might be used to research that topic. Therefore, I think it will be helpful for us, before we start, to consider what sort of notes you may want to take that will be useful in your decision-making and, eventually, in carrying out your research.*	**Using Cornell Notes During PowerPoint Presentation** *Have students title the notes: "Research Methods for Sociology" or, simply, "Research Methods."* *Then, have them divide the page vertically into two columns. With notepaper, it works well to fold the right side of the paper into the left margin line; this creates two columns, one a little narrower than the other. Have the students label the two columns as follows:* • *Subtitle the first column* Record . . . *this is where the notes go.* • *Subtitle the second column* Respond . . . *this is the column in which students can rewrite the vocabulary they are learning or questions or ideas they have as they go along.*

(Continued)

(Continued)

Unit Sequence—Curriculum of Practice	Teacher Reflections
(Provide students with a preferred note-taking strategy, or have students set up a page for Cornell notes as outlined in the next column.) *So if I say to take notes during this PowerPoint that will help you plan and conduct research, what types of things will you be looking for? What types of methodological information do you need at this point?* Allow responses from students, writing them on the board or on easel paper. Offer a few ideas to get them started, if needed, and write down any things that are relevant. After the ideas seem to fizzle, or the list below has been mostly mentioned, stop the idea-collecting phase and evaluate each of the questions. If there are some that may cause students to record unnecessary information, ask them questions about the item and help them identify when the question may not be helpful. Below are some questions they should probably generate, based on the information actually in the PowerPoint, that can be integrated into the preferred note-taking strategy. • Is there any language of the discipline we need to know to understand the methods? • What types of research methods are there? • What is each best used for? • What are the general procedures of each method? Once students are ready to take notes, work through the PowerPoint slides on research methods together. During the PowerPoint, point out or have students point out when there is something that answers one of the questions on which they decided to take notes. In addition, at the points where the presentation asks how a particular method may be used, use the students' own developing questions as examples. Perhaps just call on a student and have them read a question. Then ask, Would this method work for researching that question? Why or why not? Then, ask another volunteer to share a question that might or might not fit (whichever will provide the opposite reasoning as the first) with the given research method. Continue this questioning until it seems that the	*When the PowerPoint is finished, have students draw a line across the page where the notes end. Under that line, write the subtitle* Recapitulate. *In this space, have students summarize which of the research methods seems to be the most useful to the topic they want to research and why. Also, they could describe one that won't be useful to them and explain why not.* *The teacher will want to look at the following online reference pages to familiarize himself or herself with the research methodologies beforehand. Online research resources include the following:* • *Colorado State University. (2008). Writing guide for content analysis. Retrieved July 9, 2008, from http://writing.colostate.edu/ guides/research/content/index.cfm* • *Colorado State University. (2008). Writing guide for survey research. Retrieved July 9, 2008, from http://writing.colostate.edu/ guides/research/survey* • *Colorado State University. (2008). Writing guide for experimental and quasi-experimental research. Retrieved July 9, 2008, from http:// writing.colostate.edu/guides/research/experiment/ index.cfm* • *Colorado State University. (2008). Writing guide for observational research. Retrieved July 9, 2008, from http://writing.colostate .edu/guides/research/observe*

Unit Sequence—Curriculum of Practice	Teacher Reflections
group understands the application of the method given. Model and encourage students to use the language of the discipline from the slides to describe the reasons for using or not using a particular methodology. **Pulse Check** Have students complete a 3-2-1 Assessment Card (included at the end of this lesson) about the research question development and methodology components. **Sociological Research Plan** Students will now begin the process of developing a research plan. Distribute copies of the "Management Plan for Sociological Study Development" that are included at the end of this lesson, and instruct students to just read it over for a minute, paying attention to all of the parts and what goes in each one. Then, direct them back to Part 1 and let them know that, if they can multitask, they can write in the plan while it is being discussed. Encourage them to use pencil so that they can make revisions as needed. Then tell the students: *Part 1 begins with content. Content is the focus of your study, which will be "humor and . . . " or "humor in . . . " Next, there is the question of audience. Ask yourself, Who might benefit from or be interested in the study? What types of people might you write here? (Call on students to respond.) You may want to write a title now, or later.* *Look at the Draft Synthesis Statement. Notice the word* **Draft**. *Draft a sentence or two that explains why what you are going to study is going to be interesting or helpful to a particular audience. For instance: This study of animal characters in humorous children's stories might help people who want to develop positive, but respectful, attitudes toward animals, like the American Society for the Prevention of Cruelty to Animals (ASPCA) or naturalist-educators.*	*Modification for Learner Need:* To reduce complexity for some students, teachers may want to limit the number of methodologies introduced. *Review the responses to the 3-2-1 cards as soon as possible, before proceeding to the next phase. If this activity falls into the middle of instructional time, collect the cards and go through the questions, either answering them immediately, or placing them in a "next time" pile. Some of the questions may be answerable by posing them to the class and having them work out the answers together. The goal is to ease students into the upcoming complex task.* *The management plan given is fairly generic, and it can be used, with minor modifications, for many types of independent research, study, and production. Science teachers may have a format for designing experiments that students are familiar with and that would provide an equally useful scaffold for students.* *If technology is available, the teacher may want to upload the document online to a Portal or Blackboard system, so that students may access the scaffold electronically. Doing this encourages fluency of writing and willingness to revise.* *Give some time to start working on the plan (the time needed will vary based on the students). After 10 to 15 minutes, have students get together to share their research plans; pair up so that one group's or individual's plan can be shared with another group or individual. Before they begin the discussion, instruct students to focus on asking clarifying questions or the other research plan; by doing this, they will improve the quality of each*

(Continued)

(Continued)

Unit Sequence—Curriculum of Practice	Teacher Reflections
Part 2 is the actual research development plan. First, list things you already know about the topic; these are facts, like "Children like to laugh at funny animals." Things you understand will be more abstract: "I understand that children are influenced by the images they see." Finally, list the skills you already have related to research. *These three columns are meant to have you consider the knowledge and skills that you can draw from and build on as you research. You may have a lot of knowledge or a little; some of the columns may have little or nothing in them. Take a little time right now to jot down some things in this section. Allow about four minutes, and then ask some students to share what they wrote in each column.* Continue to tell students: *Material and human resources are a list of things and people that you will need to conduct your experiment. And the last section is a list of steps you will take to carry out your research. Spend some time now to complete this research plan. You do not have to fill it out in order, and if you need to do some pre-planning-planning, then brainstorm some ideas on another piece of paper. Look over the four-square we have been using to develop questions. If you are going to work with a team, you may move to sit with the group.* **In-Depth Study of Research Methods** Have students review the Web site that explains the methodology they have selected for use. A modified Frayer Research Methodology Diagram provides a scaffold for focusing students' attention on important information. To provide additional support, students could work together in pairs or small groups based on shared methodology needs of their research questions.	*other's research. Remind students of clear operational definitions, independent and dependent variables, and the variety of research methods that might be used. (Ask questions to help them remember and write words and phrases on the board to remind them to look for and question each other about these things.)* *The following are the suggested Web sites for analysis. Because they are from the same source, the formats are similar, allowing for use of one graphic organizer, no matter the methodology being investigated.* **Content Analysis** - *Colorado State University. (2008). Writing guide for content analysis. Retrieved July 9, 2008, from http://writing.colostate.edu/ guides/research/content/index.cfm* **Survey Research** - *Colorado State University. (2008). Writing guide for survey research. Retrieved July 9, 2008, from http://writing.colostate.edu/ guides/research/survey*

Unit Sequence—Curriculum of Practice	Teacher Reflections
	Experimental Research • *Colorado State University. (2008). Writing guide for experimental and quasi-experimental research. Retrieved July 9, 2008, from http://writing.colostate.edu/guides/research/experiment/index.cfm* **Observation Research** • *Colorado State University. (2008). Writing guide for observational research. Retrieved July 9, 2008, from http://writing.colostate.edu/guides/research/observe* **Online Writing Guides for Sociology** • *The Writing Center, University of North Carolina at Chapel Hill. (2007). Sociology. Retrieved July 9, 2008, from http://www.unc.edu/depts/wcweb/handouts/sociology.html (Novice Source)* • *Department of Sociology, USC-Berkeley. (2008). Writing for sociology. Retrieved July 9, 2008, from http://sociology.berkeley.edu/documents/student_services/WritingforSociologyJan2008.pdf (Intermediate Source)*
Monitoring the Learning From this point forward, students will need a variety of levels of support to successfully conduct their research. Conversations with students need to occur as to the individual support or group mini-lessons they might need to continue. Some possible steps might be: • Teacher approval of research plans for feasibility. • Small-group instruction on various research methods. This would involve such skills as helping groups set up their recording system for content analysis, writing and delivering survey questions, designing an experiment, and taking observational notes. • Writing mini-lessons. Some students have experience writing scientific reports or even doing expository writing. Included in the supporting materials for this unit, there are guides for writing sociology. They can provide resources for both teachers and students on the structure and	

(Continued)

(Continued)

Unit Sequence—Curriculum of Practice	Teacher Reflections
style of writing reports. Understanding the big picture, the teacher can modify and scaffold according to students' readiness and needs. • Time and opportunity to research. Will students do this on their own outside of class, or can class time and structures be provided for conducting research during the school day? Some students without home resources and support will need time within or after the school day to conduct research. Some advanced students may need some mentors or advanced resources for conducting research. • Check-ups on student progress. Whether students are working outside of or within the school setting, students should report on their progress and have the opportunity to reflect and problem-solve with a partner, small group, or during a teacher-student conference, depending on their independence level and readiness to tackle a complex task. • Writing process opportunities within the classroom: drafting, peer-editing, and revising. Use writing workshop procedures with which students are familiar.	
Sharing Results—Sociological Symposium When it is time for students to consider how they will share their results, show students the word *symposium*. Have them identify the word parts that help them figure out what the word means: • Sym = together; related words: sympathy (feeling along with someone), symphony (the sounds work together) • Pos = place; related words: juxtapose (place beside in contrast), position (the place where something is) • ium = noun suffix; related words: helium, auditorium A symposium, then, is a place and opportunity for people to gather together and share ideas. Explain to students that they are going to share their research with their fellow sociologists in a symposium. There are a	**Symposium Options** *Students might enjoy setting up a professional symposium using multiple spaces. In the middle school, other teachers on the team may be willing to forgo the regular schedule to arrange for "product fair" space, a keynote presentation (either by a professional or a student with a particular talent in this area and an advanced product), presentation options, panel discussions, and so on, as might occur at a real-world symposium. A program could be produced and community members and professionals could be invited to attend.* *Such a large-scale event would not be necessary, however, to give students the feeling of professionalism in their presentation. If standards demand that students develop public speaking and presentation skills, it would be reasonable to require everyone to present to the class; however, consider offering multiple presentation options. Sharing these presentations and products with a*

Unit Sequence—Curriculum of Practice	Teacher Reflections
variety of ways that this sharing can occur. These may include, but are not limited to, a formal presentation, a panel discussion, or a product fair. Depending on teacher, student, and facility needs and opportunities, any of these, or others, could be used. Discuss as a class the preferred method. Should we all do the same thing? Could we have multiple options? More than one panel discussion, grouped topically? How might we schedule, plan, and carry out our symposium?	*real audience would provide more authentic venues that mirror the work that sociologists prepare for as a way to communicate their findings.* *Another helpful thing to consider is that scientists often present preliminary results of their research. This is important because some students may not completely finish before the deadline, and they could present what they have found out so far; explaining the challenges and successes of their process even without final or definitive results.*
Closure	
Use the Sociological Research Report Evaluation handout at the end of this lesson to assess student levels of success on the research task. The squares are left blank to provide space for student and/or teacher comments. At the end of the Sociological Symposium, have students use the Self-Evaluation and Reflection handout, also included at the end of this lesson, to answer these questions about what they have learned from conducting the research: • How did you, as a sociologist, decide which approaches and methods would be effective in conducting your research? • To what extent do you feel that your work as a sociologist was successful? Please explain. • What is the wisdom that sociology contributes to the world? How has that wisdom affected you? To what degree can you see yourself contributing to that wisdom?	*A note on grading: Consider that "Meets Expectations" represents what a reasonably motivated typical student at a given grade or knowledge level would produce, and make this a B. Give extra points for exceeding, and subtract for not meeting expectations—maybe 3 or 4 percentage points. This achieves the effect of both lessening the threat of failure and rewarding initiative.* *These questions are designed to help students see themselves in relation to the discipline both now and with possibilities for the future; understand the discipline more fully by connection with their lives and experiences; increase awareness of their preferences, strengths, interests, and need for growth; and think about themselves as stewards of the discipline. These questions are aligned to the purposes of the Curriculum of Identity.*

DEVELOPING A RESEARCH QUESTION

Types of Research	Concepts Related to Humor
• Case-study description • Classifying • Comparing • Finding relationships • Finding causes and effects • Measuring and estimating • Mapping structures	Society Interaction Freedom Conflict Power Change Others?
Places Where Humor Might Be Found Comic pages	**Sociological Issues Related to Humor** Ethnic stereotypes

We will use this chart to help identify possible research topics. You may try to purposely match items in the categories, or "force-fit" them. Work on your own (for now) to write at least five possible research questions, phrasing them in a way that makes it clear that the boxes have interacted to create the questions you developed.

Example: By classifying the types of jokes made in comic pages with references (visual or verbal) to ethnic groups, I could examine whether negative stereotypes are being presented.

Copyright © 2010 by Corwin. All rights reserved. Reprinted from *Parallel Curriculum Units for Social Studies, Grades 6–12*, edited by Jeanne H. Purcell and Jann H. Leppien. Thousand Oaks, CA: Corwin, www.corwinpress.com. Reproduction authorized only for the local school site or nonprofit organization that has purchased this book.

3-2-1 ASSESSMENT CARD

Name: _____   Class: _____

Things I learned about sociological research:

3
1.
2.
3.

Thoughts I have about conducting my own sociological research:

2
1.
2.

Question I have about sociological research:

1
1.

Copyright © 2010 by Corwin. All rights reserved. Reprinted from *Parallel Curriculum Units for Social Studies, Grades 6–12*, edited by Jeanne H. Purcell and Jann H. Leppien. Thousand Oaks, CA: Corwin, www.corwinpress.com. Reproduction authorized only for the local school site or nonprofit organization that has purchased this book.

MANAGEMENT PLAN FOR SOCIOLOGICAL STUDY DEVELOPMENT

Part I: Problem Finding and Focusing

Content: Humor in ──────────────────────────────

Audience (Who cares?):

Title:

Draft Synthesis Statement (Why is this project important to you and your audience?):

Part II: Research and Development

Knowledge I Already Have on This Topic:
Research Questions:

I know:	I understand:	I can:

Human and Material Resources:

I need to know:	I want to understand:	I want to learn:

Getting Started (What is the process I will follow or have followed to complete this task?):

Material Resources	Human Resources

1. ──────────────────────────────────────
2. ──────────────────────────────────────
3. ──────────────────────────────────────
4. ──────────────────────────────────────
5. ──────────────────────────────────────
6. ──────────────────────────────────────

Evaluation (After finishing the product, reflect on the effectiveness of your project and process, as well as areas of weakness, strengths, and areas for future research):

Copyright © 2010 by Corwin. All rights reserved. Reprinted from *Parallel Curriculum Units for Social Studies, Grades 6–12*, edited by Jeanne H. Purcell and Jann H. Leppien. Thousand Oaks, CA: Corwin, www.corwinpress.com. Reproduction authorized only for the local school site or nonprofit organization that has purchased this book.

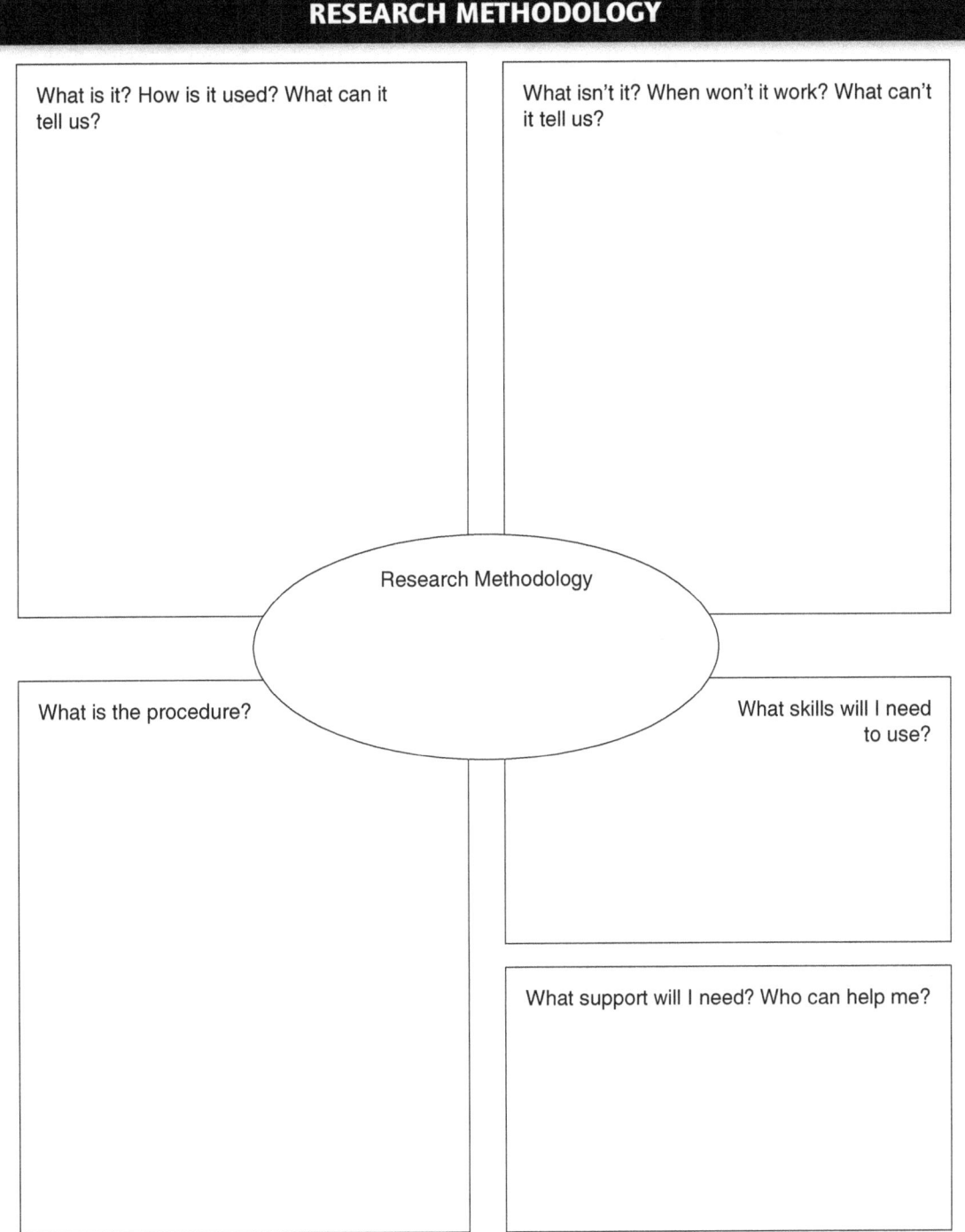

Copyright © 2010 by Corwin. All rights reserved. Reprinted from *Parallel Curriculum Units for Social Studies, Grades 6–12*, edited by Jeanne H. Purcell and Jann H. Leppien. Thousand Oaks, CA: Corwin, www.corwinpress.com. Reproduction authorized only for the local school site or nonprofit organization that has purchased this book.

SOCIOLOGICAL RESEARCH REPORT EVALUATION

Expectation	Does Not Meet	Meets	Exceeds
Student develops a research question that relates to issues of how use of humor impacts society.			
Student develops a reasonable research plan that makes use of a research methodology relevant to the field of sociology.			
Student is clear on what is being researched (including use of good operational definitions and clarifying independent and dependent variables).			
Student exhibits scholarly behaviors for successful research: creating and maintaining a schedule, using time wisely, setting and adjusting goals, maintaining records, and seeking resources to solve problems.			
Student synthesizes information in order to develop generalizations about the relevance of the essential questions of sociology.			
Student produces a quality, professional product.			
Student reflects thoughtfully on the learning process and product.			

Name: _____ Class: _____

SELF-EVALUATION AND REFLECTION

Refer to the evaluation page, and read the descriptors of the expectations. For each, place a small (but not too small) check in the box that best describes how you feel you did in each area. If you want to add explanatory notes, please do so; however, these three questions will be thoughtfully considered as your personal reflection. If you feel better with lines, feel free to write your responses on your own loose-leaf paper.

- How did you, as a novice sociologist, decide which approaches and methods would be effective in conducting your research?
- To what extent do you feel that your work as a sociologist was successful? Please explain.
- What is the wisdom that sociology contributes to the world? How has that wisdom affected you? To what degree can you see yourself contributing to that wisdom?

Copyright © 2010 by Corwin. All rights reserved. Reprinted from *Parallel Curriculum Units for Social Studies, Grades 6–12*, edited by Jeanne H. Purcell and Jann H. Leppien. Thousand Oaks, CA: Corwin, www.corwinpress.com. Reproduction authorized only for the local school site or nonprofit organization that has purchased this book.

LESSON 5: CURRICULUM OF IDENTITY CREATIVE EXTENSION (2 CLASS PERIODS)

Concepts

M1: Society
M2: Interaction
M5: Freedom

M3: Conflict
M4: Power
M6: Change

Principles

P1: Society is a process of interactions among individuals and groups.
P2: Every society develops a system of rules, norms, values, and sanctions that guides the behavior of individuals within society.
P3: Individuals are shaped by social factors.
P4: Conflicts between the individual and society often reflect beliefs about balance of power and the value of freedom.
P5: People use various means of communication in order to make sense of conflict and promote change.
P6: A speaker or writer's attempt to communicate with a given audience through humor can reveal genuine themes as the reader or listener interprets conflict, language, character, and symbolism as shaped by cultural and historical influence.

Skills

GB1 Grade 8 Goal: To develop an understanding of systems of knowledge, themes, issues, and problems that frame the external world, gifted students will

- reflect on issues that impact society, noting personal biases and prejudices;
- justify personal perspectives on a given concept, theme, or issue;
- analyze and interpret appropriate solutions to real-world problems;
- recognize their role in the systems of issues and problems occurring in the external world; and
- develop generalizations related to major systems, themes, issues, and problems.

GB2 Grade 8 Goal: To develop critical thinking, creative abilities, and problem-solving skills, gifted students will

- apply various problem-solving techniques to problem situations (e.g., mathematical, scientific, literary, technological);
- construct generalizations and synthesize across data, concepts, and perspectives; and
- apply the cognitive processes of application, synthesis, analysis, and evaluation to the research process.

GB3 Grade 8 Goal: To develop metacognitive skills that foster independent and self-directed learning in order to develop self-understanding, gifted students will

- plan, conduct, and complete complex assignments independently;
- exhibit scholarly skills and behaviors; and
- demonstrate openness and respect for diverse viewpoints.

Standards

SD7.5: The student will read, write, respond to, and demonstrate comprehension of a variety of fiction, narrative nonfiction, and poetry.

   c. Describe the impact of word choice, imagery, and poetic devices.
   f. Make inferences based on explicit and implied information.

SD7.8: The student will develop narrative, expository, and persuasive writing.

   b. Elaborate the central idea in an organized manner.
   e. Revise for clarity and effect.

Unit Sequence—Curriculum of Identity	Teacher Reflections
Introduction and Teaching and Learning Activities	
Have students refer to the inquiry questions and give them some time to comment on them. This does not have to be a formal conversation. Ask students what they think about the value of essential questions, rather than what the answers are. As the conversation starts to die down, but before it fizzles out completely, transition into the video as follows: *This seven-minute video is available from UnitedStreaming. It explains the collaborative behavior of an illustrator and writer who create political cartoons together.* *As you watch the video, pay attention to the following questions.* (Post these clearly or hand out slips of paper with these questions on them.): • Why do these men create humor? • How do these men collaborate to create humor? • What do these men say about the essential elements of humor? **Production Task** For this activity, use the Humor Creative Production Task handout included at the end of this lesson. In this learning activity, students are given the opportunity to create their own brand of humor. The performance task instructions are as follows: *You are a middle school student who has recognized complexity in the lives of adolescents in your community, in the United States, and in the world. Understanding that humor offers a means of wrestling with such complexities, you have decided to share your perspective on one of these complex issues with a relevant audience through a written, oral, and/or visual product. Your product must show consideration for these essential questions and their personal relevance to you:* • What purposes does humor serve? How has humor served you well in the past or in the future? • How do rules, norms, and sanctions guide behavior? How have these ideas shaped who you are?	*To allow students to express internalization of the principles and concepts related to humor, the unit may be enriched or extended by allowing students to create their own examples of humor.* *The video suggested for this activity can be accessed through the UnitedStreaming online resource that is perhaps located in your media center. The video is called the* **Lighter Side of Writing** *and is by Discovery Channel Schools (2005).* *Allowing for creative production encourages students to incorporate what they have learned in the study of sociology into their own practice, encouraging them to reflect on sociology by applying concepts and principles as a humorist makes use of them in order to recognize interactions and gain further insights.* *Help students plan for this project by reviewing the types of humor that have been studied in this unit and the ways in which humor is presented. Ideas for student products or performances include:* • *Writing: narratives, poetry, editorial, satirical news article, parody, or other nonfiction piece.* • *Oral pieces: stand-up routines, original or parody songs, or dramatic presentations.* • *Visual: comics, videos, sculpture, photography, or other artistic piece.* *The questions posed to the students are built on the purposes posed in the Curriculum of Identity. They require students to use what they have learned by looking outward to the disciplinary ideas as a means to look inward toward self.*

Unit Sequence—Curriculum of Identity	Teacher Reflections
• How do people cope with the challenges of living within a society? What challenges exist in your world and how do you propose to wrestle with these conflicts? • What can humor reveal about the status and structure of groups within society? How do these structures and groups affect your life? You must submit the following: • The product you have chosen to create; • A record of the series of steps or plan you followed to create the product; and • Your personal reflection on the success of your venture and the extent to which your product and process allowed you to answer the essential questions.	*The rubric outlined at the bottom of the Humor Creative Production Task handout can be used to guide and support students as they create their products.*
Closure	
To culminate this final activity, ask students to share their products in small groups. After students share these products, the class will be asked to suggest some final remarks or ideas regarding the types of impact these disciplinary ideas had on the shaping of their lives.	*The teacher should use this time to rotate around to view the products that are being presented. The purpose of this closing discussion is to have students discuss the role that disciplinary ideas and skills have in shaping who they become and what this means to them in terms of learning.*

HUMOR CREATIVE PRODUCTION TASK

You are a middle school student who has recognized complexity in the lives of adolescents in your community, in the United States, and in the world. Understanding that humor offers a means of wrestling with such complexities, you have decided to share your perspective on one of these complex issues with a relevant audience through a written, oral, and/or visual product. Your product must show consideration of these essential questions:

- To what extent is written text conservative, and to what extent is it dangerous?
- How can literature serve as a catalyst for change?
- Does literature primarily shape culture or reflect it?

You must submit:

1. The product you have chosen to create.
2. A record of the series of steps or plan you followed in order to create the product.
3. Your personal reflection on the success of your venture and the extent to which your product and process allowed you to answer the essential questions.

	Does Not Meet Expectations	*Meets Expectations*	*Exceeds Expectations*
The product presents a complex issue that is personally relevant to the student in his or her world and wrestles with the issue through the format or genre selected.	Student selects a topic that is rather straight-forward and/or has an obvious answer. The topic is not personally relevant to the student, as evidenced by lack of engagement in task.	Student identifies and wrestles with the issue by addressing multiple perspectives that must be considered when making choices related to the issue. The issue is something in which the student is interested.	Student identifies and wrestles with a complex issue, *revealing less-than-obvious complications and drawing insightful conclusions about the issue*. The student feels passionate about the topic.
The product is appropriate for the audience of a chosen format or genre and communicates effectively with that audience to achieve the student's purpose.	Student creates a generic project that does not show consideration for an effective relationship between genre or format, purpose, and audience.	Student creates a project that shows some consideration for how to best achieve a purpose for a given audience using the conventions of a genre or format.	Student creates an *innovative* project that *skillfully manipulates conventions* of a genre or format to connect to audience, allowing student to *successfully achieve a valuable purpose*.

	Does Not Meet Expectations	Meets Expectations	Exceeds Expectations
The student engages in meaningful self-reflection concerning the extent to which the design and plan of the product was sufficient to allow the student to meet the conceptual and creative criteria of the task.	Student's self-reflection does not demonstrate an honest, constructively critical self-analysis about process or product. Length may not be sufficient to allow for thorough analysis.	Student's self-reflection offers a report of process and summation of learning related to producing process and product, with limited mention of student's learning profile.	Student's self-reflection explains his or her process and demonstrates awareness of his or her own strengths and limitations as a learner and identifies how their unique profile benefits him or her while also providing opportunities for growth.

Copyright © 2010 by Corwin. All rights reserved. Reprinted from *Parallel Curriculum Units for Social Studies, Grades 6–12*, edited by Jeanne H. Purcell and Jann H. Leppien. Thousand Oaks, CA: Corwin, www.corwinpress.com. Reproduction authorized only for the local school site or nonprofit organization that has purchased this book.

4

True Story-Telling

How Historians Construct the Past

Grade 10

Catherine Little

BACKGROUND INFORMATION

This unit is intended to focus on the work of the historian and on some of the considerations of context that influence history, including observation, interpretation, and perspective. The lessons use the lens of the Progressive Era in American history as the context for exploring these key ideas and for helping students to understand the concept of historical significance and how it emerges over time.

The unit is designed as a companion piece to a high school history class's study of the Progressive Era. The examples, activities, and projects of the unit are linked to the period of 1900–1920 in American history, and they include both an overview study of key concepts of the period and specific attention to selected issues, including immigration, the experiences of children in the period, and several specific events. However, the unit is not a comprehensive study of this period and needs to be accompanied by other instruction to ensure content coverage. The primary focus of the unit objectives and concepts is on the discipline of history itself and on the historical process in general; with revision of the examples and some of the specific activities, these major ideas could also be used to study a different period.

This unit may be used at the same time as a more comprehensive study of the Progressive Era, or after such a study. Lesson 2 of this unit is designed to provide students with an overview of the period, but the lesson could also be approached as a review of details of the period if it has already been studied. It is recommended that the unit be used in conjunction with other study of the period, with these lessons inserted at appropriate moments, but depending on the teaching context, teachers may prefer to use it as a follow-up.

Within the Parallel Curriculum Model, the unit primarily reflects the parallel of Practice, with its emphasis on the work of the historian in critically examining the artifacts and documents of another era to develop new interpretations that might illuminate our present understanding of the past. The Core parallel is also addressed through the specific content of the unit and through the emphasis on key historical analysis skills that are central to history standards as well as to the work of the professional historian; these skills provide a strong bridge between the Core parallel and the parallel of Practice. The unit also addresses the parallel of Identity through an emphasis on memory and personal experience as a way of demonstrating for students their own place and role in making, interpreting, and recording history.

Activities of the unit include the review of a variety of primary and secondary sources about the period, including documents and textbooks with varying degrees of period detail; extensive opportunities for discussion in small groups as well as in a larger group; and writing activities, including journal responses to key ideas about history. Several lessons use source analysis worksheets to build the students' capacity to ask and answer key questions about a source they explore; all source analysis worksheets are built from a central set of key analysis questions, and where appropriate, the worksheets are differentiated to respond to differences in student readiness.

What the Teacher Needs to Know Before Starting

The expectation is that students should enter this unit within a roughly chronological study of American history, having covered or at least been introduced to key aspects of American society in the late 19th century, including the growth of business, urbanization, the emergence of labor unions, and the increase in immigration. Several of these topics, which are central to any study of the Progressive Era, will be used as lesson and project emphases within this unit, connecting the Core and Practice parallels through emphasis on the historian's work. Therefore, previous study of the topics noted will allow students to have the background needed to understand how the Progressives emerged and the types of societal issues they confronted in this period.

The unit focuses considerable attention on how historical accounts are constructed, including both primary and secondary sources. Students should have some familiarity with the distinctions between primary and secondary sources and should have a sense of the basic questions a historian might ask when first viewing a source. Guiding questions for working with sources are provided within the unit, but students will have a stronger basis for interacting with the sources if they have some experience with primary sources already. If students do not have experience with drawing distinctions between primary and secondary source documents, teachers may wish to provide a mini-lesson on this topic. Several online resources are listed for teacher and student reference.

Teachers will need to gather several resources before the start of the unit. Resources should include texts and links to online sources, and they should be drawn from the following categories:

- General American history texts and Web sites that include sections on the Progressive Era
- Texts and Web sites that focus specifically on the Progressive Era (examples are provided throughout)
- Texts and Web sites that approach history in unique ways (examples are provided throughout)
- Texts and Web sites that explain and explore primary sources
- Photographs and/or sample objects that represent daily life and major events of the period
- "Year in Review" types of articles or lists from magazines or newspapers over several recent years (see Lesson 5)
- Information on the work of historians and journalists; contact with guest speakers from these professions

CONTENT FRAMEWORK

Organizing Concepts

Macroconcept	Discipline-Specific Concepts: 3 to 5 Concepts	Principles
M1: Perspective	C1: History	P1: Written history is a human construction, relying on interpretation and judgment to make sense of the past.
	C2: Historical narrative	P2: Individuals are selective in what they see, remember, and record about events they witness or study; the selective recording of events in the past influences our understanding of those events.
	C3: Reliability	P3: Developing an understanding of a historical period or event requires exploring multiple sources from multiple perspectives.
	C4: Chronology	P4: Understanding historical sources requires exploring the purpose for their creation and their intended and actual influence on those who read or viewed them.
	C5: Memory	P5: Personal and group identities are influenced by history, and personal and group perspectives influence how we think about and record history.
	C6: Significance	

Skills

S1: Observation

S2: Inference

S3: Analyzing significance

S4: Summarizing details

S5: Comparing and contrasting

S6: Sequencing

S7: Determining point of view

S8: Identifying details

S9: Assessing and predicting significance

National Standards (from National Standards for Historical Thinking, Grades 5–12)

SD1: Historical comprehension: Identify the central question(s) the historical narrative addresses.

SD2: Historical analysis and interpretation: Differentiate between historical facts and historical interpretations.

SD3: Historical analysis and interpretation: Consider multiple perspectives.

SD4: Historical analysis and interpretation: Compare competing historical narratives.

SD5: Historical analysis and interpretation: Hypothesize the influence of the past.

SD6: Historical research capabilities: Formulate historical questions, obtain historical data, and interrogate historical data.

UNIT ASSESSMENTS

The unit incorporates a variety of formative assessment opportunities throughout and a pre- and postassessment for the unit overall.

Preassessment

The preassessment asks students to identify an event in their own lifetime that they feel is both memorable and historically significant and to explain why they think the event is memorable and significant. They are then asked to do the same thing with an idea, movement, or change—something historically significant that is not an event. For one or the other, they are asked to describe an example of how it might be presented to people learning about it—a textbook write-up, documentary, film, a work of historical fiction, and so on. Finally, the preassessment presents two sources, a photograph and an excerpt of a book written in the time period, and asks students to explain what they can learn from the sources and what other kinds of sources they would wish to explore.

The primary purpose of the preassessment is to give the teacher a sense of the students' understanding of *historical significance* and of the value of different kinds of sources in studying history, as well as the idea of using multiple sources to corroborate historical findings. The preassessment should not be specifically graded but rather reviewed against the key criteria to gain a sense of student understanding to support instructional planning.

For some students who struggle with reading, writing, and/or the study of history, an abbreviated version of the preassessment may be given to provide information without placing impossible demands on the student. Two abbreviations are suggested: one is to reduce the reading on Question 4 by providing only the first paragraph of the Riis excerpt, and the second possible abbreviation, only for students who really would struggle extensively, is to eliminate Question 2 and revise Question 3 to focus only on the response to Question 1.

Formative Assessments

Formative assessments will include ongoing journal entries in which student responses to quotes about history will be used to determine their understanding of key principles from the unit. Projects within the unit, including a brief history of some aspect of the Progressive Era written for a specific audience and an analysis of the distinctions between journalism and history, will also be used as formative assessments that demonstrate understanding of historical content and disciplinary content.

Postassessment

The postassessment is a project that includes individual and small group contributions to an overall class assignment. Students will be asked to work in groups to develop a list of historically significant events, ideas, or people from the period under study. Then, individually, students will work to develop a write-up for one event, idea, person, or group of people; in this write-up, students will be asked to explain multiple perspectives, use sources from the period, and explain historical significance.

Teachers may also choose to administer the preassessment again as a posttest to obtain another measure of students' developing historical understanding.

OVERVIEW OF KEY LESSON IDEAS/PURPOSES

Lesson 1 is an introduction to the key ideas about selective observation and personal experiences of history. The focus is on these important ideas: (a) individuals make choices, consciously or unconsciously, about what they see, remember, and record about events they witness or portray; and (b) selective observation and selective recording play a role in the historical record.

Lesson 2 explores the historian's role in arranging historical events into a sequence in order to report them. The focus is on the complexity of history, whether history can be explored just chronologically, and on figuring out how to tell a story in a way that makes sense. This lesson includes exploration of various secondary sources and their reporting on the Progressive Era as a way of providing an overview of the era and also a basis for discussing how history is put together. A unit project is introduced in this lesson.

Lesson 3 explores multiple perspectives in history and the responsibility of the historian to gather multiple perspectives. Using the lens of immigration as a major issue in the Progressive Era, the lesson invites students to explore different documents from the time and then to look at how the issue has been reported *over* time (looking at the writer's perspective in both primary and secondary sources).

Lesson 4 focuses on human construction of history and on the difference between reporting events of a time and explaining them with a historical viewpoint. The lesson uses a specific example, the newspaper reporting that occurred upon the sinking of the *Titanic*, as the launching pad for comparing the roles of the journalist and the historian. This lesson ideally entails interviews with professional journalists and historians to help students understand the distinctions between the roles and the tensions that each role faces in trying to report events with accuracy and timeliness.

Lesson 5 focuses on defining and describing historical significance. Students are asked to consider recent events that may or may not be memorable over time and then to apply this understanding to looking at the past. Sources used in the lesson demonstrate that the people who were present at major events could not have fully known the consequences and implications of an event, and students are asked to consider what elements contribute to an understanding of historical significance.

LESSON 1: SELECTIVE MEMORY (APPROXIMATELY 2 DAYS)

Lesson 1 is an introduction to the key ideas about selective observation and personal experiences of history. The focus is on these important ideas: (a) individuals make choices, consciously or unconsciously, about what they see, remember, and record about events they witness or portray; and (b) selective observation and selective recording play a role in the recording of history.

As noted in the introduction, this unit is intended to be a companion to other study of the Progressive Era. It is recommended that Lessons 1 and 2 be conducted near the beginning of the study of the period; Lesson 2 invites students into an overview of the period and thus should be conducted near the beginning, and Lesson 1 should precede Lesson 2.

Concepts

M1: Perspective

Discipline-Specific Concepts
C1: History
C5: Memory

Principles

P2: Individuals are selective in what they see, remember, and record about events they witness or study; the selective recording of events in the past influences our understanding of those events.
P5: Personal and group identities are influenced by history, and personal and group perspectives influence how we think about and record history.

Skills

S1: Observation
S2: Inference
S3: Analyzing significance

Standards

SD2: Historical analysis and interpretation: Differentiate between historical facts and historical interpretations.
SD4: Historical analysis and interpretation: Compare competing historical narratives.

Guiding Questions

- What makes an object, person, or event memorable?
- How are memory and history related?
- What are some of the factors that might change how we feel about or remember an event in the past?

Unit Sequence	Teacher Reflections
Introduction	
Tell students that you are going to share some pictures with them that are representative of the time period you will be studying. Put about 20 pictures out on the table, and share stories about a few of them. (You might include pictures of early automobiles or airplanes, advertisements from the period, photographs of major figures such as Taft and Roosevelt, etc.) Invite students to look at the pictures and think about how they may be related to the time period. Cover the pictures and ask students to write down as many as they can remember. Invite the students to compare their lists in pairs, and then share the full list of items and ask students to comment on how many they remembered. Encourage students to share briefly what they think might have helped them remember certain items. Ask students the following questions: Were any of the items particularly meaningful to you personally? Why? In what ways do you think these items capture or represent the time period?	The purpose of this introductory activity is to prompt students to begin thinking about the possibilities and limitations of memory. Throughout the unit, they will be exploring how individual perspectives influence written history, including exploration of the reliability of memory and the emphasis that different individuals may place on events based on their own experiences and values. It might be preferable to use actual sample objects that are representative of the period, or a combination of pictures and objects. Pictures are suggested here because they are easier to obtain than period artifacts might be. You might want to consider playing music in the background if you can get some recordings of music of the period. The activity should be brief; it is introductory and meant only to inspire thinking about the individual connections that help to promote memory. At the same time, it provides an introduction to the period in a visual format, which might help to increase appeal and interest.

(Continued)

(Continued)

Unit Sequence	Teacher Reflections
Teaching Strategies and Learning Experiences	
DAY 1 Explain to students that in the course of this unit, they will be exploring history in a different way, focusing on how history is written and what kinds of questions the historian must consider in studying and writing history. Tell students that to begin the unit, they will be completing a preassessment that will provide you with some information about how they think about history and how the work of a historian is done. Distribute the Preassessment and ask students to complete it. If students complete the task and have extra time, invite them to explore the pictures or objects from the Progressive Era further. When all students have completed the preassessment, hold a brief class discussion about the questions, inviting students to share their ideas about memorable events and movements in their own lifetimes and how they would plan to share those events. Day 1 closure: Ask students to write a journal response to the following question: How do you think our introductory activity about remembering objects is related to the questions you answered on the preassessment?	*The lesson plan is written here as though this lesson is preceding entry into the study of the Progressive Era.* *All students should be able to respond to the questions on the preassessment, but their level of response in terms of understanding historical significance will vary. Teachers will be able to draw some inferences from the class discussion, as well as from the written preassessments about students' understanding of the key concepts. Key criteria to examine in reviewing the preassessment are provided on Assessment Criteria; also see suggestions in the introduction about abbreviating the preassessment for students who might struggle with reading and writing.* *Throughout the unit, students will be asked to respond in writing to journal questions that primarily probe their understanding of history as a discipline and of historical thinking. For this initial journal question, students should be beginning to show attention to the idea that events and ideas become memorable or important based on the degree to which they are meaningful to the people involved and the people they affect, as well as for the magnitude of change these ideas or events may bring. Students may not yet have crystallized these ideas, but this is the direction toward which their thinking should begin to go.*
DAY 2 Ask students to discuss briefly in pairs the following two questions: What might make an event, occasion, or activity memorable to those who were there? What might make an event, occasion, or activity worth reporting to and remembering by others who were not there? Invite the pairs to share their ideas with the class, and write a few responses on the board. Ask students to think about how the concepts of *history* and *memory* are related and to write down statements to describe the relationships. List	

Unit Sequence	Teacher Reflections
student statements on the board. Encourage a discussion of the following questions: • How is a participant's memory of an event different from a history of an event written by someone else? • To what degree does our understanding of history rely on the memories of people who were there? • How reliable would you consider each of the following accounts: the account of an event written by a witness, the account of an event written by a journalist who interviewed those there at the time, or the account of a historian who wrote about the events based on studying documents years later? Why? What factors might make an account more or less reliable?	
[Optional jigsaw approach to this last set of questions: Divide the class into groups of three to four students. Explain that the groups will be assigned a type of account of an event, and they are to talk about in what ways such an account would likely be considered reliable and in what ways it might not be reliable. Assign some groups to consider observer/participant accounts of an event, some groups to consider journalists' reporting of an event, and some groups to consider a historian's presentation of an event. Tell the groups that each member should make notes on the key points of the discussion. Then reshuffle the class into groups of three, such that each group has one member who discussed observers' accounts, one member who discussed journalists' accounts, and one member who discussed historians' accounts. Tell students to share their key points within their new groups and to discuss the advantages and disadvantages of each in terms of understanding an event.]	*This optional jigsaw is presented as an option for classes that are large and/or have many students who are less likely to participate in whole-class discussions. This approach may also be useful for students who may have less experience thinking about different kinds of accounts of events. The jigsaw allows a longer exploration of the key ideas that different sources might be created for different purposes and will have different kinds of reliability based on the information available to the person constructing the source. In arranging groups, it is advisable to ensure that the final groupings are arranged by readiness, such that three more advanced students are together to discuss the different types of sources, three students who struggle more are together, and so on. Students may then remain in these groups for the following activity.*
Have students form groups of three to four people. Once in their groups, the students should select a recent event, related to this class, at which all members of the group were present. This might be the previous day's class session (or another recent class session), a recent test or other assessment situation, an assembly, a field trip, and so on. The event should have taken place within the last two weeks.	*Arrange groups for this activity based on student readiness in critical thinking as observed over time and in the preassessment. Although all students will be able to participate in this activity, they will bring different levels of complexity to the discussion, and the grouping will allow all students to participate at a level that allows them to contribute.*

(Continued)

(Continued)

Unit Sequence	Teacher Reflections
Once each group has selected an event, the group members should separate and work *individually* to write an account of the event, providing as much detail as possible. Encourage students to try to convey the details as completely and accurately as possible, using text as well as diagrams or other visuals they feel to be appropriate.	As the students work individually to write their accounts, circulate among them and ask guiding questions of students who seem to be struggling. Encourage students to consider starting with a list of the key pieces of the event and then to elaborate.
Have students return to their groups to share and compare the individual accounts. Each group should complete a Compiled Account chart.	
Bring the class back together to debrief the activity. Ask students to share some of the differences that emerged in various accounts of the events that were selected. Invite students to comment on why they think some of the differences emerged.	
Wrap up the activity by bringing the discussion back to thinking about history. Ask students to summarize factors that might change or influence how different participants might describe an event and how descriptions might change over time. Explain that these factors are some of the things a historian must consider in reviewing sources from the past and in planning how to share information about the past.	In this discussion, guide students to identify the following key factors (others might also emerge from their thinking): different perspectives, subsequent events, subsequent actions by the people involved, emergence of new information, unreliability of memory, passage of time, and changing feelings about an event.
Closure	
Explain to students that as they progress through this unit, they will be asked to respond in writing to some quotes about the nature of history and how it is used in the world. Explain that in some cases they will be responding to specific questions about the quotes, and in other cases they will be asked just to write about what they think the quote means and how it might link to their own lives and experience of history. **Journal Prompt** Consider and respond to the following quote: "The past is malleable and flexible, changing as our recollection interprets and re-explains what has happened." (Peter Berger) Here are some questions to get you started: How is *history* different from *the past*? Give an example from your own life in which your understanding of a past event changed over time.	Throughout the unit, students will be asked to respond to quotations about history. These quotes have been selected to promote reflection about the specific concepts and issues addressed within each lesson, but they may be presented in a different order at your preference. The purpose of the Berger quote is to introduce or reinforce the idea that the past is knowable only through the interpretations of those who lived or remembered it, or through interpretation of the artifacts they left behind, and therefore interpretation plays a great part in understanding of the past. Such understanding of the individual human influence on history—from personal history to the history of civilizations—is important for students to understand and forms a central part of the unit.

PREASSESSMENT

Read each of the following questions carefully, and write your responses below. Be sure to try to respond to all parts of each question.

1. Think of an event that has occurred in your lifetime and that you think will be remembered as historically significant. (In other words, think of an event that has occurred during your life that students of the future will read about in their history classes!) Identify the event, and explain why you think it will be remembered as historically significant.

2. Think of an idea, movement, or change that has emerged in your lifetime and that you think will be remembered as historically significant. This is different from Question 1! You should choose something for this question that has been important within your lifetime but cannot be clearly identified as a particular *event*. Examples from the past might include industrialization, increasing movement to cities, the Civil Rights movement, or increasing numbers of women in professional positions. Identify the idea, movement, or change, and explain why you think it will be remembered as historically significant.

3. Choose either the event you described in Question 1 or the idea or change you described in Question 2. Imagine that you are a historian 15 years from now who is working to create a history of whatever you chose. Your history will be used by high school history classes to study the topic. Describe what this history will look like. Include attention to these questions in preparing your response:

    - What kinds of sources would you, as the historian, explore for information? Why?
    - What individuals or groups of people might you talk to in order to learn more? Why did you choose these people?
    - What format might you use to present your history? Would you write a textbook, a biography, a novel, an article? Or would you use some other format, such as a documentary, a feature film, or a Web site? Explain your reasoning for your choice.

4. Look at the 1912 photograph of a tenement yard in Providence, Rhode Island (http://memory.loc.gov/service/pnp/nclc/02700/02730v.jpg), and read the excerpt that follows from Jacob Riis's book *How the Other Half Lives*, published in 1890. Answer the following questions:

    - What details can you learn about tenement life in this period from the two sources?
    - Jacob Riis was a journalist who was trying to bring public attention to what he saw as major social problems in the city. Give specific examples to show how this excerpt from his book reflects this purpose.
    - How are these sources different from something you might read in your history textbook? What advantages or disadvantages do these sources provide for learning about the topic?
    - List at least three questions that you have about these sources or the time period. What other kinds of sources would you want to explore to understand more about the topic?

Reading

The hall is dark and you might stumble over the children pitching pennies back there. Not that it would hurt them; kicks and cuffs are their daily diet. They have little else. Here where the hall turns and dives into utter darkness is a step, and another, another. A flight of stairs. You can feel your way, if you cannot see it. Close? Yes! What would you have? All the fresh air that ever enters these stairs comes from the hall-door that is forever slamming, and from the windows of dark bedrooms....The sinks are in the hallway, that all the tenants may have access—and all be poisoned alike by their summer stenches. Hear the pump squeak! It is the lullaby of tenement-house babes. In summer, when a thousand thirsty throats pant for a cooling drink in this block, it is worked in vain.... Listen! That short hacking cough, that tiny, helpless wail—what do they mean? They mean that the soiled bow of white you saw on the door downstairs will have another story to tell—Oh! a sadly familiar story—before the day is at an end. The child is dying with measles. With half a chance it might have lived; but it had none. That dark bedroom killed it....

... A hundred thousand people lived in Tear tenements in New York last year. Here is a room neater than the rest. The woman, a stout matron with hard lines of care in her face, is at the wash-tub. "I try to keep the children clean," she says, apologetically, but with a hopeless glance around. The spice of hot soap-suds is added to the air already tainted with the smell of boiling cabbage, of rags and uncleanliness all about. It makes an overpowering compound. It is Thursday, but patched linen is hung upon the pulley-line from the window. There is no Monday cleaning in the tenements. It is wash-day all the week round, for a change of clothing is scarce among the poor. They are poverty's honest badge, these perennial lines of rags hung out to dry, those that are not the washerwoman's professional shingle. The true line to be drawn between pauperism and honest poverty is the clothes-line. With it begins the effort to be clean that is the first and the best evidence of a desire to be honest.

From Jacob Riis's (1890) *How the Other Half Lives*, http://www.cis.yale.edu/amstud/inforev/riis/title.html

Copyright © 2010 by Corwin. All rights reserved. Reprinted from *Parallel Curriculum Units for Social Studies, Grades 6–12*, edited by Jeanne H. Purcell and Jann H. Leppien. Thousand Oaks, CA: Corwin, www.corwinpress.com. Reproduction authorized only for the local school site or nonprofit organization that has purchased this book.

PREASSESSMENT CRITERIA

General criteria are provided below for reviewing student responses to preassessment questions. Levels of performance are given as "high," "medium," or "low" to indicate levels of developing historical understanding and recognition of the skills of the historian. The preassessment should not be graded, but rather reviewed to provide evidence of the students' developing understanding; this evidence can be used to guide instruction and grouping throughout the unit and to assess progress at the conclusion of the unit.

Read each of the following questions carefully and write your responses below. Be sure to try to respond to all parts of each question. Think of an event that has occurred in your lifetime and that you think will be remembered as historically significant. (In other words, think of an event that has occurred during your life that students of the future will read about in their history classes!) Identify the event, and explain why you think it will be remembered as historically significant.

	High	*Medium*	*Low*
Event choice (note: assessment relies to some extent on the teacher's own judgment of events in recent history and their likely significance)	Event occurred during student lifetime and has strong likelihood to be recognized as significant by historians and the public in general (e.g., major political event, change in power, or policy change at national or international level; major humanitarian crisis; incident with significant economic implications; large-scale conflict; major scientific or artistic achievement).	Event occurred during student lifetime and may be recognized by some as significant but unlikely to be remembered by many in the general public (e.g., event that may be significant locally but not in a broader scope; event that is currently dominating news but is likely to be ignored in histories of the period).	Event occurred outside student lifetime and/or is unlikely to be recognized as historically significant (e.g., events in popular culture that receive extensive news attention but result in no real change or influence in society; events significant in a student's own life but not for general public).
Explanation of historical significance	Explanation includes such factors as attention to the event's direct influence on large numbers of people; indirect influence through policy change, etc.; effect on shifting attitudes, behaviors, or perspectives; or effects on everyday life. Explanation should give attention both to the memorable nature of the event itself and to the event's effect or influence on some aspect of people's lives, thereby making distinctions between events that are merely *widely memorable* versus those that are *historically significant*.	Explanation attempts to show how the event was influential in creating some kind of change, but may be limited in discussion of the scope of change or how influence and significance are related; explanation may focus more on the memorable nature of an event than on its influence or significance for people over time.	Explanation is limited in terms of the scope of influence discussed; explanation may not give attention to any key elements of historical significance.

1. Think of an idea, movement, or change that has emerged in your lifetime and that you think will be remembered as historically significant. This is different from Question 1! You should choose something for this question that has been important within your lifetime but cannot be clearly identified as a particular *event*. Examples from the past might include industrialization, increasing movement to cities, the Civil Rights movement, or increasing numbers of women in professional positions. Identify the idea, movement, or change, and explain why you think it will be remembered as historically significant.

	High	*Medium*	*Low*
Topic choice (note: assessment relies to some extent on the teacher's own judgment of ideas, movements, and changes in recent history and their likely significance)	Topic described emerged during student lifetime and has strong likelihood to be recognized as significant by historians and the public in general (e.g., major social or environmental movement, major technological change, major perspective shift within the general public).	Topic emerged during student lifetime and may be recognized by some as significant but unlikely to be noted as significant by many in the general public (e.g., change that may be significant locally but not in a broader scope; issue that is currently dominating news but is likely to be ignored in histories of the period).	Topic emerged outside student lifetime and/or is unlikely to be recognized as historically significant (e.g., changes in popular culture that receive extensive news attention but result in no real change or influence in society; topics significant in a student's own life but not for general public).
Explanation of historical significance	Explanation includes such factors as attention to the topic's direct influence on large numbers of people; indirect influence through policy change, etc.; effect on shifting attitudes, behaviors, or perspectives; or effects on everyday life. Explanation should give attention both to the memorable nature of the topic itself and its effect or influence on some aspect of people's lives, thereby making distinctions between topics that are merely *widely memorable* versus those that are *historically significant*.	Explanation attempts to show how the topic was influential in creating some kind of change, but may be limited in discussion of the scope of change or how influence and significance are related; explanation may focus more on the memorable nature of the topic than its influence or significance for people over time.	Explanation is limited in terms of the scope of influence discussed; explanation may not give attention to any key elements of historical significance.

2. Choose either the event you described in Question 1 or the idea or change you described in Question 2. Imagine that you are a historian 15 years from now who is working to create a history of whatever you chose. Your history will be used by high school history classes to study the topic. Describe what this history will look like. Include attention to these questions in preparing your response:

   - What kinds of sources would you, as the historian, explore for information? Why?
   - What individuals or groups of people might you talk to in order to learn more? Why did you choose these people?

- What format might you use to present your history? Would you write a textbook, a biography, a novel, an article? Or would you use some other format, such as a documentary, a feature film, or a Web site? Explain your reasoning for your choice.

	High	Medium	Low
Sources (Questions A and B)	Response mentions both primary and secondary sources and describes sources and individuals specific to the event or topic chosen, rather than only generic sources. Response includes attention to primary accounts of key events/ideas and to individuals who would be knowledgeable based on expertise and experience. Response elaborates on source choices by explaining aspects of experience of the topic/event, expertise, and multiple perspectives.	Response mentions use of both primary and secondary sources as well as individuals who experienced an event/idea, but response gives these sources as general source categories rather than providing sample sources and individuals specifically linked to the chosen topic or event. Response is limited in explanation of why varied sources are important for studying and preparing a history.	Response does not mention primary and secondary sources specifically or identify individuals linked to an event or idea as key sources. Explanation is minimal and does not address the need for varied sources or sources close to the actual occurrence of a topic or event.
Format (Question C)	Response describes a format appropriate to the topic or event. Emphasis in response is given to the reasoning component, in which student links the format choice directly to the need to communicate certain aspects of the topic and/or to engage and inform the audience. Reasoning about format choice is logical and appropriate to the topic.	Response describes a format appropriate to the topic or event. Emphasis in response is primarily on describing the format and how the topic or event will be depicted, rather than on reasoning for format selection; or, reasoning is provided but is weak or limited in logic connecting format to topic and purpose.	Response includes a format inappropriate to the topic or event; no explanation or reasoning is provided.

3. Look at the 1912 photograph of a tenement yard in Providence, Rhode Island (http://memory.loc.gov/service/pnp/nclc/02700/02730v.jpg), and read the attached excerpt from Jacob Riis's book *How the Other Half Lives*, published in 1890. Answer the following questions:

- What details can you learn about tenement life in this period from the two sources?
- Jacob Riis was a journalist who was trying to bring public attention to what he saw as major social problems in the city. Give specific examples to show how this excerpt from his book reflects this purpose.

- How are these sources different from something you might read in your history textbook? What advantages or disadvantages do these sources provide for learning about the topic?
- List at least three questions that you have about these sources or the time period. What other kinds of sources would you want to explore to understand more about the topic?

	High	Medium	Low
Observation of detail (Questions A and B)	Responses highlight specific details from sources that link directly to the questions asked; response to Question A compares and synthesizes details across both sources to demonstrate how they provide information when examined together. Responses may highlight the negative aspects of tenement life but are primarily analytical and descriptive rather than emotional in nature.	Responses list details that link to the specific questions asked, but may draw upon too many or too few details to show focus. Response to Question A lists observations but provides only limited comparison or synthesis across sources. Responses may be more emotional in nature than descriptive or analytical.	Limited details are drawn from the sources, and some misconceptions or inaccuracies emerge in inferences made. Response may include details from only one of the sources. No comparison or synthesis across sources provided for Question A.
Connection of text and purpose (Questions B and C)	Response to Question B draws upon specific examples that directly demonstrate author purpose; details clearly demonstrate author's point of view. Response to Question C may highlight distinctions between a history text as a secondary source provided long after an event versus as primary sources provided at the time; some attention to the purposes of these different sources.	Response to Question B shows understanding of Riis's perspective but provides limited or ineffective examples showing point of view. Response to Question C does not really focus on the possible purposes of primary and secondary sources. Overall attention in response to purpose of sources is limited.	Specific examples are not provided for Question B or do not connect to author purpose. Response to Question C gives no indication of distinctions in purpose of different sources.
Primary/ secondary sources (Questions C and D)	Responses demonstrate an understanding that primary sources may provide direct accounts of experiences while secondary sources may provide a broader perspective and a different kind of historical context; attention is given to the value for the historian of understanding multiple	Responses demonstrate an understanding of the difference between primary and secondary sources and a recognition that historians should explore primary sources in studying a	Response demonstrates limited understanding of primary sources versus secondary sources and the historical perspectives offered by either. The issue of multiple

	High	Medium	Low
	perspectives. Response to Question D includes both types of sources and recognition of the value of exploring multiple sources.	period. Responses may have limited explanation of the different kinds of perspectives offered by primary and secondary sources, and limited attention is given to the value of exploring multiple perspectives. Response to Question D highlights using sources but may not identify much source variety.	perspectives is not addressed, and response to Question D does not indicate an understanding of the need for exploring multiple sources.
Questions about period (Question D)	Response provides several questions relevant to the period based on the sources provided; response may demonstrate good understanding of the general types of questions a historian may ask about life during a particular period. Sources suggested are logically linked to the questions given.	Response provides questions that may have only tenuous links to the sources and time period or are generic or peripheral in nature. Sources suggested are also generic and provide limited clear connection to the questions asked.	Response does not provide questions that would result in any historical understanding of the period. Sources are not listed or are not connected to the questions.

Copyright © 2010 by Corwin. All rights reserved. Reprinted from *Parallel Curriculum Units for Social Studies, Grades 6–12*, edited by Jeanne H. Purcell and Jann H. Leppien. Thousand Oaks, CA: Corwin, www.corwinpress.com. Reproduction authorized only for the local school site or nonprofit organization that has purchased this book.

COMPILED ACCOUNT

As a group, discuss the accounts each person wrote of the class event. Answer the questions below in your discussion.

Work together to make a list of the key details of the event. Using highlighters of two different colors, highlight those aspects of the event that were originally listed by more than one group member in one color and those that were included by only one member in another color. If needed, use a third color to highlight details on which the accounts *disagreed*.
Look at the details that two or more group members included. What do these details have in common? How are they different?
Look at the details that were included by only one group member. Discuss why these details might have been important to the person who remembered them.
Look at the details on which group members disagreed. Did members disagree on *facts* that could be verified or on *interpretations* or ways of thinking about what occurred? How might you resolve the truth of the event?
If your group was writing an account of the event for readers who were not present (for example, for an article for the school newspaper), which details would you include and which would you leave out? Why? What additional details would you need to include?

Copyright © 2010 by Corwin. All rights reserved. Reprinted from *Parallel Curriculum Units for Social Studies, Grades 6–12*, edited by Jeanne H. Purcell and Jann H. Leppien. Thousand Oaks, CA: Corwin, www.corwinpress.com. Reproduction authorized only for the local school site or nonprofit organization that has purchased this book.

LESSON 2: CONSTRUCTING HISTORY (APPROXIMATELY 2 DAYS)

Lesson 2 explores the historian's role in arranging historical events into a sequence in order to report them. The focus is on the complexity of history, whether history can be explored just chronologically, and on figuring out how to tell a story in a way that makes sense. This lesson includes the exploration of various secondary sources and their reporting on the Progressive Era as a way of providing an overview of the era and also as a basis for discussing how history is put together. A unit project is introduced in this lesson, and it is to be completed over the course of the remaining time of the unit.

Concepts

Discipline-Specific Concepts
C1: History
C2: Historical narrative
C4: Chronology

Principles

P1: Written history is a human construction, relying on interpretation and judgment to make sense of the past.
P2: Individuals are selective in what they see, remember, and record about events they witness or study; the selective recording of events in the past influences our understanding of those events.
P3: Developing an understanding of a historical period or event requires exploring multiple sources from multiple perspectives.
P4: Understanding historical sources requires exploring the purpose for their creation and their intended and actual influence on those who read or viewed them.

Skills

S4: Summarizing details
S5: Comparing and contrasting
S6: Sequencing

Standards

SD1: Historical comprehension: Identify the central question(s) the historical narrative addresses.
SD2: Historical analysis and interpretation: Differentiate between historical facts and historical interpretations.
SD4: Historical analysis and interpretation: Compare competing historical narratives.

Guiding Questions

- What kinds of decisions do historians need to make in figuring out how to present the past to readers/viewers?
- What are the advantages of presenting or reading history chronologically? What are the disadvantages?
- What are some of the different approaches a historian might take in presenting details of a historical period?

Unit Sequence	Teacher Reflections
Introduction	
Ask students to explain the purpose of a timeline. Show or point to examples of timelines that you might have in the classroom or in students' history books. Ask students to identify what the timelines have in common and to explain ways in which they might differ and how these differences affect the purpose and possible uses of the timelines.	*This lesson should follow very shortly upon Lesson 1 because it moves from the idea of recalling events that have occurred to organizing those events for others to read—in other words, to writing a sort of history. This lesson also serves as an introduction into the study of the Progressive Era because it includes opportunities for students to read overviews of the history of the era.*
Tell students that they are going to prepare a draft timeline of their own lives. Provide long strips of paper and rulers. Ask students to document on the timeline key events that occurred in their lives. Invite students to share their timelines with a partner.	*As students are preparing their timelines, teachers may wish to challenge students of higher ability to incorporate both world events they recall and personal events on their timelines. This will allow students to begin to see how world history and individual histories may interact.*
Have students discuss the following questions in small groups: In what ways does your timeline capture the history of your life effectively? In what ways is it lacking as a history of your life? What important aspects of your life does the timeline not capture?	*The purpose of this introductory discussion is to help students see that a chronological listing of events is not sufficient for a full history of a life or a period. From the small group discussion and/or the large group debriefing, students should begin to develop the understanding that some important parts of history do not occur as events to be identified on a timeline, but rather as ideas, movements, influences, or other forces of change that emerge over time rather than at a specific point.*
Ask each group to write a sentence or two to explain the advantages and disadvantages of a timeline in telling a history. Have each group share their conclusions about advantages and disadvantages by writing them on the board or overhead, and have a brief discussion about their statements.	
	The questions raised here, at the end of the introduction, are presented for a brief response at this point, but they should be addressed in more detail later in this and other lessons.
Raise the following questions for students to consider, and invite them to write down brief responses individually as a lead-in to the lesson: How are history and chronology related? In what ways is chronology important to a historian trying to tell about history? In what ways does a chronological view limit our picture of history?	*The focus on differentiating history from chronology here has emerged from several influences. One is a quote from The College Board in a vertical teaming handbook (AP Vertical Teams in Science, Social Studies, Foreign Language, Studio Art, and Music Theory: An Introduction [New York: College Entrance Examination Board, 1999]): "All too often, social studies students are required to memorize answers rather than explore questions, regurgitate decisions rather than comprehend choices, and understand chronology rather than wrestle with concepts" (p. 21). Another influence is some recent research that has demonstrated the degree to which American students, in particular, have difficulty even with some aspects of chronology, in part because the narrative approach to history seems to have influenced a narrowing view of time, space, and the*

Unit Sequence	Teacher Reflections
	scope of historical events. An interesting discussion of this issue, including discussion of some of the research comparing U.S. students with others, may be found in Teaching History for the Common Good, by Keith Barton and Linda Levstik.
Teaching Strategies and Learning Experiences	
Explain to students that they will be exploring the question of how historians arrange their information for sharing with an audience. Provide a variety of American history textbooks that include chapters or sections on the Progressive Era. Include print and online sources if possible, and include books written for general audiences, for younger students, for students of the age of the class, and so on. Ensure that each group of students has at least two different sources to explore. Explain that students will be using these textbooks to explore different ways historians have chosen to write about the Progressive Era when they presented it within the context of a larger survey of American history. Have students work in groups to read the sections within the textbooks about the Progressive Era. As they work in groups, have students complete The Progressive Era—General History Sources handout to document what they have found.	*This portion of the lesson has a twofold purpose. The primary purpose within the context of the outcomes of the unit is to help students to recognize that historians choose different ways to organize information in order to write it, and that, in particular, when studying a period less marked for particular events than for the overall spirit of the time, the writing is likely to take a variety of forms and not to be very chronological in organization. The second purpose is to provide students with some background knowledge about the period.* *If the unit is being presented as a follow-up to the study of the Progressive Era instead of as a companion to it, this lesson may be used as a review of key ideas, perspectives, individuals, and events.* *For a class with a wide range of readiness levels, sources should be carefully assigned to groups to respond to those different levels. Students who are more capable readers or more advanced in their historical knowledge may be provided with more advanced texts, perhaps even college-level textbooks. Students who need more support in their reading and/or historical background may be presented with materials written at a less demanding reading level. Several sample sources are identified in the resources section; however, any American history textbook should have a section on the period and will serve as a source for this activity.*

Invite students to share some of their findings with the whole class and debrief. Some guiding questions for the whole group discussion are as follows:
 	
    In what ways were your sources similar?
    In what ways were they different?
    Did your sources arrange details more chronologically or more by key ideas? Give an example to support your answer. Did your sources seem to judge the priorities of the Progressives as positive or negative for the country at the time? How can you tell?
	Note that the charts to be completed in this lesson will have the same questions for both groups; differentiation in this activity occurs through varying complexity in the sources that are reviewed. Teachers should circulate around the room to facilitate as students work, providing assistance as needed with reducing the textual information to key points for the chart.

(Continued)

(Continued)

Unit Sequence	Teacher Reflections
Next, have students work in their groups to explore two sources written specifically about the Progressive Era. Students do not need to read the entirety of these texts; they should browse through them to explore what information is presented and how it is organized. Have students complete The Progressive Era: Sources About the Period as they review their sources. Again, invite students to share some of their findings with the whole class and debrief. You may use some of the same guiding questions, with a few additional ones (given below): In what ways were your sources similar? In what ways were they different? Did your sources arrange details more chronologically or more by key ideas? Did your sources seem to judge the priorities of the Progressives as positive or negative for the country at the time? How can you tell? Across all the specific sources, how did the major topics relate to the topics addressed in the more general sources? Explain to students that as they work through their unit on this period, they will be working in groups to create a history of one aspect of the time period. They will explore a variety of general and specific sources to discover how other historians have treated the topic, and they will also use primary sources to find out further details about the people who lived through the time and their perspectives. Introduce the project, in which students will develop a history of how young people lived in the Progressive Era and how life changed for young people during this time. Distribute "Young Peoples' Lives" and go over project details with students. Invite students to begin working on their project by exploring their sources from the earlier parts of the lesson for details on the lives of children in the period.	*As with the previous activity, this is another spot for differentiation by level of readiness. Several texts about the Progressive Era are suggested in the resource section, covering a variety of levels of complexity. Different groups should be assigned different sources to explore based on readiness.* *As students share and discuss their findings, it is important for them to begin to recognize that the ideas of the Progressives were not shared by everyone in the country at the time, and nor were the concerns of the Progressives the only things happening in the history of the country at the time. The activity and discussion are intended both to help students get a grasp of key concepts of the era and to help them recognize the complexity of reporting widespread movements, ideas, and time periods in history.* *Over the subsequent days, provide time and opportunity for students to work on their projects.*
<div align="center">**Closure**</div>	
Journal Prompt Have students consider and respond to the following quote:	*Questions that may help start students' thinking about this quote are as follows: What did our exploration of sources about the Progressive Era show you about interpretations of the past?*

Unit Sequence	Teacher Reflections
"History is not a recipe book; past events are never replicated in the present in quite the same way. Historical events are infinitely variable and their interpretations are a constantly shifting process. There are no certainties to be found in the past." (Gerda Lerner) **Extension to Lesson** A possible extension to this lesson, with the purpose of expanding student knowledge and understanding of the Progressive Era, would be to invite students to work in groups to examine and summarize for one another segments of the Progressive Party platform from the election of 1912. This activity would serve to corroborate with a primary source some of the conclusions students drew from secondary sources about major themes of the Progressive Era. The platform is available at http://www.pbs.org/wgbh/amex/presidents/index.html, listed under "primary sources" on the page about Theodore Roosevelt. This Web site also includes more extensive information on the election of 1912.	*Consider this extension within a variety of scenarios. If this unit is not being taught in conjunction with a broader study of the Progressive Era, the document will provide additional background information to help students with this unit. On the other hand, the document could also be used as an enrichment activity for students who may benefit from additional challenge in the unit.*

THE PROGRESSIVE ERA—GENERAL HISTORY SOURCES

	Source 1	Source 2	Observations about similarities and differences
Make a list of the major topics covered in each of your sources in its section on the Progressive Era. List the topics in the order in which they were presented in the source.			
Make a list of key individuals from the Progressive Era that are discussed in each source. For each individual, write a brief explanation of why the person is important to the history of the era.			
From each source, identify two or three specific events or accomplishments of the period that were important in the Progressive movement.			
From each source, describe one source of opposition to the ideas of the Progressives and explain the rationale behind the opposition.			
Based on your reading of *both* sources, identify one major *theme* or central *idea* that historians seem to have focused on as they talk about the Progressive Era. Write 1 to 2 sentences explaining this major theme.			

Copyright © 2010 by Corwin. All rights reserved. Reprinted from *Parallel Curriculum Units for Social Studies, Grades 6–12*, edited by Jeanne H. Purcell and Jann H. Leppien. Thousand Oaks, CA: Corwin, www.corwinpress.com. Reproduction authorized only for the local school site or nonprofit organization that has purchased this book.

THE PROGRESSIVE ERA: SOURCES ABOUT THE PERIOD

	Source 1	Source 2	Observations about similarities and differences
Make a list of major topics covered in each of your sources. You may want to use the Table of Contents (if available) and headings to guide you. Use a highlighter to mark the topics that were also given attention in your general history sources.			
Make a list of 2 to 3 key individuals whose lives and work are given substantial attention in each source. Provide a brief explanation of how the source presents each individual—are there full chapters, various sections, and so on, on each person? Check to see if individuals highlighted in one of your sources are also included in the other source and in your general history sources.			
Return to the major theme of the Progressive Era you wrote about on your other chart. Read an excerpt from each of your new sources (you may want to read an introductory chapter) and explain whether and how you see that theme reflected in each source.			

Copyright © 2010 by Corwin. All rights reserved. Reprinted from *Parallel Curriculum Units for Social Studies, Grades 6–12*, edited by Jeanne H. Purcell and Jann H. Leppien. Thousand Oaks, CA: Corwin, www.corwinpress.com. Reproduction authorized only for the local school site or nonprofit organization that has purchased this book.

YOUNG PEOPLE'S LIVES

In this assignment, you will be constructing your own history of how young people lived in the Progressive Era and how the time period represented change for them. Your project goal is to prepare a secondary source that explores some aspect of the lives of young people in the Progressive Era. You will have many options for the format of your history, but all formats will have to demonstrate thorough research into the specific content and the connections between the specific content and one or more of the larger themes of the Progressive Era discussed in class.

Possible Topics (note that several topics overlap)

- Working conditions and laws related to child labor
- Public education
- The lives and experiences of immigrant children and U.S.-born children of immigrants
- Leisure activities for young people
- Young women in the suffrage movement
- A specific event affecting children/young people (with background to help show the significance of the event)
- Topic of your choice (subject to teacher approval)

You must select the following:
- A topic
- An audience
- A format

Possible Audiences

- General audience
- History students your age
- Younger students

Possible Formats

- Textbook chapter
- Stand-alone (short) book
- Picture book
- Web site
- Short documentary film
- Photo essay
- Museum display
- Format of your choice (subject to teacher approval)

Criteria

- Accurate detail on the topic with thorough coverage appropriate to the chosen format
- Connections made to one or more Progressive Era themes
- At least three secondary and three primary sources used in developing product and appropriately referenced
- Appropriate format, language, and content for chosen audience
- Satisfactory reflection on process and product

Steps in the Process

1. Do some background reading. Explore some of the general and specific sources on the Progressive Era for the content they present on young people and children in the period.

2. Decide on a topic you would like to explore, either from the previous list or from something you find in your exploration of sources.

3. Write a summary (narrative or list) of what you already know about your topic. Then list questions you have about the topic.

4. Search for answers to your questions in a variety of sources. As you explore, keep notes on what you find out from each source to answer your questions and also what new information and questions emerge for you as you conduct your research.

5. You should use at least three primary and at least three secondary sources in your research. Along with your informational notes, also keep track of quotations that might help to illustrate some of your key points in your own secondary source that you develop.

6. Once you have developed your own understanding of your topic, develop an outline for the key elements you will want to include in your history of the topic. Carefully consider the type of product you will be developing, and look at some samples of similar products for a sense of key features. Remember that your history should focus primarily on your topic but should also show connections to the larger themes of the Progressive Era.

7. Develop your secondary source using the information you have gathered and your understanding of what features are important to your product format.

8. Present your final product with a written reflection that discusses your choice of topic and format, what you feel to be the strengths of your product, and what you found to be the most interesting and the most challenging about the process.

9. Notes to teacher: This project is intended to be completed by students working in groups that are based loosely on ability and also organized by interest. It may also be completed individually by students, either by their choice or by yours. The choice of product formats, topics, and audiences allows students to incorporate their own interests and learning preferences into the process, while still organizing all students around the key content of the Progressive Era and around a focus on how historical content is presented. At the conclusion of the project, conduct a debriefing discussion to invite students to share the experience of collecting and organizing information to present to an audience of history learners.

LESSON 3: THE PAST THROUGH MANY EYES (MULTIPLE SESSIONS)

Lesson 3 explores multiple perspectives in history and the responsibility of the historian to gather multiple perspectives. Using the lens of immigration as a major issue in the Progressive Era, the lesson invites students to explore different documents from the time and then to look at how the issue has been reported *over* time (looking at the writer's perspective in both primary and secondary sources). This lesson also has a focus on contrasting history as a biography of famous individuals with history as collections of stories of the nonfamous.

Concepts

M1: Perspective

Discipline-Specific Concepts

C1: History
C3: Reliability

Principles

P1: Written history is a human construction, relying on interpretation and judgment to make sense of the past.
P2: Individuals are selective in what they see, remember, and record about events they witness or study; the selective recording of events in the past influences our understanding of those events.
P3: Developing an understanding of a historical period or event requires exploring multiple sources from multiple perspectives.
P4: Understanding historical sources requires exploring the purpose for their creation and their intended and actual influence on those who read or viewed them.
P5: Personal and group identities are influenced by history, and personal and group perspectives influence how we think about and record history.

Skills

S1: Observation
S2: Inference
S5: Comparing and contrasting
S7: Determining point of view

Standards

SD1: Historical comprehension: Identify the central question(s) the historical narrative addresses.
SD2: Historical analysis and interpretation: Differentiate between historical facts and historical interpretations.
SD3: Historical analysis and interpretation: Consider multiple perspectives.
SD4: Historical analysis and interpretation: Compare competing historical narratives.
SD5: Historical analysis and interpretation: Hypothesize the influence of the past.

Guiding Questions

- In what ways is history the story of famous people rather than that of nonfamous people? How do primary sources reflect the perspectives of the people who wrote or created them?
- How do secondary sources reflect the perspectives of the people who wrote or created them?

Unit Sequence	Teacher Reflections
Introduction	
Explain to students that in this lesson they will be focusing on the work of the historian as they explore one of the major influences on United States history in the time they are studying: immigration. Ask students to share what they know about what was happening with immigration around the turn of the 19th and 20th centuries.	*Key points to know at this time are that immigration patterns were changing in the late 19th century and that concerns about immigration included opposition to particular groups and the degree to which education should work to "Americanize" immigrants, among others.*
Tell students that you will start this lesson's exploration of immigration by looking at some photographs that were taken of immigrants arriving in the United States. Divide the class in half, and then into smaller groups within each half. Give half of the class copies of the picture labeled "Landing at Ellis Island" (taken 1902) and the other half "Immigrants on an Atlantic Liner" (taken 1906). In their small groups, students should complete Questions 1 to 3 on Source Analysis: Response to Photographs (be sure that each student completes a copy).	*The photographs for this activity may be found at http://www.loc.gov/rr/print/list/070_immi.html.* *Note that (at the time of unit development) there is an incorrect link on the page; for the picture "Landing at Ellis Island," click on the title, not the thumbnail image—the thumbnail links to a different picture.* *Circulate among the students as they complete both parts of the analysis sheet. Ask guiding questions to assist students who may be struggling, and encourage students to be specific in the supporting details they provide in their responses. You may want to allow students to choose their groups for the initial grouping, but then consider assigning the pairs for the second portion to be roughly ability-based. Among the specific details students should be focusing on about these photographs are the crowded conditions on the ship and the limited possessions the immigrants had with them, as well as the range of emotion apparent in some of the faces.*
Then, have students find a partner from the other half of the class, and have the pairs work together to share their responses to Questions 1 to 3 and then to complete Questions 4 through 6.	
Bring the class back together and invite a few comments on what students learned from looking at the photographs and what questions they have about immigration based on their discussion.	
Teaching Strategies and Learning Experiences	
PART ONE	
Explain to students that in this lesson they will be looking at multiple perspectives in history and the historian's responsibility for learning from a variety of perspectives. They will spend part of the lesson focusing on the topic of immigration as a way of understanding these ideas.	
Ask students to jot down a definition in their own words of the word *perspective*. Encourage them to also think of at least two examples of how the word might be used. Invite them to	*This portion of the lesson may be abbreviated if the concept of perspective has already been extensively addressed with students in your study of history. If*

(Continued)

(Continued)

Unit Sequence	Teacher Reflections
share their definitions and uses of the word in pairs, and have each pair choose one example of the use of the word to share with the class. Use questions such as the following to guide discussion: How are the examples similar and different? In the examples, if you replace the word *perspective* with *point of view*, does the meaning remain the same? Explain the meaning of the following phrases: "Keep things in perspective," "Look at the situation from my perspective."	*this is the case, review the concept and discuss some of the questions given, but move on quickly toward the remaining portions of the lesson.*
Provide the following definitions of *perspective* (from *The American Heritage Dictionary*): • a mental view or outlook • the ability to perceive things in their actual interrelations or comparative importance • subjective evaluation of relative significance; a point of view (from the *Merriam-Webster Dictionary*): • the interrelation in which a subject or its parts are mentally viewed • the capacity to view things in their true relations or relative importance	
Ask students to relate these definitions to the definitions they wrote. Summarize the discussion by explaining that one way of thinking about *perspective* is that it is one's way of seeing a scene, a situation, or an idea and that different *perspectives* or ways of seeing may be presented by individuals.	
Ask students the following question: Based on our discussion of perspective, what do you think it means when we say that historians have to explore multiple perspectives in history? Would all of the witnesses to a particular event be likely to have the same point of view about the event? Would all of the people who lived through a major change in society have the same perspective on whether that change was good or bad for the country?	*This discussion may be linked back both to the discussion from Lesson 1, showing that individuals might have different memories and perspectives on a past event, and the discussion from Lesson 2, showing that multiple points of view were present on issues of the Progressive Era.*
Present students with the following quote, and ask them to jot down their initial response to the quote in their journals: "There is properly no history; only biography." (Ralph Waldo Emerson)	*Suggested starter questions if students have difficulty thinking about a response to the question: What is biography? How is it similar to history? In what ways is history the story of individuals, and in what ways is it not?* *During this discussion, look for students to be thinking about and commenting on the degree to*

Unit Sequence	Teacher Reflections
Ask students to share their initial responses to the quote, and then use questions such as the following to discuss further: In what ways are history and biography similar? In what ways are they different? Who are the individuals we tend to learn about in history? What different kinds of understandings of history can we obtain by learning about the individuals who are not famous? How do the photographs from the first part of this lesson teach us about history without focusing on famous people? Recall for students the previous lesson, in which they were to explore different textbooks and how they arranged the events and concepts of history. Ask students to identify individuals who emerged from their reading as key figures of the Progressive Era and to explain why these individuals were important. Then, ask students to identify *groups* of people whose influence was important to the history of the era, even if we do not know the individual names of those people (workers, immigrants, child laborers, etc.). Introduce the term *social history* and ask students to think of examples from their study of history this year in which they have focused on social history (as opposed to political history, etc.). Return to the topic of immigration during the early part of the 20th century. Ask students to talk about what they already know about immigration in the period and what questions they have. Invite students to return to their notes from Lesson 2 to review what they learned about immigration while looking at the different histories of the Progressive Era. Explain that in the next portion of the lesson, students will be exploring a variety of sources to learn about the experiences of immigrants as they traveled to and began living in the United States around the turn of the century. Place students in groups of two or three, based roughly on their readiness levels. Provide each group with the appropriate level copy of Picturing the Past: Immigration (Red group: high level; green group: on level; blue group: below level). All students will need Internet access for this set of activities, so you may wish to conduct this portion of the lesson in a	*which they have learned about famous people in history instead of those who are not famous. Encourage them to think about what they know about everyday life for people at different stages of the past. Tie this back to the photographs from the introduction to the lesson by asking students to consider whether those people's stories are important to history and why or why not.* *Each Picturing the Past guide engages students in four different activities related to exploring immigration and historical sources about immigration. The first activity continues the introduction's exploration of pictures and photographs; depending on their level, students compare drawings and photographs for the perspectives they present, or they compare drawings offering different perspectives on*

(Continued)

(Continued)

Unit Sequence	Teacher Reflections
computer lab or library if sufficient computers are not available. The activities are set up as though they could be learning stations; you may wish to allow students to rotate through activities in different orders based on their groups, or to allow them to work at their own pace through the activities. At the conclusion of the immigration station activities, debrief with the whole group by inviting students to share some of their ideas from the final activity.	*immigration. In the second activity, students read firsthand accounts of the experiences of immigrants traveling in steerage to the United States. These accounts differ somewhat in terms of their authors, length, and complexity. In the third activity, students explore additional pictures and text about immigration and touch upon the immigration laws that were emerging over the period. Finally, students are asked to select one of the photographs they have viewed and explain how it is representative of what they have learned about immigration. For each activity, a variety of questions are presented; all student groups complete the same total number of questions, but the specific questions, as well as the sources, vary in complexity from one group to another.* *During students' work on these activities, circulate among the students to facilitate their work and maintain a relatively even pace across the tasks.* *Note that the Picturing the Past activity for the red group already introduced these ideas to them; therefore, the discussion that follows here will extend and deepen their learning while introducing the ideas to the other two groups.*
PART TWO Remind students that our work to this point has focused on the ways in which the perspectives of different individuals can give us a more complete understanding of history. Remind students also, from earlier lessons, that historians make choices in how they present history. Propose this question: In what ways does the perspective of the historian influence his or her presentation of history? Ask students to try to identify some important perspective shifts that have happened in American history. Propose American attitudes toward Great Britain as one example, and invite students to suggest other examples. Then ask students to think about what shifts in thinking were occurring for some Americans during the Progressive Era, based on their study of the period. Ask students to identify some of the major issues pursued by the Progressives and to explain what kinds of opinions they were trying to change. Explain to students that secondary sources, as well as primary sources, tell us something about	*During this portion of the lesson, encourage students to explore their prior knowledge of American history to discuss ways in which perspectives have changed over time. You might choose to invite students to consider how perspectives have changed about racial groups, about women, and so on.* *A recommended source for this activity is Kyle Ward's book* History in the Making *(see resource list for bibliographic details). In this book, Ward has collected textbook excerpts on a variety of topics and periods in American history, drawing the texts themselves from a variety of periods in American history. The chapter on immigration contains textbook excerpts from 1905, 1916, 1933, 1936, 1950, 1961, and 1986. You may choose to search for and put together your own collection of textbook accounts, but this book has many collected in one place that will illustrate the key points for this lesson. Ward and a colleague also published another book,* History Lessons, *that uses the same approach but includes selections from textbooks*

Unit Sequence	Teacher Reflections
the period in which they were written through their contents and tone. Provide students with excerpts about immigration from various older textbooks (see recommended source at right). Allow students to continue working in the groups from the earlier part of the lesson, and give each group at least two textbook excerpts to read. For each excerpt, students should keep notes on the point of view conveyed about immigration and the details that demonstrate this point of view. Create a large chart on the board or on chart paper with the dates of the various sources, and invite the students to write their responses on these charts. Then, hold a discussion in which you invite students to compare and contrast the perspectives on immigration presented over time.	*from other countries; this book also has a section on immigration that may be used in this activity.*

Closure

Two quotes are provided for a journal response to this lesson, one for each of the major parts of the lesson. A third quote is presented as an option for students who wish to explore the history/biography idea further.

Journal Prompt for Part One

Respond to the following quote:

> *"We can learn from history how past generations thought and acted, how they responded to the demands of their time and how they solved their problems. We can learn by analogy, not by example, for our circumstances will always be different than theirs were." (Gerda Lerner)*

Journal Prompt for Part Two

As a closing for the last portion of the lesson, share the following quote from Mark Twain and follow-up questions with students and invite them to respond in their journals:

> *"To arrive at a just estimate of a renowned man's character one must judge it by the standards of his time, not ours." (Mark Twain)*

- How does Twain's comment relate to what we found in reviewing textbook accounts over time?
- Why might our perspectives today be different from textbook authors writing 20, 50, or 100 years ago?

Optional Additional Journal Prompt

> *"History will be kind to me for I intend to write it." (Winston Churchill)*

SOURCE ANALYSIS: RESPONSE TO PHOTOGRAPHS

Question	Response With Supporting Details
Photograph:	
Describe the photograph. What details does it show? What can you tell about the time period from looking at the photograph?	
What feelings does the photograph give you as you study it? What can you infer about how the people in the photograph are feeling?	
How does this source change what you already knew about the topic, event, person, or period? Does the source *add new information, corroborate (or support) previous evidence, present a different perspective,* or some combination of these and other effects?	
What similarities and differences did you and your partner find in your responses to the two photographs?	
What questions do you have about immigration after looking at the two photographs?	
What other kinds of sources might you want to explore to understand these photographs more fully or to corroborate details?	

Copyright © 2010 by Corwin. All rights reserved. Reprinted from *Parallel Curriculum Units for Social Studies, Grades 6–12*, edited by Jeanne H. Purcell and Jann H. Leppien. Thousand Oaks, CA: Corwin, www.corwinpress.com. Reproduction authorized only for the local school site or nonprofit organization that has purchased this book.

PICTURING THE PAST: IMMIGRATION (RED GROUP)

In this set of activities, called *immigration stations*, you will view a variety of pictures and documents and keep notes on what you learn about immigration in the late 19th and early 20th centuries. Work in groups of two or three to complete the activities, and be prepared to share your responses in a whole-class debriefing.

Immigration Station 1

Visit the Library of Congress collection titled "Selected Images of Ellis Island and Immigration, ca. 1880–1920" at http://www.loc.gov/rr/print/list/070_immi.html, and browse through the pictures. Select and view the picture titled "Welcome to the Land of Freedom." Then, answer the following source analysis questions using details from the picture:

Question	Response With Supporting Details
Describe the *content* of the source. What is it about? What are its main features, points, or message?	
What can you tell about the *point of view* of the person who created the source? How did the person feel about the topic or issue that the source addresses?	

Next, visit this Library of Congress site: http://www.loc.gov/rr/print/list/picamer/paImmig.html, and click to enlarge the picture labeled "Unrestricted immigration and its results." Examine the details of the picture and the full title at the bottom of the picture. Answer the following questions based on this picture and on comparisons with the picture examined previously:

Question	Response With Supporting Details
Describe the *content* and *point of view* of the second picture. What is it about? What are its main features, points, or message?	
How do the two pictures compare to one another in terms of their message? How do the two pictures compare in terms of the impressions they give of immigrants?	

(Continued)

(Continued)

Question	Response With Supporting Details
Beyond the central content of the sources, what else do they show you about the time in which they were created?	
How does this set of sources change what you already knew about the topic, event, person, or period? Do the sources *add new information, corroborate (or support) previous evidence, present a different perspective,* or some combination of these and other effects?	
What other kinds of sources might you want to explore to understand these more fully or to corroborate details?	

Immigration Station 2

Visit this Web site from the Balch Institute for Ethnic Studies in Philadelphia: http://www.balchinstitute.org/resources/destinationusa/html/intromigration.html. Click on "Steerage Experience," and then on "Reports of the Immigration Commission–Steerage Conditions, United States Senate." Skim through the introductory material, and then read a portion of the firsthand account of a member of the commission who went undercover as a steerage-class passenger. Note that the document is quite lengthy; you may select a sample to read. Page 3 of the document is a good representative sample. You may also choose to skim some of the other pages. As you read, answer the source analysis questions below.

Question	Response With Supporting Details
Describe the *content* of the source. What is it about? What are its main features, points, or message?	
What do you find to be especially interesting, surprising, or disturbing about the account? What specific details drew your attention?	

Question	Response With Supporting Details
How does this source change what you already knew about the topic, event, person, or period? Does the source *add new information, corroborate (or support) previous evidence, present a different perspective,* or some combination of these and other effects?	
What other kinds of sources might you want to explore to understand this one more fully or to corroborate details?	

Immigration Station 3

Read these most famous lines from Emma Lazarus's poem "The New Colossus" (inscribed on a tablet in the pedestal of the Statue of Liberty [http://www.libertystatepark.com/emma.htm]):

> ... Give me your tired, your poor,
>
> Your huddled masses yearning to breathe free,
>
> The wretched refuse of your teeming shore.
>
> Send these, the homeless, tempest-tost to me,
>
> I lift my lamp beside the golden door!

Think about the pictures you have viewed and the primary source account you read. In what ways does this poem describe or differ from the immigration experience as you have seen it in these sources?

Visit this Web site from "Digital History": http://www.digitalhistory.uh.edu/photo_album/photo_album.html, and go through the pages of text and pictures. Note that the text quotes from and summarizes what was written in the original book, which was published in 1906, and also adds some additional information about immigration history. After you browse through the pages, reread the text in italics at the top of each page. Note that this text in italics is from the original 1906 source. Then, answer the following questions:

Question	Response With Supporting Details
What attitudes and perspectives on immigrants are conveyed in the author's words? What point of view do you think the author had about the people coming to the United States? Based on other sources you have explored, do you think this point of view was common?	

(Continued)

(Continued)

Question	Response With Supporting Details
Review the picture and text on page 7 on the site. In what ways does this reflect or differ from what you read about traveling in steerage?	
What did you find to be surprising or interesting about the information provided on this Web site? Does the source *add new information, corroborate (or support) previous evidence, present a different perspective,* or some combination of these and other effects?	
What other kinds of sources might you want to explore to understand this one more fully or to corroborate details?	

Immigration Station 4

Work independently on this activity.

Browse through the pages on the Digital History link again. Select one of the pictures given in the slideshow that you think shows something that is important in conveying information or a message about immigration. Write a description of the key details of the picture, and then write an explanation of what you think the picture represents in trying to understand immigration.

Copyright © 2010 by Corwin. All rights reserved. Reprinted from *Parallel Curriculum Units for Social Studies, Grades 6–12*, edited by Jeanne H. Purcell and Jann H. Leppien. Thousand Oaks, CA: Corwin, www.corwinpress.com. Reproduction authorized only for the local school site or nonprofit organization that has purchased this book.

PICTURING THE PAST: IMMIGRATION (GREEN GROUP)

In this set of activities, called *immigration stations*, you will view a variety of pictures and documents and keep notes on what you learn about immigration in the late 19th and early 20th centuries. Work in groups of two to three to complete the activities, and be prepared to share your responses in a whole-class debriefing.

Immigration Station 1

Visit the Library of Congress collection titled "Selected Images of Ellis Island and Immigration, ca. 1880–1920" at http://www.loc.gov/rr/print/list/070_immi.html and browse through the pictures. Select and view the picture titled "Welcome to the Land of Freedom." Then, answer the following source analysis questions, using details from the picture:

Question	Response With Supporting Details
Describe the *content* of the source. What is it about? What are its main features, points, or message?	
What can you tell about the *point of view* of the person who created the source? How did the person feel about the topic or issue that the source addresses?	

Next, look again at the picture we already studied, titled "Immigrants on Atlantic Liner," and at the picture titled "Emigrants coming to the 'land of promise.'" Answer the following questions based on the exploration of all three pictures:

Question	Response With Supporting Details
What do the three pictures have in common in terms of their *content*? How are they different?	
Beyond the central content of the source, what else do the sources show you about the time in which they were created?	
How *reliable* are the sources? In what ways might a photograph be more or less reliable than a drawing? What different kinds of messages are sent by each type of source?	

(Continued)

(Continued)

Question	Response With Supporting Details
How does this set of sources change what you already knew about the topic, event, person, or period? Do the sources *add new information, corroborate (or support) previous evidence, present a different perspective,* or some combination of these and other effects?	
What other kinds of sources might you want to explore to understand these more fully or to corroborate details?	

Immigration Station 2

Visit this Web site from the Balch Institute for Ethnic Studies in Philadelphia: http://www.balchinstitute.org/resources/destinationusa/html/intromigration.html. Click on "Steerage Experience" and then on "Russian-East Asian Steamship Company, Russian-American Line, emigrant account." Read the firsthand account, including some observations about a journey in steerage class on a ship to the United States. As you read, answer the source analysis questions below.

Question	Response With Supporting Details
Describe the *content* of the source. What is it about? What are its main features, points, or messages?	
What do you find to be especially interesting, surprising, or disturbing about the account? What specific details drew your attention?	
How does this source change what you already knew about the topic, event, person, or period? Does the source *add new information, corroborate (or support) previous evidence, present a different perspective,* or some combination of these and other effects?	
What other kinds of sources might you want to explore to understand this one more fully or to corroborate details?	

Immigration Station 3

Read these most famous lines from Emma Lazarus's poem "The New Colossus" (inscribed on a tablet in the pedestal of the Statue of Liberty):

> ... Give me your tired, your poor,
>
> Your huddled masses yearning to breathe free,
>
> The wretched refuse of your teeming shore.
>
> Send these, the homeless, tempest-tost to me,
>
> I lift my lamp beside the golden door!

Think about the pictures you have viewed and the primary source account you read. In what ways does this poem describe or differ from the immigration experience as you have seen it in these sources?

Visit this Web site from "Digital History": http://www.digitalhistory.uh.edu/photo_album/photo_album.html, and go through the pages of text and pictures. Note that the text quotes from and summarizes what was written in the original book, which was published in 1906, and also adds some additional information about immigration history. After you browse through the pages, reread the text given on page 6 and page 9, and then answer the following questions:

Question	Response With Supporting Details
What was the *intent* of the immigration laws that are described on this page? What attitudes and perspectives on immigrants do the laws reflect?	
In what ways are these laws similar to or different from the perspective given in Emma Lazarus's poem?	
What did you find to be surprising or interesting about the information provided on this Web site? Does the source *add new information, corroborate (or support) previous evidence, present a different perspective,* or some combination of these and other effects?	
What other kinds of sources might you want to explore to understand this one more fully or to corroborate details?	

Immigration Station 4

Work independently on this activity.

Browse through the pages on the Digital History link again. Select one of the pictures given in the slideshow that you think shows something that is important in conveying information or a message about immigration. Write a description of the key details of the picture, and then write an explanation of what you think the picture represents in trying to understand immigration.

PICTURING THE PAST: IMMIGRATION (BLUE GROUP)

In this set of activities, called *immigration stations*, you will view a variety of pictures and documents and keep notes on what you learn about immigration in the late 19th and early 20th centuries. Work in groups of two to three to complete the activities, and be prepared to share your responses in a whole-class debriefing.

Immigration Station 1

Visit the Library of Congress collection titled "Selected Images of Ellis Island and Immigration, ca. 1880–1920" at http://www.loc.gov/rr/print/list/070_immi.html, and browse through the pictures. Select and view the picture titled "Welcome to the Land of Freedom." Then, answer the following source analysis questions using details from the picture:

Question	Response With Supporting Details
Describe the *content* of the source. What is it about? What are its main features, points, or messages?	
What can you tell about the *point of view* of the person who created the source? How did the person feel about the topic or issue that the source addresses?	

Next, look at the picture titled "Emigrants coming to the 'land of promise.'" Answer the following questions based on this picture and on exploring the two pictures together:

Question	Response With Supporting Details
Describe the *content* of the second picture. What is it about? What are its main details?	
What do the two pictures have in common in terms of their *content*?	
How are the two pictures different? What different feelings do the two pictures seem to show?	

(Continued)

(Continued)

Question	Response With Supporting Details
Which is a more *accurate* type of source, a photograph or a drawing? Explain your answer. Can a photograph convey a message the way a drawing can? Why or why not?	
How does this set of sources change what you already knew about the topic of immigration? Do the sources *add new information, corroborate (or support) previous evidence, present a different perspective,* or some combination of these and other effects?	
What other kinds of sources might you want to explore to understand these more fully or to corroborate details?	

Immigration Station 2

Visit this page at the "Eyewitness to History" Web site: http://www.eyewitnesstohistory.com/immigrating.htm. Read the introduction section to give you background, and then read the section under the heading "We saw the big woman with the big spikes on her head." As you read Sadie's story, answer the source analysis questions below.

Question	Response With Supporting Details
Describe the *content* of the source. What is it about? What are its main features, points, or messages?	
What do you find to be especially interesting, surprising, or disturbing about the account? What specific details drew your attention?	

Question	Response With Supporting Details
How *reliable* is the source? How does the passage of time (three years since arrival in America) affect memory? Do you think Sadie's memories are trustworthy? Why or why not?	
What other kinds of sources might you want to explore to understand this one more fully or to corroborate details?	

Immigration Station 3

Read these most famous lines from Emma Lazarus's poem "The New Colossus" (inscribed on a tablet in the pedestal of the Statue of Liberty):

> ... Give me your tired, your poor,
>
> Your huddled masses yearning to breathe free,
>
> The wretched refuse of your teeming shore.
>
> Send these, the homeless, tempest-tost to me,
>
> I lift my lamp beside the golden door!

Make a list of (or underline) the words used in the poem to describe the immigrants. Give at least two examples of ways in which the sources you have explored have shown similar images of immigrants.

Visit this Web site from "Digital History": http://www.digitalhistory.uh.edu/photo_album/photo_album.html, and go through the pages of text and pictures. Note that the text quotes from and summarizes what was written in the original book, which was published in 1906, and also adds some additional information about immigration history. After you browse through the pages, reread the text given on page 6, and then answer the following questions:

Question	Response With Supporting Details
What was the *intent* of the immigration laws that are described on this page? What attitudes and perspectives on immigrants do the laws reflect?	
In what ways are these laws similar to or different from the perspective given in Emma Lazarus's poem?	

(Continued)

(Continued)

Question	Response With Supporting Details
What did you find to be surprising or interesting about the information provided on this Web site? Does the source *add new information, corroborate (or support) previous evidence, present a different perspective,* or some combination of these and other effects?	

Immigration Station 4

Work independently on this activity.

Browse through the pages on the Digital History link again. Select one of the pictures given in the slideshow that you think shows something that is important in conveying information or a message about immigration. Write a description of the key details of the picture, and then write an explanation of what you think the picture represents in trying to understand immigration.

Copyright © 2010 by Corwin. All rights reserved. Reprinted from *Parallel Curriculum Units for Social Studies, Grades 6–12,* edited by Jeanne H. Purcell and Jann H. Leppien. Thousand Oaks, CA: Corwin, www.corwinpress.com. Reproduction authorized only for the local school site or nonprofit organization that has purchased this book.

LESSON 4: WHO WRITES HISTORY? (MULTIPLE SESSIONS)

Lesson 4 focuses on the human construction of history and on the difference between reporting the events of a time and explaining them with a historical viewpoint. The lesson uses a specific example, the newspaper reporting that occurred upon the sinking of the *Titanic*, as the launching pad for comparing the roles of the journalist and the historian. This lesson ideally entails interviews with professional journalists and historians to help students understand the distinctions in the roles and the tensions that each role faces in trying to report events with accuracy and timeliness.

Concepts

M1: Perspective

Discipline-Specific Concepts

C1: History
C2: Historical narrative
C3: Reliability

Principles

P4: Understanding historical sources requires exploring the purpose for their creation and their intended and actual influence on those who read or viewed them.
P1: Written history is a human construction, relying on interpretation and judgment to make sense of the past.
P3: Developing an understanding of a historical period or event requires exploring multiple sources from multiple perspectives.
P5: Personal and group identities are influenced by history, and personal and group perspectives influence how we think about and record history.

Skills

S8: Identifying details
S2: Inference

Standards

SD2: Historical analysis and interpretation: Differentiate between historical facts and historical interpretations.
SD3: Historical analysis and interpretation: Consider multiple perspectives.
SD4: Historical analysis and interpretation: Compare competing historical narratives.

Guiding Questions

- In what ways are journalism and history similar and different, both as disciplines and professions?
- How can misinformation about the past be corrected in the minds of those who have read incorrect accounts?
- What are the responsibilities of the journalist and the historian for representing events accurately?

Unit Sequence	Teacher Reflections
Introduction	
Explain to students that although most of the time in this unit has been spent exploring movements, ideas, and broader social change, this lesson will focus more specifically on an event in history and how that event was represented at the time. Share with students the front page headline from the *New York Times* on April 16, 1912. The text of the headline was as follows: *Titanic sinks four hours after hitting iceberg; 866 rescued by Carpathia; probably 1250 perish; Ismay safe; Mrs. Astor maybe; noted names missing* Ask students to share briefly what they know about this event. Present a brief summary of the event from a secondary source if necessary, in order to provide students with brief background information. Then, present the following headlines that also appeared in newspapers in the day or two immediately following the sinking of the *Titanic*: • Passengers Safely Moved and Steamer Titanic Taken In Tow; *Christian Science Monitor* (Boston, MA), 4/15/1912 • Titanic Sunk, No Lives Lost; *Daily Mail*, London, England, 4/16/1912 • Repair Problem, No Dock Large Enough in America; *Daily Mail*, London, England, 4/16/1912 Remind students of the details of the event, and ask how these headlines might have come about. If students' discussion does not lead in this direction, ask the following question: In what ways might *accuracy* and *timeliness* create a tension for the people who report the news? (Possible follow-up questions to guide discussion: What happens if a news story is reported before the reporters have all of the details? What happens if a news story is not reported until after all the details and perspectives on the event have been collected?)	*If possible, share the actual image of the New York Times headline—the image may be found at http://www.nytimes.com/slideshow/2001/11/14/ dining/20MCFA.slideshow.ready_3.html. This URL accesses the front page within a slideshow demonstrating the newspaper's use of its largest headlines over time (the Titanic tragedy marked the Times' first-ever banner headline). This link also accesses an image of the front page from April 16: http://www.nytimes.com/learning/general/ onthisday/big/0415.html#article* ***Note:*** *The collection of error headlines, along with a larger collection of headlines reporting the* Titanic's *sinking, may be found at http://www.lva.lib.va.us/whoweare/exhibits/titanic/ index.htm. On the site, the error headlines may be viewed as images from the original newspaper pages; if possible, use these images as opposed to only the headline texts as a way to engage interest and draw students more directly into an understanding of the issue. This site also includes a summary of the tragedy, which may be useful in providing students with background information as needed.* *The focus of this discussion should be on helping students to recognize the tension between a journalist's job to report events quickly and his or her responsibility to try to ensure the accuracy of information. If students begin to bring the discussion into the current context by talking about the immediacy of the news media today, encourage them to consider to what degree the information systems we have today increase or decrease the potential for error in reporting the news. This is the focus for the next section of the lesson below, but it may be emphasized here instead if students begin moving that way in discussion.*

Unit Sequence	Teacher Reflections
Teaching Strategies and Learning Experiences	
Tell students that the newspapers, of course, did soon learn the truth of what had occurred with the *Titanic*. Share several of the newspaper headlines that did get the details correct (see http://www.lva.lib.va.us/whoweare/exhibits/titanic/index.htm). Ask students the following question: What do you think happens when a newspaper or (today) TV station or Internet site needs to correct previously reported news? Explain to students that newspapers, magazines, and other sources will often print retractions or updated stories to correct information errors (share examples of this if possible); invite students to discuss what difficulties might emerge as media sources try to correct misinformation.	*The questions for brief discussion here are intended to get students to think about the difficulty of correcting misinformation that has been shared in the news. As students discuss the issue, ask them to consider how they might feel if they were involved in a major event but the newspapers and other media published details that were incorrect. This perspective will lead them into the primary source discussion that follows.*
Put students in groups of two or three, establishing groups based on readiness. Have students read James B. McGough's account of the sinking of the *Titanic*. Encourage them to highlight key points in the document as they read. Have the groups complete the appropriate Source Analysis: Titanic sheet for the reading. As groups complete their analysis sheets, have students write a response to one of the following questions in their journals (assign questions based on which analysis sheet students completed): (Source Analysis Sheet 1 group): How does McGough's account change your understanding of the event? In what ways does it make the history of the event more real to you? (Source Analysis Sheet 2 group): In what ways does reading an observer's perspective help a historian to understand an event? What role does emotion play in understanding events of the past?	*McGough's affidavit is available at http://www.titanicinquiry.org/USInq/AmInq18McGough01.php. His message to his mother immediately upon arriving in New York is also available as a document on the event; it is included in the primary source collection* Our Nation's Archives: The History of the United States in Documents *(see list of resources). More advanced students should complete Source Analysis: Titanic (2), and students who are less advanced should complete Source Analysis: Titanic (1). The analysis sheets address the same major emphases, but Sheet 2 has more complex and abstract questions. Circulate among the groups as they work on the analysis sheets.*

(Continued)

(Continued)

Unit Sequence	Teacher Reflections
Hold a short debriefing of the charts and journal responses. Then explain that to follow upon the *Titanic* discussion, students will be thinking about the jobs of the historian and the journalist, and they will develop some questions to use in an interview of people who pursue these roles professionally.	
Share the following quote with students and ask them to jot down a response explaining what they think the quote means: "News is the first rough draft of history" (attributed to Philip L. Graham, once the publisher of *The Washington Post*).	*The lesson will need to be split into multiple class sessions, and this spot might be an appropriate place to split the activities. Depending on time and the discussion patterns of the students, consider debriefing the charts at the end of one day's lesson or the beginning of the next day's class.*
Explain to students that they will be learning more about both history and journalism and how professionals in each discipline see their responsibilities for learning and telling about events and ideas. Invite students to describe their understanding of the jobs of the journalist and the historian. Then have students begin brainstorming questions that they might want to ask of a journalist or a historian, based on the categories on the chart or going beyond these categories.	*Some suggested questions, if students need prompts to guide their response to the quote:* • *How are history and the news related? How are they different?* • *In what ways is the news a rough draft? When you hear the words* rough draft, *what do you think of?*
Have students share their questions, and compile a class list of questions. These questions should be used as the basis for interviewing a guest journalist and a guest historian.	
Following the visit of your guest speakers, ask students to return to their response to the quote about news as the first rough draft of history and to expand on this response.	
Questions for discussion: What role does passage of time play for the journalist and the historian? What kind of errors can both make? What role does writing and storytelling play for each?	
Closure	
Journal Prompts These journal prompts invite students to think about the degree to which a written historical account can capture the truth of an experience, either because of the issue of misinformation or	

Unit Sequence	Teacher Reflections
because of the difficulty of capturing experiences in words. Invite students to choose the quote that they find most interesting or connected to their own thinking about history and to write a response to that quote. *"A historian who would convey the truth must lie. Often he must enlarge the truth by diameters, otherwise his reader would not be able to see it."* (Mark Twain) *"History, a distillation of rumour."* (Thomas Carlyle) *"Future years will never know the seething hell and the black infernal background, the countless minor scenes and interiors of the secession war; and it is best they should not. The real war will never get in the books."* (Walt Whitman) **Extension** For students who are advanced in their history work and/or who show a particular interest in the roles of journalist and historian, share the following article as an extension to this lesson: • "Whose Turf Is the Past?" by Andie Tucher, from the September/October 2004 issue of *Columbia Journalism Review*, available at http://cjrarchives.org/issues/2004/5/ideas-essay-tucher.asp?	

SOURCE ANALYSIS: *TITANIC* (1)

Question	Response	Evidence to Support Response
Describe the *content* of the source. What is it about? What are its main features, points, or messages? What does the author assume his audience already knows about the event?		
What can you tell about the *point of view* of the person who created the source? What are the author's feelings about the event? How can you tell?		
Beyond the central content of the source, what else does the source show you about the time in which it was created?		
What other kinds of sources might you want to explore to understand this one more fully or to corroborate details?		

Copyright © 2010 by Corwin. All rights reserved. Reprinted from *Parallel Curriculum Units for Social Studies, Grades 6–12*, edited by Jeanne H. Purcell and Jann H. Leppien. Thousand Oaks, CA: Corwin, www.corwinpress.com. Reproduction authorized only for the local school site or nonprofit organization that has purchased this book.

SOURCE ANALYSIS: *TITANIC* (2)

Question	Response	Evidence to Support Response
What can you tell about the *point of view* of the person who created the source? How did the person feel about the topic or issue that the source addresses?		
What does the author assume his audience already knows about the event? Why do you think it was important to him to provide his own eyewitness account?		
How does this source change what you already knew about the topic, event, person, or period? Does the source *add new information, corroborate (or support) previous evidence, present a different perspective*, or some combination of these and other effects?		
What other kinds of sources might you want to explore to understand this one more fully or to corroborate details?		

Copyright © 2010 by Corwin. All rights reserved. Reprinted from *Parallel Curriculum Units for Social Studies, Grades 6–12*, edited by Jeanne H. Purcell and Jann H. Leppien. Thousand Oaks, CA: Corwin, www.corwinpress.com. Reproduction authorized only for the local school site or nonprofit organization that has purchased this book.

LESSON 5: WHAT MAKES THE HISTORY BOOKS? (4–5 CLASS PERIODS)

Lesson 5 focuses on defining and describing historical significance. Students are asked to consider recent events that may or may not be memorable over time and then to apply this understanding to looking at the past. Sources used in the lesson demonstrate that the people who were present at major events might not have known that major events were occurring at the time, and students are asked to consider what elements contribute to an understanding of historical significance.

Concepts

M1: Perspective

Discipline-Specific Concepts

C1: History
C5: Memory
C2: Historical narrative
C6: Significance

Principles

P1: Written history is a human construction, relying on interpretation and judgment to make sense of the past.
P2: Individuals are selective in what they see, remember, and record about events they witness or study; the selective recording of events in the past influences our understanding of those events.
P3: Developing an understanding of a historical period or event requires exploring multiple sources from multiple perspectives.
P5: Personal and group identities are influenced by history, and personal and group perspectives influence how we think about and record history.

Skills

S2: Inference
S9: Assessing and predicting significance

Standards

SD1: Historical comprehension: Identify the central question(s) the historical narrative addresses.
SD3: Historical analysis and interpretation: Consider multiple perspectives.
SD5: Historical analysis and interpretation: Hypothesize the influence of the past.

Guiding Questions

- Is a memorable event always a significant event?
- What characteristics make an event or idea historically significant?

Unit Sequence	Teacher Reflections
Introduction	
Ask students to think about an event in history they would like to have witnessed. Encourage them to choose something that happened during the period of 1900–1920 if they wish, but do not necessarily require it. Have students imagine that they were present for this event, and invite them to work individually or in pairs to write a brief letter home to a loved one that describes the event as if they were there. Emphasize that students should try to imagine that they are writing the letter immediately after the event, and therefore with no knowledge of what occurred after it.	*Give students the choice of working individually or in pairs of their choice as a way of increasing motivation and engagement in the activity. The task is not meant to be a fully developed writing project, just a hook to lead students into the discussion of historical significance.*
Invite each student or pair of students to exchange the draft letter with another student or pair. Ask the reader(s) to review the letter and to highlight or make notes on where and how in the letter the writer(s) showed the following: • emotions about the event • whether and why the event was important • what the implications of the event might be	*As students are writing and reviewing, note the specific events students chose to describe. At the conclusion of the introductory section, when students share, it is ideal to include some events that were perhaps not recognized as highly significant when they happened but were deemed significant later, as well as some events that were clearly recognized as highly significant when they happened. Therefore, if you can find examples of both among the students' work, encourage those students to share in the later part of the lesson.*
Have the students gather in small groups with their peer-review partners, and encourage them to share what they found in their reviews and to discuss the following question: How did your knowledge of events subsequent to the event you described affect your writing? In what ways did it make the writing harder or easier to do?	*Circulate among the groups as they hold this discussion to listen for hints of key understandings about hindsight and how it may change perspective on events.*
Ask a few students to share with the class what event they described and why they chose to describe it. Then invite students to comment on their small group follow-up discussion.	
Teaching Strategies and Learning Experiences	
Explain to students that sometimes when we look for primary source evidence related to a particular event, we often find that the event's	

(Continued)

(Continued)

Unit Sequence	Teacher Reflections
significance was not fully recognized at the time because, of course, the observers and participants in an event did not know what the consequences and subsequent events would be. Present students with a copy of the excerpt from Orville Wright's diary recounting the first flight on December 17, 1903 (available at http://www.eyewitnesstohistory.com/wright.htm) and a copy of Source Analysis: First Flight.	
Ask students to think about what characteristics of an event might indicate that people will be talking about it long after the event occurred. Explain that in this lesson, they will be exploring the concept of historical significance.	*Encourage students to think about such characteristics as the degree of change or novelty that an event represents, the number of people likely to be affected by it, and subsequent significant events linked back to an initial event.*
Obtain copies of various magazines' "year in review" types of articles from the previous year and from three to four years ago. Divide students into small groups and give each group at least one list or article from the previous year and one list or article from a year slightly further in the past. Have students work in their groups to review the articles and to highlight things they remember and things that they think are going to be memorable for a long time. Use What Will We Remember? as an organizer for this activity.	*This activity may be approached in a variety of ways. The most straightforward would be to obtain articles from newsmagazines such as* Time, Newsweek, *or* U.S. News and World Report; *each of these generally provides, in late December, some year-end lists of important events or discussion of the most memorable moments of the year. By providing each group of students with one list or article from the previous year and one from a year slightly further into the past, you allow a variety of perspectives to emerge and therefore promote some good conversations across different groups. You might also choose to tap further into students' interests by providing a year-end article from a newsmagazine and then some from entertainment or sports magazines. The point of the activity is to help students begin to understand that across longer and longer periods of time, it becomes clearer which events are likely significant and memorable in history and which are not.*
After students have worked in their groups, invite them to share briefly their two or three items from Question 3. Discuss what the items have in common across the class and how they differ. Ask students why they think certain items did not show up on anyone's "most memorable" list. Return to the ideas described in the previous discussion about what might make an event significant, and encourage students to add to or modify their ideas about the concept.	*Grouping for this activity may be approached in a variety of ways, depending on the materials you use and your understanding of your group. You may wish to group by ability and provide articles from more and less advanced sources for different groups. You may also wish to allow students to group themselves by interest, especially if you are providing lists from entertainment and sports sources as well as newsmagazines.*
Explain to students that in trying to gain an understanding of historical significance on a large scale, they must first gain an	

Unit Sequence	Teacher Reflections
understanding of how individuals and groups perceive events as memorable and significant in their own lives.	
Ask students to think about the events and periods in their own lives that have been most memorable to them. Have students think back to the timeline of their own lives that they created in Lesson 2 and consider why they chose particular events for the timeline. Invite a few students to share examples of memorable events from their lives with an explanation of why these events were memorable.	*Leading into this lesson, it would be interesting to invite students to ask their families about events in the family's history that are memorable and important to each member.*
Draw a Venn diagram on the board and ask students to draw one on their own paper. Write the word *memorable* in one of the circles and *significant* in the other. Invite a few students to share aloud what they think each word means, and then share dictionary definitions for each. *significant* (from *Merriam-Webster Dictionary*) 1: having meaning; especially : suggestive <a significant glance> 2 a: having or likely to have influence or effect : important <a significant piece of legislation> (from *American Heritage Dictionary*) Having or likely to have a major effect; important *memorable* (from *Merriam-Webster Dictionary*) worth remembering : notable (from *American Heritage Dictionary*): worth being remembered or noted; remarkable	*Throughout this discussion and Venn diagram activity, guide students to recognize the distinctions between the definitions of the two terms—especially the emphasis in definitions of* significant *on having some kind of an effect. This will help them in developing an understanding of historical significance.*
After sharing the definitions, ask students the following question, and invite them to work in pairs to make notes on their Venn diagrams as they think about the question: When we think about the events that happen to us as individuals or in the world around us, what is the difference between *memorable* and *significant*?	*[See note above regarding the effect aspect of significance]*

(Continued)

(Continued)

Unit Sequence	Teacher Reflections
Invite students to share their ideas about the distinctions between the two terms. Encourage them to identify events that might have been memorable but not necessarily significant. Ask students if this distinction works the other way (Can events be significant but not memorable?) and help students to see the difference.	
Then ask students to give a definition for the following term: *historical significance*. Ask questions such as the following to prompt discussion: How might we be able to know the significance of an event when it happens? How do we know what will and will not be memorable? What kinds of events can you think of that might have been recognized as significant when they happened, versus those whose significance might not have been recognized until later? What are the implications for historians of the time lag that might occur between an event and its recognition as something significant?	*The scope of this unit does not encompass direct attention to the events of World War I; however, most classes will study this as part of the broader study of the period. The assassination of Archduke Francis Ferdinand is a good example of an event whose significance was not recognized immediately when it happened, and it would be a good connection back to this lesson when that topic is covered.* *In discussing the final question here, encourage students to think about the preservation of records of an event and to recognize that an event that is immediately seen as significant is more likely to have more records preserved.*
Tell students that just as every year newsmagazines, and so on, review the events of that year, such reviews for significant events happen to an even greater degree at the end of a decade or a century. Have students work in groups of two or three to create a list of five events of the 20th century that they think were the most significant, given their own knowledge of the century. Have students share their ideas, and keep a record of what events the student lists had in common.	*The purpose of building this lesson from a discussion of key events of the recent past to key events of the last century is to encourage students to recognize that levels of historical significance vary, depending on the degree of focus we are bringing to a study of a particular period. To help illustrate this idea further, remind students of the degree of detail provided on the Progressive Era in the general textbooks and in specific texts back in Lesson 2.*
Introduce the online exhibit from the Newseum at http://www.newseum.org/century/index.htm. Allow students time to explore the voting results and the events that were selected by journalists and the public as the most significant events of the 20th century. Have students check to see which of the events they listed as significant above are on the list, and in what places. Then ask students to look at the timelines on the site and to identify the events that occurred within the time period they have been	*This portion of the lesson may be done in a computer lab to allow all students access to the site at the same time, or else the site may be displayed to the class using a projector. Giving all students access at once allows more exploration and hands-on connection, but the site is primarily used here as a stimulus for the following questions and activity, so a lengthy individual exploration of the site is not necessary to the lesson.*

Unit Sequence	Teacher Reflections
studying in this unit. Discuss their findings, using questions such as the following:	
How are the events from 1900-1920 similar to or different from other items on the total list? Which of the items from this period have we studied in our unit on the Progressive Era? What aspects of our study of the period are not represented by the list? Why do you think some of our topics of study are not listed?	
Remind students of other portions of the unit in which they have focused on specific events versus movements or ideas in history and on the lives of famous people versus nonfamous people. Ask students which of these (in both pairings) are more likely to make it onto a list of most important historical details, and why.	
Explain that the class is going to put together a collection of historically significant aspects of the period they have been studying, based on the class's developed understanding of historical significance. The students will work in groups to decide on several of the items that should be included on a "most significant" list from the period, and then students will work individually to explain one entry for the list. Divide the class into four groups of similar size, organized approximately by ability in critical thinking and conceptual understanding as demonstrated throughout the unit. Assign each group one type of historical information to explore, as follows:	*The activity discussed here is a culminating activity that invites students to bring their developing understanding of historical significance into a discussion of important ideas, events, and people from the Progressive Era. The activity involves creating a "most important" list as a group and then developing individual write-ups of the individual entries on this list. Grouping by readiness is used to differentiate the level of complexity of the types of list entries students will be organizing and studying. The more advanced groups are asked to list and study ideas or movements and groups of people, while the less advanced groups are asked to list and study the types of entries that are more common for "year-end" lists of this type: specific events and famous individual people. However, although the topics are different in level of complexity, all students are asked to use sources from the period, to explore multiple perspectives, and to explain historical significance. Therefore, the major historical thinking objectives are required of all students, but some students are asked to pursue them using more concrete topics and some using more abstract topics.*
Yellow group (most advanced): Significant movements or ideas of the period from 1900–1920	
Green group (next most advanced): Significant groups of people whose lives and experiences are important in understanding the period and subsequent history	
Red group (next most advanced): Significant individuals whose lives were particularly important and influential during the period	
Blue group (least advanced): Significant specific events that occurred during the period	

(Continued)

(Continued)

Unit Sequence	Teacher Reflections
Each group should discuss their topic and review all of the materials they have explored in the unit thus far (and in their broader study of the Progressive Era). Each group should come up with a list for their category, including as many entries as there are group members, and each group should determine a preliminary order for their list (as though they are creating an end-of-year type of list as examined in the magazines). Have the groups share and then post their preliminary lists in the classroom.	
Following the group determination of a list of items in their category, each individual in each group should select an entry or item from the list for which he or she will develop the write-up for the class's "historically significant" list. Using the resources from throughout the unit as well as other resources the students might access, students are to prepare a one to two page write-up for the list item. The write-up should accomplish the following:	
• Identify and explain or define the item and its place in American history 1900–1920. • Explain to what degree the significance of the item was recognized at the time and what people at the time thought of the event, idea, person, or group. • Provide at least two quotations from different sources from the time period that refer to the item, preferably in ways that demonstrate one or more perspectives and/or comment on historical significance. • Explain why this item may be seen today as historically significant, using the characteristics of historical significance that were developed in class discussion.	*These specific expectations are designed to ensure that the write-ups focus on aspects of historical significance and include attention to multiple perspectives and use of sources.*
After students develop a draft of their write-up, they should meet again in their original groups to share and offer peer feedback. The groups should also revisit the order in which they listed their items originally and revise the order as they feel is appropriate based on their work. Students may then revise their write-ups.	*Another way to approach this group meeting would be to regroup students based on topical similarity—for example, students from all groups whose topics focused in some way on immigration or on political activity might be put into groups together. This obviously prevents the re-ordering part of the activity, so that piece should be accomplished by*

Unit Sequence	Teacher Reflections
Once completed, all write-ups should be shared across the whole class, either through oral presentations or sharing in a booklet or posted format. Finally, the project should be wrapped up with a discussion in which students are invited to revisit the concept of historical significance and to explain their understanding of it after having examined specific events, ideas, and people from the period. In this discussion, invite students to share different perspectives on which items on the class list they think are more or less significant (or should go higher or lower on the list). Ask students to explain their point of view, and remind them that the work of a historian is always influenced by the historian's own perspective and interests and that the work of history requires a balance that uses individual interests and strengths but also tries to maintain objective distance.	*another brief group meeting of the original groups. The grouping should be determined by the topics chosen by various students and on the degree to which regrouping would create dramatic differences across ability levels, rendering true mutual peer collaboration too difficult.*
Finally, if desired, administer the preassessment again as a postassessment of student understanding of the key concepts of the unit.	*The final activity above is designed to cover the major concepts of the unit overall (in combination with the unit project on Young People's Lives, which addresses the objective of focusing on how historians present their work). However, if the collaborative nature of the project makes individual assessment more complicated, teachers may choose to re-administer the preassessment at the end of the unit in addition to completing the project.*
\multicolumn{2}{c}{**Closure**}	

Unit Sequence	Teacher Reflections
Journal Prompt Invite students to write a response to the following quote. Encourage them to use examples from their own lives and/or from their study of history to illustrate points in their response. *"The main thing history can teach us is that human actions have consequences and that certain choices, once made, cannot be undone. They foreclose the possibility of making other choices and thus they determine future events."* (Gerda Lerner)	*This journal prompt is intended to prompt further student thinking about the concept of historical significance. Encourage students to think about the concept as they write their response.*

SOURCE ANALYSIS: FIRST FLIGHT

Question	Response With Supporting Details
Describe the *content* of the source. What is it about? What are its main features, points, or messages?	
What can you tell about the *point of view* of the person who created the source? How did the person feel about the topic or issue that the source addresses?	
Beyond the central content of the source, what else does the source show you about the time in which it was created?	
How *reliable* is the source? Did the person who created the source know enough about what the source describes? Did the person witness or attend what is being described? Was the source created during or soon after the event, or a long time later?	
How does this source change what you already knew about the topic, event, person, or period? Does the source *add new information, corroborate (or support) previous evidence, present a different perspective,* or some combination of these and other effects?	

Copyright © 2010 by Corwin. All rights reserved. Reprinted from *Parallel Curriculum Units for Social Studies, Grades 6–12*, edited by Jeanne H. Purcell and Jann H. Leppien. Thousand Oaks, CA: Corwin, www.corwinpress.com. Reproduction authorized only for the local school site or nonprofit organization that has purchased this book.

WHAT WILL WE REMEMBER?

The questions and directions on this sheet will guide your group discussion of "year in review" articles.

1. Individually, use a highlighter to mark three to five events that you remember from each "year in review" article or list. Answer the questions below about your highlighted items:

   - What do you think made each item or event memorable to you?
   - What do your highlighted items have in common? How are they different?

2. Have each member of the group share his or her highlighted items, then discuss the following questions. Make some notes as you discuss so that you can share some of your discussion with the class later.

   - What highlighted items did group members have in common?
   - What differences appeared in group members' lists?
   - Did group members have similar reasons for why certain events were memorable to them? Be prepared to share examples.

3. As a group, discuss which items from your lists or articles are likely to make it into the history books or be remembered far into the future. Select the two to three items your group feels are most likely to be remembered for a long time, and be prepared to share your responses with the class.

Copyright © 2010 by Corwin. All rights reserved. Reprinted from *Parallel Curriculum Units for Social Studies, Grades 6–12*, edited by Jeanne H. Purcell and Jann H. Leppien. Thousand Oaks, CA: Corwin, www.corwinpress.com. Reproduction authorized only for the local school site or nonprofit organization that has purchased this book.

RESOURCES

Web Resources on Primary Sources and Primary Source Analysis

http://www.lib.washington.edu/Subject/History/RUSA. Good resource for defining and evaluating primary sources on the Web.

http://www.primarysourcelearning.org. Web site on primary source teaching, developed in conjunction with the Library of Congress.

http://lcweb2.loc.gov/learn/lessons/psources/pshome.htm. Library of Congress set of lesson plans on primary sources.

http://historymatters.gmu.edu. A "gateway" to a variety of history sources on the Web; provides useful annotations of each linked source and a search engine allowing searches by topic, type of source, and other criteria.

http://digitalgallery.nypl.org/nypldigital/index.cfm. New York Public Library site containing several different types of collections, including images and audio-visual collections as well as textual documents.

http://www.ourdocuments.gov. Web site that includes a variety of American history sources and also guidelines for teaching with documents; cooperative effort with National History Day, the National Archives and Records Administration, and USA Freedom Corps.

http://www.digitalhistory.uh.edu. Digital history source from the University of Houston; includes a large collection of primary sources and teaching/learning modules on many periods of American history; specific modules available on Progressivism and immigration.

http://www.library.yale.edu/instruction/primsource.html. Yale University site on primary sources, with links to digital collections.

Web Resources Used in Specific Lessons

Lessons 1 and 2:

http://www.pbs.org/wgbh/amex/presidents/26_t_roosevelt/psources/ps_tr progress.html. Progressive Party platform from the election of 1912.

Lesson 3:

http://www.loc.gov/rr/print/list/070_immi.html

http://www.loc.gov/rr/print/list/picamer/paImmig.html

http://www.balchinstitute.org/resources/destinationusa/html/intromigration.html

http://www.digitalhistory.uh.edu/photo_album/photo_album.html

http://www.eyewitnesstohistory.com/immigrating.htm

Lesson 4:

http://www.nytimes.com/slideshow/2001/11/14/dining/20MCFA.slideshow.ready_3.html

http://www.lva.lib.va.us/whoweare/exhibits/titanic/index.htm

http://www.titanicinquiry.org/USInq/AmInq18McGough01.php

http://cjrarchives.org/issues/2004/5/ideas-essay-tucher.asp?

Lesson 5

http://www.newseum.org/century/index.htm

http://www.eyewitnesstohistory.com/wright.htm

Web Resources on Unit-Specific Topics

http://memory.loc.gov/learn/features/port/start.html. Library of Congress learning center on immigration.

http://www.eyewitnesstohistory.com/20frm.htm. Source that includes a variety of primary source excerpts from various events in the early 20th century.

http://bss.sfsu.edu/cherny/gapesites.htm#documents. Links to a variety of sources on the Progressive Era.

http://library.duke.edu/digitalcollections/eaa. Web site from Duke University on the emergence of advertising in America; includes sample advertisements from 1850–1920.

http://memory.loc.gov/ammem/vshtml/vshome.html. Library of Congress page on vaudeville and popular entertainment around the turn of the century.

http://elections.harpweek.com. *Harper's Weekly* page on elections; includes a focus on the election of 1912.

http://www.pbs.org/wgbh/amex/wilson/sfeature/sf_election.html. Special feature on the election of 1912 from PBS's *American Experience* site on the presidents.

http://www.ilr.cornell.edu/trianglefire. Cornell University Library site on the 1911 Triangle factory fire.

http://www.memorialhall.mass.edu/home.html. American history and art from New England; includes a chronology function that allows searching of different chronologies over specified time periods.

http://www.titanicinquiry.org. Site on the *Titanic* disaster, including affidavits from survivors.

http://www.tntech.edu/history/gilprog.html. Extensive list of links on the Gilded Age and Progressive Era.

http://cehs.unl.edu/ushistory/online/american/primary.html. Links and descriptions for a variety of Web sites covering U.S. history from 1877 to 1929.

Selected General Texts and Primary Source Collections

Bruun, E., & Crosby, J. (1999). *Our nation's archive: The history of the United States in documents.* New York: Tess Press.

Hoose, P. (2001). *We were there, too! Young people in U.S. history.* New York: Farrar, Straus & Giroux.

Lindaman, D., & Ward, K. (2004). *History lessons: How textbooks from around the world portray U.S. history.* New York: The New Press.

Mintz, S. (2004). *Huck's raft: A history of American childhood.* Cambridge, MA: The Belknap Press.

Ward, K. (2006). *History in the making.* New York: The New Press.

Selected Texts on the Progressive Era

Chambers, J. W. (1992). *The tyranny of change: America and the Progressive Era, 1890–1920.* New York: St. Martin's Press.

Cooper, J. M. (1992). *Pivotal decades: The United States, 1900–1920.* New York: W. W. Norton.

Daniels, R. (2002). *Coming to America: A history of immigration and ethnicity in American life* (2nd ed.). New York: HarperCollins.

Diner, S. J. (1998). *A very different age: Americans of the Progressive Era.* New York: Farrar, Straus & Giroux.

Rosenszweig, R. (1983). *Eight hours for what we will: Workers and leisure in an industrial city, 1870–1920.* New York: Cambridge University Press.

Index

American Civil War unit, 4–8
Anticipation Guide Worksheet, 70, 72
AP Vertical Teams in Science, Social Studies, Foreign Language, Studio Art, and Music Theory: An Introduction (College Board), 172–173
AP Vertical Team strategies, 128–129
Ascending levels of intellectual demand, 2, 6, 110
Assessment
   for Becoming a Geographer unit, 15, 17, 34
   defined, 3
   Jamestown Critical Reading series and, 62
   learning journals for, 28, 42
   "possible sentences" strategy and, 29
   for Subversion and Controversy unit, 106–107, 108–109, 111, 131
   for Through the Looking Glass unit, 50–51, 52
   for True Story-Telling unit, 156–157

Balch Institute for Ethnic Studies, 188, 192
Barrymore, Ethel, 127
Barton, Keith, 173
Become a Climate Expert assignment sheet, 23
Become a Climate Expert Rubric, 24
Becoming a Geographer unit, 10, 15–16
   assessments for, 15, 17, 34
   content framework for, 14
   foundational skills needed for, 13
   Lesson 1: Climate and Seasons, 16–24
   Lesson 2: Investigating World Populations, 25–29
   Lesson 3: Shop Around the Globe, 30–38
   Lesson 4: Culture of Geography, 39–44
   national standards for, 15
   parallels addressed, 16
   skills addressed in, 15
Berger, Peter, 162
Biographies, 66–68. *See also* The Past Through Many Eyes (True Story-Telling unit)
Brooks, Mel, 127
Burke, Heather, ix, 10, 13–44
Burnett, Carol, 127

Careers, 28, 31
Carlyle, Thomas, 203
Causes and Effects of Individual and Group Behaviors (graphic organizer), 113–116
Census, U.S., 27
Chaplin, Charlie, 127
Character Identity Poems Handout, 62, 64
Children of the Dust (Henshaw), 86
Churchill, Winston, 185
CIA World Fact Book, 29
Circle maps, 79
Civil War (American) unit, 4–8
Climate and Seasons (Becoming a Geographer unit)
   Become a Climate Expert assignment sheet for, 23
   Become a Climate Expert Rubric for, 24
   Climate Map Project in, 22
   closure for, 21
   concepts in, 16
   differentiation for, 19
   guiding questions for, 16
   national standards for, 16
   preassessment for, 17
   principles of, 16
   skills addressed in, 16
   unit sequence for, 17–21
   Web sites for, 23
Climate Map Project, 22
Closure, defined, 3
Compiled Account chart, 162, 170
Concept maps for Becoming a Geographer unit, 17, 21
Concepts for each unit
   Authentic Authors (Through the Looking Glass unit), 65
   The City (Through the Looking Glass unit), 77
   Climate and Seasons (Becoming a Geographer unit), 16
   Constructing History (True Story-Telling unit), 171

Culture of Geography (Becoming a
    Geographer unit), 39
Curriculum of Identity Creative Extension
    (Subversion and Controversy unit), 147
The Great Depression (Through the
    Looking Glass unit), 83
Humor in Communication (Subversion and
    Controversy unit), 126
Humor in Society (Subversion and
    Controversy unit), 117
Investigating World Populations
    (Becoming a Geographer unit), 25
The Past Through Many Eyes
    (True Story-Telling unit), 180
Persuade Me! (Through the Looking
    Glass unit), 94
Planet Earth (Through the Looking
    Glass unit), 97
Pursuit of Happiness (Through the
    Looking Glass unit), 60
Selective Memory (True Story-
    Telling unit), 158
Shop Around the Globe (Becoming a
    Geographer unit), 30
Sign of the Times (Through the
    Looking Glass unit), 90
Sociocentrism (Through the Looking
    Glass unit), 68
Sociological Research (Subversion and
    Controversy unit), 132
Subversion and Controversy unit,
    generally, 110
What Makes the History Books?
    (True Story-Telling unit), 206
"Who Am I?" (Through the
    Looking Glass unit), 53
Who Writes History? (True Story-
    Telling unit), 199
Concept walls, 52, 54
Conformity. *See* Sociocentrism (Through the
    Looking Glass unit)
Connections, Curriculum of, 5–6
    Becoming a Geographer unit and,
        17, 34, 39, 40–41, 43
    hypotheses and, 18
    Through the Looking Glass unit, 51
Constructing History (True Story-Telling unit),
    overview of, 171
    concepts in, 171
    differentiation for, 172, 173, 174
    extension activities for, 175
    guiding questions for, 171
    national standards for, 171
    principles for, 171
    The Progressive Era—General History Sources
        (handout) for, 173, 176
    The Progressive Era—Sources About the
        Period (organizer) for, 174, 177
    skills addressed in, 171
    unit sequence for, 172–175
    Young Peoples' Lives assignment for,
        174, 178–179
Content, defined, 3
Content framework
    for Becoming a Geographer unit, 14
    for Subversion and Controversy unit, 104
    for Through the Looking Glass unit, 46–47
    for True Story-Telling unit, 155–156
Content maps, 110
Core Curriculum, 4–5
    Through the Looking Glass unit and, 51
    True Story-Telling: How Historians Construct
        the Past unit and, 154
Cornell Notes, 135–136
Culture of Geography (Becoming a
    Geographer unit), 39–44
Curriculum models, defined, 3

Dausel, Kelly M., ix, 11, 103–151
"Dealing with Differences" (video), 113
Debates, 94–97
Definitions, group development of, 19
Demographics. *See* Investigating World
    Populations (Becoming a Geographer unit)
Developing a Research Question (worksheet),
    133–134, 142
DIDLS (Details, Images, Diction, Language, and
    Sentence structure), 128–129, 130
Differentiated instruction
    Climate and Seasons (Becoming a Geographer
        unit) and, 19
    Constructing History (True Story-Telling unit)
        and, 172, 173, 174
    Culture of Geography (Becoming a
        Geographer unit) and, 40, 41, 43
    defined, 3
    grouping strategies and, 114
    Humor in Communication (Subversion and
        Controversy unit) and, 127–129
    Humor in Society (Subversion and
        Controversy unit) and, 120–121
    Investigating World Populations
        (Becoming a Geographer unit)
        and, 26, 29
    PCM and, 2
    reading formats and, 70
    Shop Around the Globe (Becoming a
        Geographer unit) and, 32, 33
    Sociological Research (Subversion and
        Controversy unit) and, 137
    Subversion and Controversy unit,
        generally, 108
    What Makes the History Books?
        (True Story-Telling unit) and, 211
    in Who Writes History? (True Story-
        Telling unit) and, 201

Digital History Web site, 193, 197
Discovery Education Web site, 108

Earth's orbit, weather and, 18
"Eccentrics" (Jamestown Critical
    Reading series), 62
Economics, geography and, 30
Election of 1912, 175
Ellis Island, 187
Emerson, Ralph Waldo, 182
Experts Analyze Humor (worksheet), 120, 125
Extension activities
    for ascending levels of intellectual demand, 6
    for Becoming a Geographer unit, 33, 42
    defined, 3
    for Subversion and Controversy unit,
        108, 127–128, 147–151
    for Through the Looking Glass unit,
        63, 71, 92
    for True Story-Telling unit, 175
Eyewitness to History Web site, 196

"Fishbowl" approach to presentations, 129
Fish bowl discussions, 99
Foundation for Critical Thinking, 71
4-square Scaffolds, 133, 142
Frameworks, content, 4–5
Frayer Research Methodology
    Diagrams, 112, 138

Galbraith, John Kenneth, 127
"Gallery" approach to presentations, 129
Gary, Romain, 127
Geography, mathematics and, 25, 29
Geography careers, 28
"Global Warming Issue: The Actions" (*Time*), 100
Gore, Al, 99
Graffiti boards, 78
Graham, Philip L., 202
Graphic organizers, 62, 67, 113–116
Great Depression (Through the
    Looking Glass unit)
    concepts in, 83
    guiding questions for, 84
    national standards for, 83–84
    principles for, 83
    skills addressed in, 83
    Tic-Tac-Toe and, 86, 89
    unit sequence for, 84–87
    Web activities for, 88
Great Depression Tic-Tac-Toe, 86, 89
Grouping strategies
    for Becoming a Geographer unit, 20
    differentiated instruction and, 114
    fluidity in, 6
    jigsaw, 20, 100, 161
    for Subversion and Controversy unit, 107
    for Through the Looking Glass unit, 50
    for True Story-Telling unit, 161, 181,
        208, 211, 213
Guided visualization, 112–113
Guiding questions for each unit
    Authentic Authors (Through the Looking
        Glass unit), 65
    The City (Through the Looking Glass unit), 78
    Climate and Seasons (Becoming a
        Geographer unit), 16
    Constructing History (True Story-
        Telling unit), 171
    Culture of Geography (Becoming a
        Geographer unit), 39
    The Great Depression (Through
        the Looking Glass unit), 84
    Humor in Communication (Subversion and
        Controversy unit), 126
    Humor in Society (Subversion and
        Controversy unit), 117–118
    Investigating World Populations
        (Becoming a Geographer unit), 25
    The Past Through Many Eyes
        (True Story-Telling unit), 180
    Persuade Me! (Through the
        Looking Glass unit), 94
    Planet Earth (Through the
        Looking Glass unit), 98
    Pursuit of Happiness (Through
        the Looking Glass unit), 60–61
    Selective Memory (True Story-
        Telling unit), 159
    Shop Around the Globe (Becoming a
        Geographer unit), 30
    Sign of the Times (Through the
        Looking Glass unit), 91
    Sociocentrism (Through the
        Looking Glass unit), 69
    Sociological Research (Subversion and
        Controversy unit), 133
    Subversion and Controversy unit,
        generally, 104–105
    What Makes the History Books?
        (True Story-Telling unit), 206
    "Who Am I?" (Through the
        Looking Glass unit), 54
    Who Writes History? (True Story-
        Telling unit), 199

"Harlem" (poem), 78–79
Henshaw, Betty, 86
Hesse, Karen, 86
Hinton, S.E., 70
Historians, 6–8. *See also* True Story-
    Telling: How Historians Construct
    the Past unit
History in the Making (Ward), 184
History Lessons (Ward and Lindaman),
    184–185

How the Other Half Lives (Riis), 163
Humor. *See* Subversion and Controversy: Sociological Considerations of Humor unit
Humor Creative Production Task (handout), 148–149, 150
Humor Creative Production Task rubric, 149, 150–151
Humor in Communication (Subversion and Controversy unit), 126–131
Humor in Society (Subversion and Controversy unit)
  concepts in, 117
  differentiation for, 120–121
  Experts Analyze Humor (worksheet) for, 120, 125
  guiding questions for, 117–118
  principles for, 117
  skills addressed in, 117
  standards for, 117
  Subversion and Controversy: Sociological Considerations of Humor handout for, 118, 123
  unit sequence for, 118–122
  Vocabulary Chart for, 119–120, 124

I Am Poem: Outline Worksheet, 55, 58
Identity, Curriculum of, overview of, 7–8
  for Becoming a Geographer unit, 33, 43
  for Subversion and Controversy unit, 105, 109, 134, 141, 148
  for True Story-Telling: How Historians Construct the Past unit, 154
  See also Through the Looking Glass unit
Identity concept walls, 52, 54
Imbeau, Marcia, 2
"Immigrants on an Atlantic Liner" (photo), 181
Immigration. *See* The Past Through Many Eyes (True Story-Telling unit)
An Inconvenient Truth (Gore), 99
Intervention classes. *See* Through the Looking Glass unit
Interviews, 63, 86–87
Introduction to lessons, defined, 3
Introduction to Sociology and How Sociologists Think (Subversion and Controversy unit), 110–116
Investigating World Populations (Becoming a Geographer unit), 25–29

Jamestown Critical Reading series "Eccentrics," 62
Janis, Lydia, 4–8
Jeopardy game, 86
Joel, Billy, 91
Journals. *See* Learning journals

"Knowledgeable others," 20

"Landing at Ellis Island" (photo), 181
Lazarus, Emma, 189, 193, 197
Learning activities, defined, 3
Learning contracts, 6
Learning journals
  for assessment, 28
  for Becoming a Geographer unit, 13–14, 33, 42
  for True Story-Telling unit, 157, 160, 162, 174, 185, 202–203, 213
Leppien, Jann H., vii–viii
Lerner, Gerda, 175, 185, 213
Lesson and unit closure, defined, 3
Levstik, Linda, 173
Library of Congress, 187, 191, 195
Lighter Side of Writing (video), 148
Linkages. *See* Connections, Curriculum of
Little, Catherine, ix, 11, 153–215
Looney Tunes—The Spotlight Collection (vol. 1), 121

Management Plan for Sociological Study Development (handout), 137–138, 144
Map making, 22
Map reading, 19
Material World (Menzel), 42–43
Mathematics, geography and, 25, 29
McGough, James B., 201
Memory. *See* Selective Memory (True Story-Telling unit)
Menzel, Peter, 42–43
Modifications. *See* Differentiated instruction
Myers, Walter Dean, 78

National standards
  Authentic Authors (Through the Looking Glass unit) and, 65
  Becoming a Geographer unit and, 15
  The City (Through the Looking Glass unit) and, 77–78
  Climate and Seasons (Becoming a Geographer unit) and, 16
  Constructing History (True Story-Telling unit) and, 171
  Culture of Geography (Becoming a Geographer unit) and, 39
  The Great Depression (Through the Looking Glass unit) and, 83–84
  Investigating World Populations (Becoming a Geographer unit) and, 25
  The Past Through Many Eyes (True Story-Telling unit) and, 180
  Persuade Me! (Through the Looking Glass unit) and, 94
  Planet Earth (Through the Looking Glass unit) and, 98
  Pursuit of Happiness (Through the Looking Glass unit) and, 60

Selective Memory (True Story-Telling
    unit) and, 159
Shop Around the Globe (Becoming a
    Geographer unit) and, 30
Sign of the Times (Through the Looking
    Glass unit) and, 90–91
Sociocentrism (Through the Looking Glass
    unit) and, 69
Through the Looking Glass unit and, 48–49
True Story-Telling unit, generally, and, 156
What Makes the History Books? (True Story-
    Telling unit) and, 206
"Who Am I?" (Through the Looking Glass
    unit), 53
Who Writes History? (True Story-
    Telling unit) and, 199
    See also Standards (Virginia)
Natural resources. *See* Shop Around the Globe
    (Becoming a Geographer unit)
Needs vs. wants. *See* Shop Around the Globe
    (Becoming a Geographer unit)
"The New Colossus" (Lazarus), 189, 193, 197
Newseum, 210
Newspapers, creating personal, 92

100% Writing–Persuasion (LinguaSystems), 96
Options for Considering Literature Through
    Sociological Inquiry Questions (handout),
    128–129, 130–131
*Our Nation's Archives: The History of the United
    States in Documents*, 201
Out of the Dust (Hesse), 86, 89
The Outsiders (film), 70
The Outsiders (Hinton), 70

*The Parallel Curriculum: A Design to Develop High
    Potential and Challenge High-Ability Learners*
    (Tomlinson et al.), 1
*The Parallel Curriculum: A Design to Develop
    Learner Potential and Challenge Advanced
    Learners*, 2d Ed (Tomlinson et al.), 1–2
*The Parallel Curriculum in the Classroom: Essays
    for Application Across the Content Areas,
    K–12* (Kaplan, et al.), 1
*The Parallel Curriculum in the Classroom:
    Units for Application Across the Content
    Areas, K–12* (Kaplan et al.), 1
Parallel Curriculum Model (PCM), 2
    components of, 3
    Connections, Curriculum of, 5–6
    Core Curriculum, 4–5
    defined, 3
    history of, 1–2
    how to use, 8–10
    Identity, Curriculum of, 7–8
    Practice, Curriculum of, 6–7
The Parallel Curriculum Multimedia Kit
    (Tomlinson), 2

The Past Through Many Eyes
    (True Story-Telling unit), 180
    concepts in, 180
    grouping strategies for, 181
    guiding questions for, 180
    national standards for, 180
    Picturing the Past: Immigration,
        generally, 183–184
    Picturing the Past: Immigration
        (Blue Group), 195–198
    Picturing the Past: Immigration (Green
        Group), 191–194
    Picturing the Past: Immigration
        (Red Group), 187–190
    principles for, 180
    skills addressed in, 180
    Source Analysis: Response to
        Photographs for, 181, 186
    unit sequence for, 181–185
PCM. *See* Parallel Curriculum Model (PCM)
Perfection Learning, 128
Perspective, 181–182
Persuade Me! (Through the Looking
    Glass unit), 94–97
Picturing the Past: Immigration
    (all groups), 183–184
Picturing the Past: Immigration
    (Blue Group), 195–198
Picturing the Past: Immigration
    (Green Group), 191–194
Picturing the Past: Immigration
    (Red Group), 187–190
Planet Earth—The Future (Disc 5), 99
Poetry, 55, 80–82
"Possible sentences" strategy, 26, 29
Practice, Curriculum of, 6–7
    for Becoming a Geographer
        unit, 33, 43
    for Subversion and Controversy unit,
        104, 109, 134, 135
    for Through the Looking Glass unit, 51
    for True Story-Telling: How Historians
        Construct the Past unit, 154
Preassessment (Selective Memory unit),
    160, 163–164
Preassessment Criteria (Selective Memory unit),
    160, 165–169
Principles for each unit
    Authentic Authors (Through the Looking
        Glass unit), 65
    The City (Through the Looking
        Glass unit), 77
    Climate and Seasons (Becoming a
        Geographer unit), 16
    Constructing History (True Story-
        Telling unit), 171
    Culture of Geography (Becoming a
        Geographer unit), 39

Curriculum of Identity Creative Extension (Subversion and Controversy unit), 147
The Great Depression (Through the Looking Glass unit), 83
Humor in Communication (Subversion and Controversy unit), 126
Humor in Society (Subversion and Controversy unit), 117
Investigating World Populations (Becoming a Geographer unit), 25
The Past Through Many Eyes (True Story-Telling unit), 180
Persuade Me! (Through the Looking Glass unit), 94
Planet Earth (Through the Looking Glass unit), 98
Pursuit of Happiness (Through the Looking Glass unit), 60
Selective Memory (True Story-Telling unit), 158
Shop Around the Globe (Becoming a Geographer unit), 30
Sign of the Times (Through the Looking Glass unit), 90
Sociocentrism (Through the Looking Glass unit), 68
Sociological Research (Subversion and Controversy unit), 132
Subversion and Controversy unit, generally, 110
What Makes the History Books? (True Story-Telling unit), 206
"Who Am I?" (Through the Looking Glass unit), 53
Who Writes History? (True Story-Telling unit), 199
Problem solving. *See* Practice, Curriculum of
Products (work samples), 3, 107
Progressive Era. *See* True Story-Telling: How Historians Construct the Past unit
The Progressive Era—General History Sources (handout), 173, 176
The Progressive Era: Sources About the Period, 174, 177
Purcell, Jeanne H., vii

Questioning Our Sociocentrism chart, 76
Questioning Our Sociocentrism Worksheet, 71, 75

Reader's Responses Worksheet, 70, 74
Reading formats, variety in, 62, 70
Reading Response Quotes Worksheet, 70, 73
Read, Write, Think Web site, 96
Reflection vs. summary, 99
Repplier, Agnes, 127
Research Methodology diagram, 138, 145
Research Report: We Didn't Start the Fire Rubric, 92, 93

Resources, 3, 101, 108. *See also* Web sites
Responses to Intervention (RTI) model, 45, 51
Riding the Rails (film), 85
Riis, Jacob, 163
Rubrics
    Become a Climate Expert, 24
    for debates, 96
    "eye-ball" rubrics, 52
    Humor Creative Production Task (Subversion and Controversy unit), 149, 150–151
    Preassessment Criteria (Selective Memory unit), 160, 165–169
    Research Report: We Didn't Start the Fire, 92, 93
    scoring guide, Humor in Communications unit, 131
    Theme Park Development Project, 37–38
    Web sites for, 97

Scaffolds, 4-square, 133, 142
Scoring guide, Humor in Communications unit, 131
Seasons. *See* Climate and Seasons (Becoming a Geographer unit)
Selective Memory (True Story-Telling unit), 158
    Compiled Account chart for, 162, 170
    concepts in, 158
    grouping strategies for, 161
    guiding questions for, 159
    national standards for, 159
    Preassessment in, 160, 163–164
    principles for, 158
    rubrics for preassessment, 165–169
    skills addressed in, 159
    unit sequence for, 159–162
Self-actualization. *See* Identity, Curriculum of
Self-Evaluation and Reflection (handout), 141, 146
Shop Around the Globe (Becoming a Geographer unit), 30–34
Skills for each unit
    Authentic Authors (Through the Looking Glass unit), 65
    Becoming a Geographer unit, generally, 15
    The City (Through the Looking Glass unit), 77
    Climate and Seasons (Becoming a Geographer unit), 16
    Constructing History (True Story-Telling unit), 171
    Culture of Geography (Becoming a Geographer unit), 39
    Curriculum of Identity Creative Extension (Subversion and Controversy unit), 147
    The Great Depression (Through the Looking Glass unit), 83
    Humor in Communication (Subversion and Controversy unit), 126
    Humor in Society (Subversion and Controversy unit), 117

Introduction to Sociology and How Sociologists Think (Subversion and Controversy unit), 111
Investigating World Populations (Becoming a Geographer unit), 25
The Past Through Many Eyes (True Story-Telling unit), 180
Persuade Me! (Through the Looking Glass unit), 94
Planet Earth (Through the Looking Glass unit), 98
Pursuit of Happiness (Through the Looking Glass unit), 60
Selective Memory (True Story-Telling unit), 159
Shop Around the Globe (Becoming a Geographer unit), 30
Sign of the Times (Through the Looking Glass unit), 90
Sociocentrism (Through the Looking Glass unit), 68
Sociological Research (Subversion and Controversy unit), 132
Subversion and Controversy unit, generally, 105
Through the Looking Glass unit, generally, 48
True Story-Telling unit, generally, 155–156
What Makes the History Books? (True Story-Telling unit), 206
"Who Am I?" (Through the Looking Glass unit), 53
Who Writes History? (True Story-Telling unit), 199
Sky Vista Middle School. *See* Through the Looking Glass unit
Sociocentrism (Through the Looking Glass unit)
  Anticipation Guide Worksheet for, 70, 72
  concepts in, 68
  differentiation for, 70
  extension activities for, 71
  guiding questions for, 69
  national standards for, 69
  principles for, 68
  Questioning our Sociocentrism chart for, 76
  Questioning our Sociocentrism Worksheet for, 75
  Reader's Responses Worksheet for, 70, 74
  Reading Response Quotes Worksheet for, 70, 73
  skills addressed in, 68
  unit sequence for, 69–71
Sociological Research (Subversion and Controversy unit)
  concepts in, 132
  Cornell Notes and, 135–136
  Developing a Research Question (worksheet) for, 133–134, 142

differentiation for, 137
  4-square scaffolds for, 133, 142
  guiding questions for, 133
  identity parallel and, 134, 141
  Management Plan for Sociological Study Development (handout) for, 137–138, 144
  methods for, 134–135, 136, 138–139
  practice parallel and, 134, 135
  principles for, 132
  Reader's Responses Worksheet for, 145
  Research Methodology diagram for, 138, 145
  Self-Evaluation and Reflection (handout) for, 141, 146
  skills addressed in, 132
  Sociological Research Report Evaluation (handout) for, 141, 146
  standards (Virginia) for, 132–133
  symposium and, 140–141
  3-2-1 Assessment Cards for, 137, 143
  unit sequence for, 133–141
  writing guides for, 139
Sociological research methods Web sites, 134–135, 136, 138–139
Sociological Research Report Evaluation (handout), 141, 146
Sociology. *See* Subversion and Controversy: Sociological Considerations of Humor unit
Source Analysis: First Flight, 208, 214
Source Analysis: Response to Photographs, 181, 186
Source Analysis: Titanic (1), 201, 204
Source Analysis: Titanic (2), 201, 205
Standards. *See* National standards
Standards (Virginia), 105–106
  Curriculum of Identity Creative Extension (Subversion and Controversy unit), 147
  Humor in Communication (Subversion and Controversy unit), 126
  Humor in Society (Subversion and Controversy unit), 117
  Sociological Research (Subversion and Controversy unit), 132–133
  Subversion and Controversy unit, generally, 111
  See also National standards
State frameworks, curriculum components and, 4–5
Statue of Liberty poem, 189, 193, 197
Strickland, Cindy, 2
Student logs. *See* Learning journals
Students
  as historians, 6–8
  peer teaching by, 19–20
  poetry examples by, 80–82
  presentations by, 23, 129, 178–179, 212
  symposium for sociology and, 140–141
Studenttales Web site, 56, 68

Subversion and Controversy: Sociological
    Considerations of Humor (handout), 118
Subversion and Controversy: Sociological
    Considerations of Humor: Essential
    Questions (handout), 118, 123
Subversion and Controversy: Sociological
    Considerations of Humor unit, 11, 109–110
  assessment for, 108–109
  background information for, 103
  content framework for, 104
  curriculum components for, 106–108
  differentiation for, 108
  extension activities for, 108
  identity parallel and, 105, 109
  Lesson 1: Introduction to Sociology and How
      Sociologists Think, 110–116
  Lesson 2: Humor in Society, 117–125
  Lesson 3: Humor in Communication, 126–131
  Lesson 4: Sociological Research, 132–146
  Lesson 5: Curriculum of Identity Creative
      Extension, 147–151
  practice parallel and, 104, 109
  resources for, 108
  skills addressed in, 105
Summary vs. reflection, 99

Teaching History for the Common Good
    (Barton and Levstik), 173
Teaching methods, defined, 3
Theme Park Development Project
  culture and, 43
  expectations for, 33
  instructions for, 35–36
  introduction to, 28–29
  rubric for, 37–38
3-2-1 Assessment Cards, 137, 143
Through the Looking Glass unit, 10
  assessment for, 50–51
  background information for, 51–52
  content framework for, 46–47
  curriculum components for, 49–50
  introduction to, 45–46
  preassessment for, 52
  Lesson 1: Introduction—"Who Am I?" 53–59
  Lesson 2: The Pursuit of Happiness, 60–64
  Lesson 3: Authentic Authors, 65–68
  Lesson 4: Sociocentrism, 68–76
  Lesson 5: The City, 77–82
  Lesson 6: The Great Depression, 83–89
  Lesson 7: A Sign of the Times, 90–93
  Lesson 8: Persuade Me! 94–97
  Lesson 9: Planet Earth, 97–101
  national standards for, 48–49
  resources for, 101
  skills addressed in, 48
Tic-Tac-Toe, Great Depression, 86, 89
Timelines, 172–173
Titanic, 199–205

Toggle books, 67
True Story-Telling: How Historians Construct
    the Past unit, 11, 157–158
  assessment for, 156–157
  background information for, 153–155
  concepts in, 155
  content framework for, 155–156
  Core Curriculum and, 154
  Identity parallel and, 154
  Lesson 1: Selective Memory, 158–170
  Lesson 2: Constructing History, 171–179
  Lesson 3: The Past Through Many Eyes,
      180–198
  Lesson 4: Who Writes History? 199–205
  Lesson 5: What Makes the History
      Books? 206–215
  national standards for, 156
  practice parallel and, 154
  skills addressed in, 155–156
Tucher, Andie, 203
Twain, Mark, 185, 203

Understanding. *See* Core Curriculum

Van Gogh, Vincent, 63
Venn diagrams, 31, 209–210
Vier, Dawn, ix, 10, 45–101
Visualization, guided, 112–113
Vocabulary Chart, 119–120, 124

Wants vs. needs. *See* Shop Around the
    Globe (Becoming a Geographer unit)
Ward, Kyle, 184
Ward, Lisa L., x, 10, 45–101
Web sites
  Balch Institute for Ethnic Studies, 188, 192
  census, 27
  CIA World Fact Book, 29
  circle maps, 79
  climate types, 23
  culture, 41
  "Dealing With Differences," 113
  Digital History, 193, 197
  Discovery Education, 108
  election of 1912, 175
  Ellis Island, 187
  Eyewitness to History, 196
  geography careers, 28
  "Global Warming Issue: The
      Actions" (*Time*), 100
  Great Depression, 85, 86, 88
  history, 92
  immigration photographs, 181
  Jeopardy game, 86
  Library of Congress, 187, 191, 195
  Newseum, 210
  Read, Write, Think, 96
  Riding the Rails (film), 85

for rubrics, 97
sociological research methods, 134–135, 136, 138–139
Statue of Liberty poem, 189, 193, 197
studenttales, 56, 68
tenement yard, 1912, 163
Titanic, 200–201
We Can Change the World Challenge, 100
"We Didn't Start the Fire" (song), 91
"Whose Turf Is the Past?" (Tucher), 203
Wright, Orville, 208
writing guides for sociology, 139

We Can Change the World Challenge (Sieman), 100
"We Didn't Start the Fire" (Joel), 91
What Makes the History Books? (True Story-Telling unit), 206
   concepts in, 206
   differentiation for, 211
   grouping strategies for, 208, 211, 213
   guiding questions for, 206
   national standards for, 206
   principles for, 206
   skills addressed in, 206
   Source Analysis: First Flight, 208, 214
   unit sequence for, 207–213
   Venn diagrams for, 209–210
   What Will We Remember? organizer, 208, 215

What's So Funny (Perfection Learning), 128
What Will We Remember? organizer, 208, 215
Where Am I From Poetry Handout, 55, 59
Whitman, Walt, 203
"Who Am I?" (Through the Looking Glass unit)
   concepts in, 53
   guiding questions for, 54
   I Am Poem: Outline Worksheet for, 55, 58
   Identity poems, 56
   national standards for, 53
   PowerPoint worksheet for, 57
   principles for, 53
   skills addressed in, 53
   unit sequence for, 54–56
   Where Am I From Poetry Handout for, 55, 59
Who Am I? PowerPoint Worksheet, 57
"Whose Turf Is the Past?" (Tucher), 203
Who Writes History? (True Story-Telling unit), 199–205
Work samples (products), 3, 107
Wright, Orville, 208
Writing guides for sociology Web site, 139

Young Peoples' Lives assignment, 174, 178–179

Zinsser, William K., 127

The Corwin logo—a raven striding across an open book—represents the union of courage and learning. Corwin is committed to improving education for all learners by publishing books and other professional development resources for those serving the field of PreK–12 education. By providing practical, hands-on materials, Corwin continues to carry out the promise of its motto: **"Helping Educators Do Their Work Better."**

In compliance with GPSR, should you have any concerns about the safety of this product, please advise: International Associates Auditing & Certification Limited The Black Church, St Mary's Place, Dublin 7, D07 P4AX Ireland
EUAR@ie.ia-net.com

www.ingramcontent.com/pod-product-compliance
Lightning Source LLC
Chambersburg PA
CBHW081354290426
44110CB00018B/2374